Scenic
Driving
IDAHO

Bob Clark

FALCON®

HELENA, MONTANA

A **FALCON** GUIDE ®

Falcon® Publishing is continually expanding its list of recreational guidebooks. All books include detailed descriptions, accurate maps, and all information necessary for enjoyable trips. You can order extra copies of this book and get information and prices for other Falcon® books by writing Falcon, P.O. Box 1718, Helena, MT 59624, or by calling toll-free 1-800-582-2665. Also, please ask for a copy of our current catalog. Visit our website at www.Falcon.com or contact us by e-mail at falcon@falcon.com.

Editing, design, typesetting, and other prepress work by Falcon, Helena, Montana.
All black-and-white photos by author unless otherwise noted.
Front cover photo by Fred Plughoft
Back cover photo by Leland Howard

Library of Congress Cataloging-in-Publication Data

Clark, Bob, 1950–
    Scenic driving Idaho / Bob Clark.
        p.   cm.
    "A Falcon guide"—T.p. verso.
    ISBN 1-56044-621-8 (alk. paper)
    1. Idaho—Tours.   2. Automobile travel—Idaho—Guidebooks.
I. Title.
F744.3.C58   1998
917.9604'33—dc21   98-5872
                                                                 CIP

CAUTION

All participants in the recreational activities suggested by this book must assume the responsibility for their own actions and safety. The information contained in this guidebook cannot replace sound judgment and good decision-making skills, which help reduce risk exposure; nor does the scope of this book allow for disclosure of all the potential hazards and risks involved in such activities.

Learn as much as possible about the recreational activities in which you participate, prepare for the unexpected, and be cautious. The reward will be a safer and more enjoyable experience.

♻ Text pages printed on recycled paper.

Contents

Acknowledgments

I would like to thank Jackie Johnson Maughan for her efforts in putting me together with Falcon Publishing. Without the brief message she posted on the Internet, and her encouragement and guidance, I would never have had the opportunity to do this book.

An anonymous thank you goes to the many volunteers who staff information booths and visitor centers in towns and cities throughout Idaho, particularly those in Idaho Falls, Ashton, Twin Falls, Lewiston, and Bonners Ferry. Your enthusiastic response to questions and your willingness to chat with a total stranger made some very long days more pleasant and saved me countless hours of backtracking. Also, librarians in Boise, McCall, and Denver played a key role in developing some of these drives. Thanks also to Lee Whittlesey, Yellowstone National Park historian, for answering an obscure historical question.

On a more personal note, I would like to thank my father, Robert O. Clark of Prescott Valley, Arizona, for the use of his motorhome, and for his patience when I returned it with a long list of things that I had either broken, destroyed, removed, or "improved." Thanks must also go to Chuck and Gail Howarth for their hospitality, some of it served up on short notice.

Finally, and most importantly, I would like to thank my wife, Marianne, and my children, Audrey and Ben, for putting up with the long absences, the piles of notes, brochures, maps, photos, and computer disks, and particularly for allowing me to chase my dream. Without your loyalty and support, this book might never have seen the light of day. I love you!

Locator Map

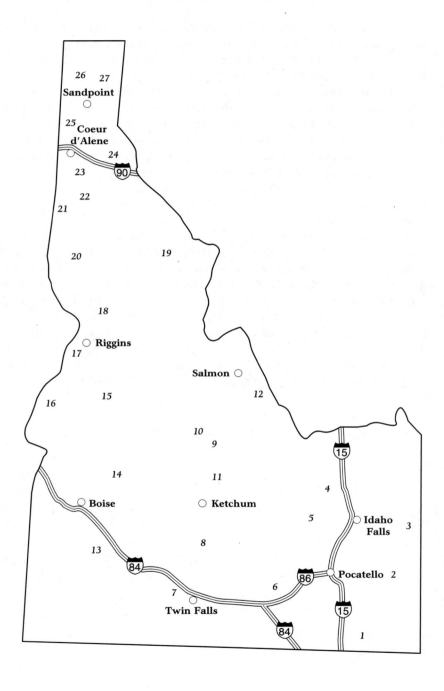

Map Legend

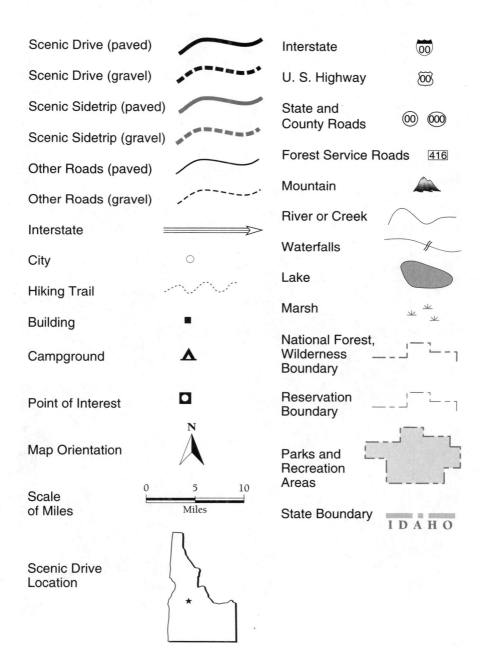

Scenic Drive (paved)

Scenic Drive (gravel)

Scenic Sidetrip (paved)

Scenic Sidetrip (gravel)

Other Roads (paved)

Other Roads (gravel)

Interstate

City

Hiking Trail

Building

Campground

Point of Interest

Map Orientation

Scale of Miles

Scenic Drive Location

Interstate

U. S. Highway

State and County Roads

Forest Service Roads

Mountain

River or Creek

Waterfalls

Lake

Marsh

National Forest, Wilderness Boundary

Reservation Boundary

Parks and Recreation Areas

State Boundary

The Salmon River above Riggins.

Introduction

Idaho is the Gem State. As many as 70 varieties of gemstones are found in the geologically young mountains and valleys of the state, and, on its surface, the nickname reflects that fact. But the real gems of Idaho are its sparkling mountain lakes, the crystalline flanks of its jagged mountains, the emerald green of its cedar and white pine forests, and the cleavage of its spectacular canyons. Add to that the friendly sparkle in the eyes of its citizens, and it's obvious why this is the Gem State.

Scenic Driving Idaho is a collection of more of Idaho's gems—more than two dozen scenic drives chosen because of their scenic beauty and human interest. This book is intended to tempt you to explore the side roads that give the state its character, and to open up the vistas of mountains and plain, forests, deserts, and water to those who might otherwise not have known what wonders are just around the bend. It will also give residents of the state an opportunity to see their home in a fresh, new light. The drives are as short as the 10-mile White Bird Battlefield Drive and as long as the two-part, 225-mile Lewis and Clark Trail, which crosses Idaho on U.S. Highway 12. There are at least as many beautiful drives not included as there are found here.

There are some excellent guidebooks available that list hotels, restaurants and shops throughout Idaho. Find one you are comfortable with and carry it along with *Scenic Driving Idaho* as you travel. The combination of the two will ensure that your excursions are enjoyable and headache-free.

Each chapter begins with general information about the drive, including a description of the drive, a listing of special attractions on the route, the general location of the drive, the highway and road numbers to be followed, advice on the best times of year to follow the route, the locations of campgrounds and tourist services, some nearby attractions that may be of interest, and an extended narrative. The narratives include specific directions to get the traveler under way, as well as stories about famous characters, information about history, geology, geography, and mythology, and other facts both relevant and trivial.

An appendix in the back of the book lists important sources of information, including addresses and phone numbers of national parks, monuments, recreation areas and wildlife refuges, Bureau of Land Management and USDA Forest Service offices, state parks, chambers of commerce, and miscellaneous sources. Use these resources to plan ahead, and to ensure that your drive will not be interrupted by an unexpected closure or other inconvenience.

The Land

Idaho's rugged, Western character is a reflection of the challenges of the land. From Basque shepherds to lumbermen, from ranchers to white-water guides, and from farmers to miners, many Idahoans make their living by challenging and confronting their natural environment. The hardships and struggles faced by early pioneers on the Oregon Trail as they crossed the state in the 1840s and 1850s were not so different from those faced by gold miners in the 1860s and 1870s, and by early farmers in the 1880s and 1890s. They all had to deal with dry, hot summers, long, cold winters, impenetrable canyons, raging rivers, and vast expanses of unyielding basalt and lava flows.

Mormon settlers in the southern part of the state began to eke out a living from the soil in the 1860s, beginning an agricultural tradition that remains today. Idaho is synonymous with potatoes, grown in the shadow of the Teton Mountains and across the southern part of the state. In Blackfoot, a town north of Pocatello, the World Potato Expo houses a museum dedicated to the popular tuber. Other crops are significant as well. Dry beans and lentils, barley, corn, and sugar beets are all grown along the Snake River, on land made fertile by a series of reservoirs which allow irrigation of the otherwise inhospitable Snake River plain. In the north, wheat and dryland crops are grown on the Palouse hills.

Idaho is sparsely populated, with little more than 1,000,000 people in the state—12 people per square mile. Almost half of those people live within the Boise metropolitan area, including the outlying communities of Nampa, Caldwell, and Meridian. Much of the rest of the state's population lives within a few miles of the interstate highways that run through the state, including Interstate 15 in the eastern part of the state, anchored by Pocatello, Blackfoot, and Idaho Falls. Burley, Twin Falls, and Mountain Home are all on Interstate 84 east of Boise, and in the Panhandle, Coeur d'Alene, Kellogg, and Wallace sit astride Interstate 90.

The largest cities off the interstate grid are Moscow, home of the University of Idaho, and Lewiston, located at the confluence of the Snake and Clearwater rivers. Other than these areas, a town with a population of 1,000 or more is a big settlement.

An old joke says that Idaho has three capitals—Boise, Spokane, and Salt Lake City. While Boise is the official capital, its distance from Panhandle communities minimizes its economic impact on the far northern reaches of the state, and the strongly Mormon southeast looks to Utah for spiritual guidance.

Geologically, large portions of the state are covered with thick deposits of basalt and other volcanic rock laid down over millions of years. Recent evidence of these natural processes can be found around Craters of the Moon National Monument, where lava flows of less than 2,000 years of age

Malad Gorge State Park.

dominate the eerily desolate landscape. A series of mountain ranges and valleys running roughly parallel from northwest to southeast define the land in the east-central part of the state, while the Idaho batholith, an enormous dome of granite, thrusts up from the Sawtooth Mountains to the Clearwater River, its flanks still being carved by the Salmon and other rivers.

In the north, the effects of the last ice age are still apparent in the glacial moraines and large lakes left behind by glaciers. Earthquakes are infrequent, although a major quake did occur near Idaho's highest mountain, Borah Peak, in October 1983.

The state's major rivers include the mighty Snake, Clearwater, Coeur d'Alene, Payette, and Salmon rivers. The Salmon River drains the entire central section of the state, flowing across almost 400 miles of Idaho before joining the Snake. The Salmon is unusual in that there are no dams along its entire length. It flows east from the high Sawtooth Mountains before heading north and then sweeping west through the pristine Frank Church/River of No Return Wilderness Area before joining the Snake River south of Lewiston.

From Bear Lake in the southeast corner of the state to Redfish Lake in the Sawtooths, and Lake Pend Oreille, Priest Lake, and Lake Coeur d'Alene in the Panhandle, the state is graced with beautiful natural lakes as well. Enormous reservoirs on the Snake River at Palisades Dam, at American Falls and Walcott dams on the Snake River plain, and at Brownlee, Oxbow, and Hell's Canyon dams generate electricity as well as provide flood control, water for irrigation, and recreational opportunities. At Ahsahka, the 717-foot-high Dworshak Dam holds back more than 50 miles of water on the North Fork of the Clearwater River.

Located on the western side of the Continental Divide, Idaho enjoys a less harsh climate than that of its neighbors on the eastern side of the divide. While Montana and Wyoming are swept by arctic air masses flowing down from Canada, Idaho's climate is more strongly influenced by its proximity to the Pacific Ocean, and by the moist air that sweeps eastward across Oregon and Washington. Temperatures generally are mild. They can be quite extreme in certain areas, however, with 100-degree Fahrenheit readings common on the Snake River plain in summer. In winter, the Stanley area is well known for its below-zero temperatures. An annual ice festival in McCall celebrates the cold with gigantic ice carvings. Annual precipitation amounts range from 10 inches or fewer in the south, to more than 40 inches in the Panhandle, much of it in the form of snow.

People and History

Native American ties to the land go back thousands of years. Early artifacts excavated in Idaho have been dated at more than 14,500 years of age. Rock paintings are found in the deserts of Owyhee County, in the southwest part of the state, as well as in various locations along the Snake River. The major tribes that inhabited Idaho at the time of the first European contact included the Shoshone, Bannock, Coeur d'Alene, and Nez Perce.

Historians say confidently that Idaho was the last of the 48 states to be visited by European-American explorers. Lewis and Clark's expedition in 1805–1806 had that honor when a small party led by Meriwether Lewis crested the Continental Divide at Lemhi Pass on August 12, 1805. When they determined that the Salmon River was, indeed, the River of No Return, the party retreated back into present-day Montana. Searching for an easier passage, they reentered Idaho at the top of Lolo Pass, and then followed the ridges north of the Clearwater River across Idaho before entering Washington on the Snake River, at the site of present-day Lewiston.

In the years following Lewis and Clark's journey, exploration was tied to the fur trade. Parties led by David Thompson, Andrew Henry, Wilson Hunt, Alexander Ross, and others crisscrossed the state in search of plentiful sources of beaver pelts. John Colter, Jim Bridger, and Jedediah Smith all explored the state at various times. When the European market for gentlemen's beaver hats crashed abruptly in the 1830s, the number of trappers passing through the state declined.

Missionaries intent on saving the souls of the native population came next. The Presbyterian minister Henry Spalding establishing a base at Lapwai, near Lewiston, in 1836. Ten years later, Jesuits, led by Father Pierre Jean DeSmet, set up a mission at Cataldo in the northern panhandle in 1846. The church, on a knoll above the Coeur d'Alene River, is the oldest building in the state.

Emigrants following the Oregon Trail westward passed through Idaho in large numbers during the 1840s and 1850s, pausing only long enough to rest their horses and oxen as they struggled across the Snake River plain in the heat of summer. The wagon trains entered the state's southeast corner near Bear Lake and intercepted the Snake River at Pocatello. The hardy pioneers followed its south bank all the way to Glenns Ferry, the first place where they were able to cross safely. From there they proceeded northwest to Fort Boise, located some 40 miles downstream from the fort's namesake city, Boise. The settlers crossed the river again, and passed on into Oregon, heading for their promised land—the Willamette Valley of western Oregon.

The most significant religious movement to impact the state came from the south. Led by Brigham Young, the Church of Jesus Christ of Latter-day Saints, whose members are commonly referred to as Mormons, expanded beyond their growing settlements around the Great Salt Lake. Franklin, on the Utah border, became the first permanent settlement in Idaho, in 1860. Many other towns in southeast Idaho got their start at Brigham Young's direction.

The discovery of gold at Pierce in 1860, and at various other locations in Idaho during the 1860s, led to the next boom and the establishment of formal government. Idaho Territory was established in 1863, with its capital at Idaho City, in the heart of the Boise Basin mining district. It was a rough and tumble place in those days, and vigilante justice was often the only "justice" to be found.

The increasing pace of white settlement soon conflicted with the interests of the native tribes. A massacre on the Bear River in 1863 was the first major documented incident; 350 Shoshone were slaughtered by the U.S. cavalry. By 1877, the push by white settlers to reclaim lands earlier given to the Nez Perce led to one of the most well known of the Native American conflicts, the Nez Perce War of 1877.

Several of the chiefs of the Nez Perce, including Chief Joseph, rebelled at being forced onto reservation lands. After some of his men killed four white settlers south of Grangeville in May of 1877, Joseph fled with about 700 followers, including many women and children. Their odyssey, as they outwitted government troops for four months and 1500 miles, took them across Idaho, Yellowstone, and Montana before they were captured 40 miles from the Canadian border and freedom.

The defeat of the Nez Perce opened all of Idaho's agricultural lands to farming. The advent of large-scale irrigation projects around the turn of the

Watch for sheep being herded along Idaho's back roads.

century assured Idaho its present reputation as a fertile and productive agricultural region.

Natural Resources

The state's natural resources include precious metals, such as gold and silver, and valuable deposits of zinc, copper, lead, antimony, and molybdenum, among others. Vast reserves of phosphate in the hills east of Soda Springs in the southeast corner of the state are mined for use in fertilizers and other everyday products.

The extensive forests of Idaho make timber one of the state's largest industries. Many years of logging have changed the face of thousands of acres of forest, and the vast tracts of white pine (Idaho's state tree) that once covered the north-central section of the state have dwindled to a fraction of their former size. Today, more selective cutting practices are having an impact on the economics of the timber industry. The conflict between conservation forces and timber interests generates never-ending arguments in the state. Since 1937, when the Sun Valley resort was opened, recreational development in Idaho has boomed. There are downhill ski areas scattered across the state, from Magic Mountain and Pomerelle south of the Snake River, to Schweitzer Mountain north of Sandpoint. Cross-country skiing is also quite popular, and the scarcity of parking at popular trailheads has led to a state-issued ski parking permit system for the coveted spaces.

The steep gradients and abundant sparkling water of the state's rivers have made river rafting a popular summer activity. Commercial river runners guide enthusiasts down some of the best whitewater in the world. The Middle Fork of the Salmon is the premiere attraction for rafters, but trips on the Lochsa, Selway, Bruneau, and Payette rivers, and even the Hell's Canyon stretch of the Snake River, are enough to thrill any river rat.

Idaho is a haven for big game. Elk, mule deer, bighorn sheep, mountain goats, and lesser numbers of mountain lions, black bears, and other more reclusive species all roam here. The contiguous United States' only population of caribou ranges through the Selkirk Mountains in the Panhandle. In 1995, timber wolves were released at various locations in the central Idaho wilderness.

Raptors, from bald and golden eagles, to ospreys, owls, and many varieties of hawks, inhabit the state. The sheer cliffs and isolation of the Snake River Canyon south of Boise have been set aside as the Snake River Birds of Prey Area. National wildlife refuges around the state house large transient populations of migrant waterfowl, including such rare species as trumpeter swans and the endangered whooping crane.

Salmon still inhabit some of the state's rivers, although extensive dam building on the Snake and Columbia rivers has reduced the numbers of the sea-going fish that make the trip to their traditional spawning grounds in Idaho. The antediluvian white sturgeon, its appearance virtually unchanged for millions of years, still inhabits deep pools in the Snake River and in the three reservoirs in the river's Hell's Canyon.

Safety Note

Remember that driving can be dangerous even in the best of conditions, and stormy weather can make it even more so. Idaho's vast size and relative emptiness mean that there can be long stretches of road without nearby help. Be sure to watch your gas gauge and plan ahead. A good rule of thumb is to think about refueling whenever the gauge drops below half-full. Be sure your car is in good mechanical condition and check oil, tires, brakes, and lights regularly. No matter what the time of year, rapidly changing weather is common in mountainous terrain. Be sure to keep food, blankets, sand, and a shovel in the car for winter driving. It is always wise to inquire locally about road and weather conditions before setting out on unfamiliar roads.

Many of the drives utilize forest roads that are also used by logging trucks. Some of these roads are narrow and have blind curves and few, if any, pullouts. The following list of suggestions for back road driving is paraphrased from a list posted at the Hell's Canyon National Recreation Area offices outside Riggins, but the list applies throughout the state.

- Stay on your side of the road; daydream only on the straightaways.
- Look ahead—watch for dust clouds.
- On curves, listen for "jake brakes" (trucker's air brakes); they may signal the approach of a logging truck.
- If you see an empty logging truck on the side of the road, don't pass it. Wait for the oncoming truck he's waiting for.
- Let empty logging trucks pass you on uphill stretches.
- Don't panic when you come across a truck on a curve: Hold your lane.
- Watch for berms (small gravel ridges) that can pull your wheels to one side or the other.
- If there's a berm in the middle, watch out—there's a road grader ahead!

The scenic drives presented here offer glimpses of all parts of the state, but they only scratch its surface. Use them as starting points for further exploration, or incorporate them into a longer vacation. Idaho is truly a gem, so explore all its facets and experience the wonder of it.

1

Franklin–Bear River Loop

General description: This 140-mile drive passes through some of the earliest settlements in Idaho, from Franklin to the Bear Lake Valley and the Bear River. Proceeding north to Soda Springs, the drive detours for a relaxing plunge at Lava Hot Springs, then makes a stop at an ice cave in a farm field, where it offers a brief geology lesson. The drive ends in Preston, just a few miles north of where it began.

Special attractions: Museum and restored buildings at Franklin; the pastoral Bear Lake Valley; Montpelier, where Butch Cassidy robbed the bank; Soda Springs, with its carbon dioxide geyser; hot springs at Lava Hot Springs; the Last Chance Canal; Niter Ice Cave.

Location: Southeastern corner of the state

Drive route numbers: U.S. Highways 91, 89, and 30, Idaho Highways 34 and 36.

Travel season: ID 36 through Emigration Canyon may be maintained only during daylight hours in winter; the remainder of the route is all-weather road. Scenic highlights include golden aspen leaves in September, and pastoral scenery in spring, summer, and fall.

Camping: Cache National Forest campground in Emigration Canyon on ID 36; camping and RV sites at Lava Hot Springs.

Services: Preston, Montpelier, Soda Springs, and Lava Hot Springs all offer food and lodging.

Nearby attractions: Grays Lake National Wildlife Refuge; fishing and sailing on Bear Lake; Minnetonka Cave.

 **The Drive**

Franklin was settled in 1860 by Mormons who moved north into this territory at the urging of Brigham Young. Franklin sits at milepost 1 on US 91, just over the border from Utah. In fact, Franklin's early settlers thought they were in Utah. Not until 1872, when an official boundary survey was completed, did they discover that they were actually in Idaho. Not only was Franklin the first settlement in Idaho, it was also the site of the first gristmill, sawmill, creamery, telegraph, telephone, and railroad stop in the state. In 1923, it became the location of the first commercial mink ranch in the country.

US 91 runs through the middle of town. On Main Street, two blocks east of the highway, stand several interesting buildings from the early settlement, including the Hatch House and the Franklin Relic Hall. The Hatch House was the residence of Lorenzo Hill Hatch, who was the town's second Mormon bishop and first mayor. He was also the first Mormon legislator in Idaho. Brigham Young himself was a frequent guest of Bishop Hatch's hospitality. The interior of the house is not currently accessible to the public because of safety considerations.

Just down the street from the Hatch House, past the old Co-op storefront, is the Franklin Relic Hall. This small museum is housed in a log cabin built in 1937 with Civilian Conservation Corps labor. It contains a collection of portraits of pioneers, hung on every available bit of wall space, as well as household and farm implements used—and in many cases made—by the early settlers. Saws, mallets, chisels, and equipment for blacksmithing, harness making, and bullet making all are represented, in glorious excess. Also on display are souvenirs collected by local residents from around the world, including a stuffed African lizard and a piece of stone from the police station in Santa Barbara, which had been damaged in an earthquake. The descendants of an early storekeeper, Elliot Butterworth, are the caretakers of this quirky and personal collection.

Return west on Main Street to US 91. Turn right (north) onto the highway, and then take the next left, at the Daughters of Utah Pioneers historic marker (just before the bridge over the Cub River) onto Parkinson Road. This is the path of the Old Yellowstone Highway. Cross under the railroad tracks. On the right side of the road are the ruins of an old flour mill. Across from the mill sits a small, welded-metal arrow on a base of yellow rock. Not much to look at, but markers like this one—thought to be the last of the many once sprinkled throughout the West—were once located along the major roads leading to Yellowstone Park. The markers were placed by enthusiastic local chambers of commerce hoping to cash in on the expected boom in travelers headed for Yellowstone Park in their new automobiles.

Double back to US 91 and turn left (north). On your left is Little Mountain, where early settlers posted scouts to watch for the approach of Native American tribesmen. Shortly you'll pass Whitney, which proclaims its fame as the birthplace of Ezra Taft Benson, Dwight Eisenhower's secretary of agriculture and president of the Church of Jesus Christ of Latterd-day Saints from 1985 until his death in 1994.

Just 3 miles north of Whitney is Preston—a peaceful, unassuming small town laid out on a neat Mormon-style grid, with streets numbered out from the center point in the four cardinal directions (100 South, 200 South, 300 South, etc.). If you understand the system, finding an address is easy in any town using the grid. Preston is a charming example of small-town America,

Drive 1: Franklin–Bear River Loop

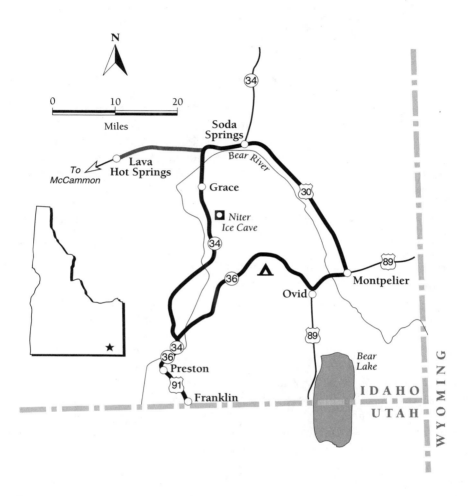

with broad, tree-lined streets and modest homes.

At the north end of Preston turn right from US 91 onto ID 34/36. Follow this road for 5 miles up the hill and back down to the crossing of the Bear River. Near here, the Bear River once entered enormous Lake Bonneville, dumping its load of sediments as its waters slowed. Notice the terraces on both shoulders of the valley, the remains of those silt and sand deposits.

Turn right on ID 36 just north of the river and head up the Hay Valley.

As ID 36 enters Cache National Forest, watch for deer. They are prevalent in this area, especially around sunup and sundown. After climbing along Strawberry Creek and passing a series of fertile hay meadows, the road climbs over and drops through Emigration Canyon. As it leaves the canyon, ID 36 follows the undulations of the landscape into the Bear Lake Valley, passing through the small community of Liberty before coming to Ovid and US 89, 39 miles from Preston.

Turn left on US 89 and continue 6 miles across the valley of the Bear River to Montpelier. This is the same Bear River that the drive left north of Preston, on the other side of the mountains. The Bear River swings around the north end of the Bear River Range at Soda Springs before turning to go back south, ultimately ending up in Utah's Great Salt Lake. Geologists speculate that a large lava flow, known as the Portneuf Flow, blocked the Bear from its then west-tending channel and sent it south, instead of allowing it to drain into the Snake River. The Portneuf River now occupies that west-tending channel.

Montpelier is on the east side of the broad, marshy Bear River Valley. The town was a center for livestock in the last century; stockyards still line the Oregon Short Line railroad tracks northwest of town. Each year at the Oregon Trail Rendezvous Pageant, held near Montpelier, the story of Mountain Fawn is retold.

Mountain Fawn was the sister of Chief Walkara of the Ute tribe, who lived in the Bear River Valley in the 1820s. She married the wild and reckless trapper, Peg Leg Smith, who earned his nickname the hard way. Smith lost his leg to an Indian arrow which shattered his ankle. Carried from the field of battle by his companions, he decided to remove the damaged leg himself. He proceeded to hack it off, interrupted occasionally by nausea, dizzy spells, and rounds of cursing his fate. Born in Kentucky, Thomas "Peg-Leg" Smith headed west at the age of 15, joining a band of Osage and selling moonshine whiskey. He came to Yellowstone country in 1823 at the age of 22. He earned the respect of the Ute tribe by riding into their camp and insisting they return mules they had stolen from his party.

After the amateur amputation job, a group of friendly Utes nursed him back to health, fashioning a poultice of tobacco, cow manure, and roots. Confounding his pals, Smith eventually recovered, fashioning himself an oaken leg. He once swung the wooden leg over his head as he rode into a camp of hostile Shoshones, who were so confused by the spectacle that they promptly retreated.

The marriage of Mountain Fawn and Peg-Leg Smith was a bit rocky. The wild frontiersman had other wives as well, fathering as many as five children in a single year. The wives' jealousy led to fighting, and Mountain Fawn was killed while Peg-Leg was away. She was buried on a hill overlooking

The Franklin Relic Hall contains a remarkable collection of portraits of early settlers.

beautiful Bear Lake, along with two horses placed in the hole for her use in the afterlife. After Mountain Fawn's tragic death, Smith continued his wild ways. He eventually died a pauper in California.

US 89 intersects US 30 just east of the center of Montpelier. At the intersection is the Oregon Trail Museum. Its exhibits detail life on the Oregon Trail and the early settlement of the valley. From US 89 in Montpelier, turn left (north) on US 30 and travel 29 miles past the small towns of Bennington and Georgetown to Soda Springs. The rejuvenating powers of the thirty-some springs in the vicinity were a welcome respite for weary travelers on the Oregon Trail.

Follow US 30 west through Soda Springs. Just outside of town is a corridor of trees and shrubs that look slightly out of place. The vegetation here, including limber pines, is typical of an elevation several thousand feet higher. The natural gap between ranges of hills to the west at Soda Point funnels the wind, making this one of the windiest spots in an already windy area. It is so cold that this area has its own micro-climate, quite different from the rest of the surrounding area.

For the emigrants of the mid-1800s, Steamboat Springs was one of the most famous features here. This spring, which made a steady huffing sound, is now covered by the waters of Alexander Reservoir. On a calm day you may be able to see the springs' bubbles from the shore by the picnic pavilion on the reservoir's western end. The spring, along with wagon ruts from the historic Oregon Trail, is also visible from the golf course that spreads along the reservoir's northern shore.

The rest of this drive follows the Pioneer Historic Byway, which is part of a statewide series of historic and scenic drives whose routes are clearly marked with distinctive signs.

From Soda Springs, continue west on US 30 to its junction with ID 34, where you will need to make a decision before you turn south. If time permits, you can follow US 30 west about 20 miles for a refreshing soak in the outdoor hot pools at the town of Lava Hot Springs. The springs here well up from the base of a cliff at the east end of town, and the pools, which range in temperature from 102 degrees F to 110 degrees F, are open year round. Or, in season, swim in the Olympic-sized swimming pool at the west end of town. Both facilities are operated by the State of Idaho, and the entrance fees are nominal. Afterward, take a stroll through the sunken gardens hidden just east of the hot pools, behind a small roadside picnic park between the highway and Main Street. After your swim, return east on US 30 to its junction with ID 34 and turn right to return to the drive.

This stretch of ID 34 is surrounded by the Gem Valley. To the west is the Portneuf Range and to the east, the Bear River Range. Much of this valley is irrigated with water from the Last Chance Canal, so named because of the pressure on citizens to perfect a claim on Bear River water before a court-imposed deadline. Just north of the town of Grace you can see the Last Chance Canal. Turn left at the sign just past milepost 47. Follow this road for about a mile to a small overlook, where a tunnel carrying Bear River water exits to a steel flume high above the Bear River. An interpretative sign explains that the tunnel solved some problems the canal company had with its wooden flumes. The 1,800-foot tunnel was dug by hand through solid basalt. Two brothers did the bulk of the work, starting from opposite ends and meeting less than one foot out of alignment. The tunnel is 12 feet high and 9 feet wide. The steel flume passes over a concrete arch that originally supported a wooden flume, also visible from this point. Debris from the old flume can be seen on the slope across the river.

Return to ID 34 and turn left. Heading south again, you will notice that the cultivated fields contain patches of volcanic rock. These outcroppings provide a constant reminder of the geological forces that shaped this region. Just before milepost 42 is an even more dramatic reminder of this land's volcanic ancestry. Turn left at the small sign for the Niter Ice Cave. Drive about 200 yards and park at the small parking lot. A lava flow from the knoll just west of the highway poured across this section of the valley. A lava tube was formed when hot lava continued to flow through a tube whose outer edges had hardened. Here a portion of the tube collapsed, opening a cave that extends almost three-eighths of a mile under the cultivated fields. Bring a flashlight with spare batteries. For any prolonged exploring, you'll want a jacket, too, since this type of cave remains cold year-round. Be very careful while exploring the cave. The floor has a thin layer of mud and icy water that can be very slippery. Notice the refreshing lack of commercialism at the site.

Back on ID 34, the road swings away from the Bear River at milepost 29 and begins a climb through some dramatic rock cuts. After passing Treasureton Reservoir, it drops into the Cache Valley and returns, 13 miles later, to the river. Here the loop is completed, rejoining ID 36. Continue south to the junction with US 91. Turn left to Preston.

The Cache Valley was, at one time, on the floor of Lake Bonneville. At Red Rock Pass, about 20 miles north of Preston on US 91, the giant lake's outlet—through the pass—carried water over a very resistant rock layer. Some 15,000 years ago this water carved through the hard rock into softer layers below, quickly opening a deeper channel through the pass. Just as in a dam break, more water moved through the opening, carving it even deeper, allowing even more water to pass through to the valley floor beyond. By the time the outlet had drained the larger lake, the shoreline was some 300 feet lower, the elevation of the valley floor at Red Rock Pass.

The town of Preston started out with the unflattering name of Worm Creek. Fortunately, it was quickly changed to honor Mormon bishop William Preston. Hay and cattle were the economic mainstays of the town, which was located on the Utah Northern rail line. Near here is the site of one of the most unfortunate episodes in the settlement of the West.

Just off US 91 about 4 miles north of Preston, a band of Northern Shoshone had settled in for the winter of 1862–1863. Colonel Patrick Connor and the Third California Infantry, assigned to protect the mail route through Utah, came north to deal with the skirmishes between this band of Northern Shoshone and the valley's Mormon settlers. The colonel and his men had requested orders to serve on the fronts of the Civil War. Having been denied their request, they were itching to fight. Coming upon the Shoshone camp in extreme cold and deep snow, they were met by taunts from the encampment. The warriors are said to have yelled in English "Come and get it, you California sons of bitches; we're ready for you!" This proved too much for the soldiers to take, and they attacked.

The battle lasted four hours, and the Shoshone were soundly defeated, caught in murderous crossfire as they tried to escape. Connor lost but 22 men, while an estimated 400 men, women, and children of the Shoshone tribe were killed. The carnage was worse by far than at later battles at Sand Creek in Colorado and Wounded Knee in South Dakota. The post office at

Preston houses a mural depicting the battle, painted by Elmon Fitzgerald. The mural contains some glaring inconsistencies, most notably the lack of clothing on the Shoshones, despite the bitter cold weather that January.

Franklin, where this drive began, is just a few miles south of Preston on US 91.

2

Grays Lake to Bear Lake

General description: This 115-mile drive passes through the quiet southeastern corner of the state. All travel is on two-lane paved roads, except for side trips to visit a pair of wildlife refuges. Pastoral landscapes and massive lava flows are both present for significant portions of the route. This drive follows a section of the historic Oregon Trail and explores the Mormon influence on the region's early settlement.

Special attractions: Grays Lake National Wildlife Refuge; a captive geyser at Soda Springs; Montpelier's Oregon Trail Museum; Bear Lake National Wildlife Refuge; the Paris Stake Tabernacle; Minnetonka Cave, and turquoise-blue Bear Lake.

Location: The southeastern corner of Idaho.

Drive route numbers: Idaho Highway 34, U.S. Highways 30 and 89.

Travel season: These are all-weather roads, but heavy winter snows can make driving hazardous. ID 34 is not heavily traveled, and help may not be readily available in case of problems. Wildlife viewing opportunities abound during spring, summer, and fall months.

Camping: The marina at Blackfoot Reservoir has camping and RV sites, as does Bear Lake State Park's East Beach Unit. Caribou National Forest campgrounds are located on ID 34 east of Wayan. Cache National Forest campgrounds are located west of Paris and St. Charles, off US 89.

Services: Food and lodging is available at Soda Springs, Montpelier, and Fish Haven.

Nearby attractions: Fishing on Blackfoot Reservoir and Bear Lake; Minnetonka Cave; hot springs pools at the town of Lava Hot Springs; scenic Logan Canyon on US 89 in Utah.

The Drive

This drive begins on ID 34 at the Wyoming border, just west of the little town of Freedom, Wyoming. This town nestles against a range of mountains on the east side of the narrow Star Valley, with the bucolic Salt River flowing through it. Just inside Idaho, you will come to a marker at milepost 112 describing the Pioneer Historic Byway, which portions of this drive follow. ID 34 climbs over Old Man Ridge on the western edge of the Star Valley and enters Caribou National Forest after 2 miles. Follow Tincup Creek, which flows alongside the road, watching it shrink before your eyes as the road climbs the valley. At milepost 105, look for a lively little waterfall on a tributary that flows down from the south.

Shortly after Tincup Creek turns away from the road, an unmarked turn to the left (south) off ID 34 leads to several remnants of the Lander Cutoff of the Oregon Trail. The Lander Cutoff was funded by the U. S. Congress in 1857 as a wagon road, and ultimately as a railroad right-of-way to aid in the settlement of the West. The completion of the transcontinental railroad line farther south across Utah in the 1860s quickly caused the use of the Lander Road to decline.

To explore traces of the old trail, turn left here, onto Lanes Creek Road (Forest Road 095). Deep in the aspen forests south of here emigrants carved their initials and dates in old-growth aspen trees; the carvings can still be seen. The grave of J.W. Lane, an emigrant who died near here in 1859 while making the long journey west to Oregon, is also near here, close to the intersection of FR 095 and Poison Creek Road (FR 107). South and east of here (but not accessible from this point) is the site of the former Oneida Salt Works. From this remote location workers shipped as many as 100,000 pounds of salt per year to Montana and the Pacific Northwest over the Lander Road. The dirt roads off ID 34 are narrow, rough, and winding, so exercise caution if you leave the highway.

ID 34 continues its slow climb as the road rides up and over the south flank of Caribou Mountain and then down to the meadows at Wayan. Near milepost 92 turn right at Grays Lake Road and travel 3 miles north to the small visitor center at Grays Lake National Wildlife Refuge.

A handful of rare and endangered whooping cranes makes Grays Lake their summer home. At 5 feet high, whooping cranes are the tallest birds in North America; they have a wingspan of almost 7 feet. The refuge is also home to a large population of greater sandhill cranes, some 200 nesting pairs. Both whooping cranes and sandhill cranes are very distinctive in appearance. Whoopers sport black wing tips at the end of large white wings, while sandhill cranes are a rich, reddish-brown color and stand almost as tall as the whoopers.

The sandhill cranes took on the role of foster parents for whooper chicks in an experiment that began in 1975. The U.S. Fish and Wildlife Service and its Canadian equivalent began work that year to establish a second viable breeding colony of whooping cranes. At that time the only other colony, which winters at the Aransas National Wildlife Refuge on the Texas coast, numbered fewer than 30 birds. Now that colony has grown to about 160 birds. The Aransas colony migrates 2,500 miles, spending its summers at Wood Buffalo National Park in Canada's Northwest Territory. The cranes at Grays Lake winter in New Mexico at the Bosque del Apache National Wildlife Refuge near Socorro, making a shorter and safer trip of

Drive 2: Grays Lake to Bear Lake

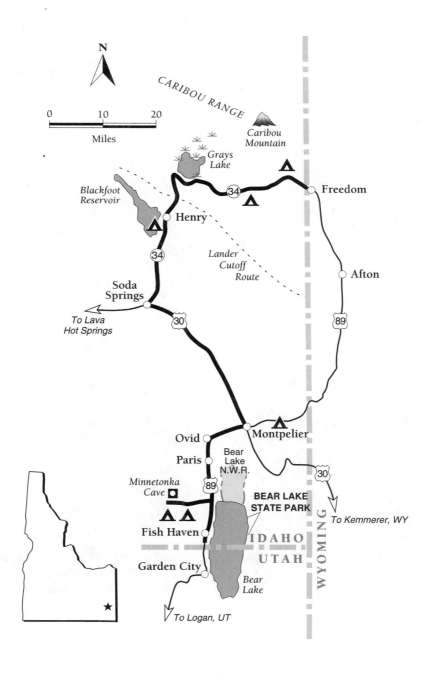

Paris Stake Tabernacle is one of the most beautiful buildings in southeastern Idaho.

only 800 miles each spring and fall.

Only about 300 whooping cranes remain in the world today, so if you are fortunate enough to see one, count yourself lucky. The foster parent program has not succeeded as well as officials had hoped, and wildlife biologists are now pursuing other methods of saving the whooping crane.

In addition to cranes, Grays Lake sustains an abundance of other waterfowl and wildlife, including mule deer, elk, and moose. If you have time, you can drive completely around the refuge on dirt and gravel roads. The loop is about 25 miles. Looming over the lake, which is more marsh than open water, is 9,803-foot Caribou Mountain. There are not now, nor were there ever, caribou in this area. The name comes from an early miner in the area named "Cariboo Jack" Fairchild. Jack was a larger-than-life character who had a reputation for spinning tall tales about his days in Canada. Fairchild finally met his match trying to subdue a wounded grizzly bear that had been terrorizing the area.

Return to ID 34 from the refuge and turn right (west). The road joins a section of the Lander Cutoff of the Oregon Trail, and parallels the pioneer trail for about 3 miles as it skirts the southern edge of Grays Lake National Wildlife Refuge. The road turns sharply south around the toe of a lava field at milepost 85. The emigrant trail continues almost due west, crossing the Blackfoot River below the site of the dam on the Blackfoot Reservoir, which is visible from the highway. The Lander Cutoff rejoins the main Oregon Trail a few miles east of Fort Hall, some 35 miles west of the Blackfoot River crossing.

The Lander Cutoff began in Wyoming at South Pass, detouring north of the main Oregon Trail to avoid 50 miles of harsh alkali desert between South Pass and Green River, Wyoming. During its heaviest use, in the late 1850s, more than 13,000 emigrants per year traveled this route, most headed to California.

Continue south through the settlement of Henry. The large cliff visible on your left, with silvery sagebrush growing in crevices and at its base, is a lava flow. Geologists think that the lava here flowed from a series of fissures aligned along a fault some 600,000 years ago, give or take a few hundred thousand years.

Henry is the home of the Chester Store, a local landmark. This general store has maintained trade in this building since 1892. Not much has changed over the years: you can still warm yourself at the pot-bellied stove, buy a cold drink or a sandwich, and get information on fishing and hunting in the area.

As you leave the reservoir to follow the Blackfoot River south on ID 34, some of Idaho's famous potato fields come into view. Note the patches of volcanic rock that intrude into almost every field. At milepost 63, east of the road, is the base of a mountain of phosphate ore that is slowly being consumed by giant shovels. Huge trucks carry the ore down a private road, crossing ID 34 at the giant Monsanto plant just north of Soda Springs. Forty percent of the country's phosphate reserves are located in this corner of Idaho. Phosphoric acid and elemental phosphorus, the end products of the processing plants, are used in fertilizer, toothpaste, matches, fireworks, soft drinks, and automobile tires.

Turn right just past the Monsanto plant, at Hooper Road. After a mile, you'll come to Hooper Springs Park, one of Soda Springs' city parks. The spring itself wells up cool and clear under a canopy of stone and wood. Early fur trappers and emigrants on the Oregon Trail knew this as the Beer Spring, so-called because of the distinctive taste of its water. While you picnic here, watch for the man-made lava flows from the phosphate plant. Workers dump molten calcium silicate slag onto the growing hills of gray, barren rock every 12 to 15 minutes, 24 hours a day.

From Hooper Springs continue 2 miles south over the railroad tracks and turn right onto US 30 and into Soda Springs, with its "tame" geyser. Municipal workers accidentally uncorked the geyser in 1937 while drilling a well to supply a municipal swimming pool. Unlike Old Faithful, the famous natural geyser in Yellowstone National Park, this geyser spews cool water, and the force is not steam, but carbon dioxide—the same gas that fizzes a soft drink. The travertine terraces around the base of the geyser are a result of the minerals in the water precipitating out of solution as the pressure is relieved. The Soda Springs area was the long-time home of a frontier woman called Six Gun Sal, supposed to have been a girlfriend of Butch Cassidy. Townspeople remember her riding in the annual Fourth of July parade up until the 1950s.

When the wind blows from the west, the city turns off the geyser so that mineral deposits do not build up on buildings and cars along Main Street. In the summer the geyser is set to erupt every half hour during daylight hours, and, in the off-season, every hour. It's on a timer, just like the ones used with sprinkler systems.

Two blocks from the geyser is Corrigan Park, which displays the Dinky Engine and the Galloping Goose—two unique rail conveyances that played important roles in local history. The miniature locomotive known as the Dinky Engine helped build Alexander Reservoir, west of Soda Springs. The engine was trapped by the rising water when the reservoir was filled in 1924 and remained underwater until 1976, when the Union Pacific Railroad recovered and restored it. The Galloping Goose, an awkward combination of streetcar, bus, and locomotive, was the only means of transportation between Soda Springs and the mining town of Conda between 1922 and 1936.

Soda Springs was an important milestone to the emigrants who came

*Hooper Spring was known to the Oregon Trail pioneers as Beer Spring,
for its peculiar taste.*

west on the Oregon Trail. It represented the end of a long stretch of tough climbs through narrow canyons and over steep hills. Soda Springs offered a chance to relax and drink from the refreshing springs. Travelers could also decide whether to veer south and head for California or to stay with the main trail to Oregon City. On the golf course west of town, foot-deep ruts from wagons traveling the Oregon Trail are still visible. Just west of Soda Springs, where the Bear River turns south, Hudspeth's Cutoff struck off to join the California Trail. Those who chose to continue to California were only about two days away from Lava Hot Springs.

Leave the center of Soda Springs and turn left onto US 30 eastbound. The road makes a short climb to Georgetown Summit before descending into Bear Lake Valley. The county seat and one of the oldest towns in Idaho, Montpelier, is 15 miles ahead. Settlers heeded the suggestion of Brigham Young, and named the town Montpelier for the capital of Vermont, where Young had been born. Montpelier is a quiet town, whose chief claim to fame is that Butch Cassidy robbed the local bank of more than $7,000 in August 1896. The town is home to the recently opened Oregon Trail Museum, at the intersection of US 89 and US 30.

To continue the scenic drive, turn right onto US 89 from US 30 and drive through downtown Montpelier. Head west across the flat pastureland of the Bear River floodplain. Bear Lake sits at the south end of this placid valley, but the Bear River does not naturally drain the lake. The river's headwaters are in the Uinta Mountains of eastern Utah, and it passes through Evanston, Wyoming, winding back and forth between Utah and Wyoming before it comes into this valley from the east. Once here, the Bear heads north through Soda Springs, makes an abrupt turnaround west of town and heads south again, ultimately emptying into the Great Salt Lake. A pumping station and canal complicate the system, linking Bear Lake, the Bear River, and Mud Lake, just north of Bear Lake. The water project holds excess Bear River water in the lake and in the marshes just north of it. A side benefit of the water project was the creation of vital habitat for migratory waterfowl, protected in the Bear Lake National Wildlife Refuge.

At Ovid, about 4 miles from Montpelier, follow the road as it bends south. After 3 miles, at the northern end of Paris, turn left on Dingle Bottoms Road for access to the Bear Lake National Wildlife Refuge. This area shelters as many as 5,000 white-faced ibis each spring, as well as many other waterfowl, including redhead and canvasback ducks. Sandhill cranes and other species that nest in bulrushes are also seen in large numbers. Mule deer, an occasional moose, coyotes, and other small mammals also frequent the refuge.

Return to US 89 via Dingle Bottoms Road to enter the town of Paris. Early Mormon emigrants settled here with the permission of the Shoshone chief Washakie. A surveyor named Frederick Perris laid out the townsite. Perris's name was ultimately given to the town, with a change of spelling.

The main attraction here is the Paris Stake Tabernacle, which dominates the center of town. Settlers quarried the stone for the tabernacle on the east side of Bear Lake and sledded it across during the winter when the lake was frozen solid. The tabernacle is open for tours in the summer. Stop and look at the two chimneys at the back of the tabernacle for a quick lesson in craftsmanship. One chimney is made of the same stone as the rest of the building, while the second chimney, added later, is of brick, and nowhere near as graceful as the rest of the structure.

Inside, the woodwork is fashioned from the region's readily available pine and fir. It has been exquisitely finished and, like the stonework outside, shows some masterful craftsmanship. The carpenter who built the tabernacle's interior was a trained shipwright from England, and the interior resembles the hull of a great sailing ship turned upside down.

At milepost 9, 6 miles south of Paris on US 89, is the turn to Minnetonka Cave. The cave is 10 miles up into the Bear River Mountains, to the west on St. Charles Creek Road. The USDA Forest Service administers the cave, and

The carbon dioxide geyser at Soda Springs spouts on a schedule.

a concessionaire gives guided tours from mid-June until Labor Day. There is a small fee for access to the cave. Unlike most of Idaho's other caves, which are volcanic in origin, this is a limestone cave, filled with stalactites, stalagmites, and other calcite formations. Damp and cold, the cave maintains a year-round temperature of 40 degrees F, so bring a jacket and sturdy shoes if you plan to do any caving. Check in Paris to verify that the cave is open before you make the drive.

After visiting the cave, return to US 89. Immediately after you turn onto US 89, on your left you will see a turn for Bear Lake State Park's North Beach. This side road skirts the southern edge of the wildlife refuge. The state park offers two beaches, one on the northern end of the lake, east of the pumping station, and the other about 6 miles farther on the eastern shore.

Back on US 89 sits the town of St. Charles, the birthplace of Gutzom Borglum, the sculptor of the presidential heads at Mount Rushmore in South Dakota. A marker commemorating Borglum's birth is located on the west side of the highway, on the grounds of St. Charles Tabernacle.

U.S. 89 skirts the western shore of Bear Lake for the next few miles. The lake's waters are a brilliant turquoise at the edges, gradually darkening toward the middle of the lake. Geologists say there is no specific reason for the spectacular color, other than the abundance of white sand and the plant life that grows in the lake. White pelicans patrol the reedy shorelines for small bait fish. The lake is also home to the Bonneville cisco, a small fish found nowhere else in the world. The sardine-like cisco is the target of ice fishers, who haul away large catches of the 7-inch fish each winter. Legends of a sea serpent in the waters of Bear Lake enliven evenings during the long, cold winters.

The drive ends here, after skirting the shore of Bear Lake and passing the neat, manicured summer homes at Fish Haven. The perfect end to this drive is a refreshing raspberry milkshake in Garden City, just over the Utah border. Choose carefully, as each and every restaurant and shop in town boasts that it is famous for its shakes. It's up to you to decide which one really is best.

3

Palisades Reservoir to Henrys Lake

General description: A pleasant, 170-mile journey through forested hills and vast fields of potatoes, with the scenic backdrop of the Tetons as accompaniment. The drive follows portions of two National Forest Scenic Byways, with spectacular waterfalls on its northern reach.

Special attractions: Palisades Reservoir; the charming Old West town of Victor; Grand Targhee Ski Area; scenic views of the "back side" of the Tetons; two powerful waterfalls and a giant natural spring on the Henrys Fork River; and Harriman State Park.

Location: Along the state's far eastern border with Wyoming.

Drive route numbers: U.S. Highways 26 and 20, Idaho Highways 31, 33, 32, and 47.

Travel season: Best times to travel are late spring through fall. Heavy snows in winter and early spring can cause hazardous driving conditions, particularly on Pine Creek Pass. The Mesa Falls section of the drive may be closed because of heavy snow at times during the winter months. Mid-September is a good time to see the changing colors of the aspens between Palisades Reservoir and Victor.

Camping: Camping is available in Targhee National Forest campgrounds at Palisades Reservoir, along ID 31 near Mesa Falls at Harriman State Park, and at Henrys Lake State Park. Private campgrounds and RV parks are located at Palisades Reservoir, Victor, Driggs, and Island Park.

Services: Motels and restaurants are available at Alpine, Wyoming, and at Victor, Driggs, Ashton, and Island Park in Idaho.

Nearby attractions: Fly fishing on the Railroad Ranch stretches of the Henrys Fork; Jackson Hole, Wyoming, just over Teton Pass east of Victor; Yellowstone National Park, less than 15 miles from Henrys Lake on US 20.

 The Drive

This drive is a good way to see what's on the "back side" of the Tetons, in conjunction with a visit to Grand Teton and Yellowstone national parks. Beginning a few miles inside Wyoming, the drive offers a variety of landscapes, from a mountain pass, to some of Idaho's rich agricultural areas, to an ancient volcanic caldera, complete with waterfalls and natural springs. The drive ends just south of the Montana border near West Yellowstone, Montana.

Drive 3: Palisades Reservoir to Henrys Lake

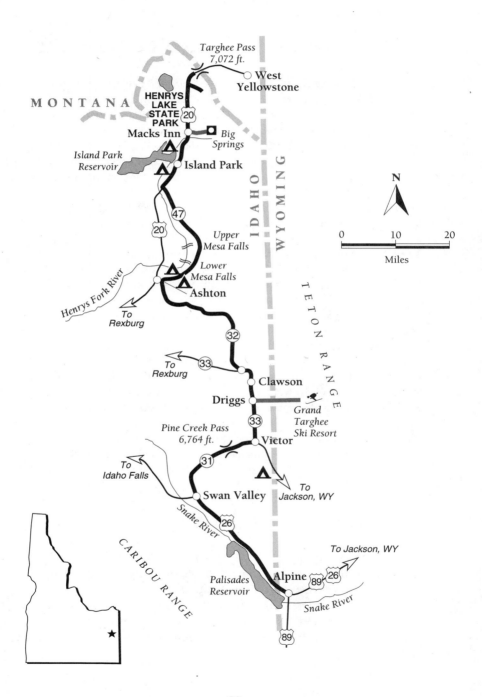

Begin on US 26 at Alpine, Wyoming, 37 miles southwest of Jackson, Wyoming. Alpine sits near the point where the Snake and Salt rivers empty into Palisades Reservoir. This small town consists of little more than tourist accommodations and fishing tackle shops. Head northwest on US 26; you'll cross into Idaho after just 2 miles.

When demands for irrigation water are low, Palisades Reservoir fills up and creeps back across the Idaho border into Wyoming. Both the Snake River and the Salt River feed the reservoir, which is part of the Minidoka water project. Minidoka's collection of reservoirs irrigates 1.1 million acres on more than 19,000 Idaho farms. As you travel along the shore of the reservoir, look for wildlife. Eagles, ospreys, and hawks are all frequently spotted here, as are moose, elk, deer, and coyotes. Bears, mountain lions, bobcats, and foxes are also common in the hills, although they are rarely seen by visitors.

The Palisades Dam is 15 miles into Idaho. The water behind this earthen dam is used to generate electricity before it is released for irrigation downstream. Pelicans cruise the tailwaters below the dam looking for fish. There is a pleasant picnic area at the base of the dam, and daytime tours of the power plant are available.

Continue on US 26 through the very small towns of Palisades, Irwin, and Swan Valley. Just past Swan Valley, turn right off US 26 and onto ID 31. This route is also designated the Teton Scenic Byway. The road begins a slow, gradual climb through highland pastures and some irrigated fields toward Pine Creek Pass. Look for llamas on a well-kept piece of property near the Targhee National Forest boundary. About 3 miles above the mouth of the North Fork of Pine Creek, the road begins a serious 1-mile climb to the summit of the pass (elevation 6,720 feet).

From the summit, the road very quickly descends 500 feet into the southern end of the Teton Valley, or as it was known to fur trappers, Pierre's Hole. Victor is the small town at the junction of highways ID 31 and ID 33. Victor is just 20 miles from the resort town of Jackson, Wyoming, over the 10 per cent grade of Teton Pass to the southeast. Early visitors to Jackson left their train here in Victor, the closest railroad access to the Jackson Hole region. The proximity to Jackson Hole is apparent in the slightly upscale restaurants and shops in town, including a restaurant in an old bank vault.

Turn left onto ID 33, which travels north from Victor in a perfectly straight line through the towns of Driggs and Clawson. The Teton River, which begins in the hills surrounding Victor and meanders north through marshes and pastures for more than 25 miles, flows over this flat valley floor. Finally, the river turns west and becomes the boundary separating Teton County and Fremont County to the north. The low range to the west, across the valley, is the Big Hole Mountains. To the right, the western foothills of the Tetons dominate the landscape.

Driggs is 7 miles north of Victor, and is the commercial center of the valley, as well as the valley's center of outdoor activity. Ski shop owners supplement their summer incomes with kayak and mountain-bike rentals. With a population of 850, Driggs is also the largest community in Teton County, and the county seat. A monument to John Colter, an early explorer who accompanied Lewis and Clark and later explored Yellowstone country, stands in front of the courthouse. A museum is housed in the American Legion hall just behind it.

Small museums in Idaho, as in other parts of the country, operate almost entirely through volunteer help, and therefore have somewhat limited hours of operation. Even during posted hours, the doors may be locked. But if you can get into these small museums, they are, without exception, charming collections of local memorabilia.

From Driggs, a 12-mile side trip east from the center of town leads to Grand Targhee Ski Resort, located high on the western slope of Wyoming's Teton Range. This side trip takes you 5 miles east to Alta, Wyoming, then another 7 miles up Teton Canyon to the ski resort, which is renowned for the prodigious quantities of snow it receives. Even though the resort is in Wyoming, the only access is through Idaho, so almost all of the cars in the parking lot have Idaho license plates. Summer season offers bluegrass music festivals and chairlift rides to the top of the mountain, where the views extend north to Sawtell Peak and into Montana, south along the spine of the Tetons, and west across Pierre's Hole.

After returning to Driggs, continue north on ID 33 through Clawson. Look back over your right shoulder at the craggy forms of the Teton spires making their appearance over the low foothills. The Tetons were named by early French fur trappers who viewed the peaks from this vicinity. Lonely after many months away from home, they were struck by the peaks' resemblance to the female breast.

The road makes a 90-degree turn left, then another to the right, and passes through Tetonia. About a mile after one more left turn, leave ID 33 and turn right onto ID 32, heading north again. Pass through Felt, a "wide spot" in the road, and enter a stretch of road that will make you wish you were in a two-seat roadster. The road climbs, dips, swoops, and twists all the way to Drummond, 16 miles ahead. Little groves of trees have been preserved in the fields, creating lush oases in the midst of neat farm crops. At Drummond, the road ceases weaving and straightens up, like kids stepping into church.

Continue to ID 32's intersection with ID 47, just east of Ashton. For fuel or a bite to eat, turn left into town. No other commercial facilities are available until ID 47 ends at US 20 at Island Park, another 25 miles.

Upper Mesa Falls.

Once you have filled your tank, backtrack along Ashton's main street and continue east on ID 47. This section of the drive is also identified as the Mesa Falls Scenic Byway. Six miles from Ashton, at an intersection with Cave Falls Road, also known as the Marysville Road, you can enjoy a side trip into the little-visited southwest corner of Yellowstone National Park. The Falls River, which the road crossed earlier, north of Drummond, begins in Yellowstone and tumbles over Cave Falls, 19 miles from here.

The main drive continues straight ahead on ID 47, and 3 miles later meets the Henrys Fork River, where Robinson Creek and Warm River enter it. The road crosses the river and climbs back into Targhee National Forest, with the Henrys Fork on the left of the road and the Warm River on the right. An overlook 2 miles farther provides a last glimpse of the Tetons to the south, just before Lower Mesa Falls. Turn left into the Lower Mesa Falls parking lot. From the parking lot, a short walk leads to a view of the falls in the distance below. It's a pretty sight, but a bit disappointing because of the distance to the falls. Upper Mesa Falls, another mile up ID 47, makes up for that, however. Turn left again from ID 47, into another, larger parking lot, 50 yards from the road.

The trail to the upper falls is a bit longer, and has a number of steps as you get close to the brink of the falls. Notice the basalt cliffs carved by the river over the centuries. The nicely finished walkways, with railings all along the water's edge, will make even the most squeamish visitors feel comfortable. The overlook is right on the lip of the falls, allowing the spray to envelop you in a cool mist. On sunny days, this is a great place to find a rainbow.

After leaving the parking lot, the road travels 12 miles through patches of open ground and logged lodgepole pine forest, until finally it bursts onto the sage-covered plain near its intersection with US 20. Prior to the construction of US 20, this scenic route served as the main highway to Yellowstone Park from eastern Idaho.

The land across US 20, behind the classic western buck fence, is part of Harriman State Park. The park was once part of the Railroad Ranch, so named because it was originally owned by the owners of the Oregon Short Line Railroad. Acquired early this century by E. H. Harriman, president of the Union Pacific Railroad, it remained in the Harriman family until 1977, when it was deeded to the state of Idaho.

The gift came with the provision that the welfare of the area's wildlife be the primary management consideration. That wildlife includes elk, deer, moose, greater sandhill cranes, and rare trumpeter swans, which nest on the park's lakes. One-third of the Rocky Mountains' trumpeter swan population winters in the park. In late summer, the vicious mosquitoes and biting flies might also be classified as wildlife.

ID 47 ends here at a T intersection with US 20. Turn right onto US 20 and enter Island Park. Within the next 30 miles, signs announce Last Chance, Island Park, and Macks Inn town limits, but the length of US 20 to Henrys Lake is dotted with scattered cabins, summer homes, and assorted small businesses.

Just before Macks Inn, there is the chance for one last side trip. Look for the Big Springs sign, and turn right before the bridge across the Henrys Fork. This is Forest Road 059. After 4.5 miles you will come to Big Springs itself, where the Henrys Fork of the Snake wells up out of the ground at the base of a basalt hillside. Clear and cold, the river begins full-grown, flowing from one of the world's largest natural springs into a sparkling pond. Where the road crosses the river, fat, well-fed trout feed on morsels thrown to them by visitors. Across the small spring pond sits the old cabin of John Sack. This hermit-like Swiss pioneer built the house by hand and developed this property, tucked between the cliff and the spring's water. Notice the small waterwheel he used to convey water to the house.

Double back on FR 059, turn right onto US 20, and head north again. The wide marshy meadow to the right is home to sandhill cranes and migratory waterfowl. The marsh is fed by Henrys Lake, nestled at the base of Black Mountain, ahead on the left. The crest of the Continental Divide, which is also the Montana state border, looms on three sides here. The drive ends 6 miles farther on, at the intersection of US 20 and ID 87. On US 20, West Yellowstone, Montana, is 14 miles from the intersection.

4

Rexburg To Island Park

General description: This 165-mile drive takes in an eclectic mix of sand dunes, lava and sagebrush, agricultural land, wildlife refuges, and forests as it passes through the sparsely settled lands between Rexburg and the Idaho-Montana border.

Special attractions: Teton Flood Museum in the college town of Rexburg; the St. Anthony Sand Dunes; Mud Lake Wildlife Management Area and Camas National Wildlife Refuge; the opal mines at Spencer; and a portion of the historic Nez Perce Trail.

Location: Eastern Idaho, along Interstate 15 north of Pocatello towards the Montana border.

Drive route numbers: Idaho Highway 33, U.S. Highway 20, West Fourth North (North Parker Road), 1900 East (Red Road or Salem-Parker Highway), local roads around the wildlife refuges, Interstate 15, Idmon Road, Clark County Road A2, Fremont County Road A2.

Travel season: Late spring, summer, and fall are the best times to take this drive, as heavy winter snows may make winter driving hazardous. The portion between Spencer and Island Park may be closed until late May or June because of lingering winter snows.

Camping: Targhee National Forest campgrounds at Island Park Reservoir.

Services: Rexburg and St. Anthony offer all tourist services. Fuel is available at Rexburg, St. Anthony, Dubois, Spencer, and Island Park.

Nearby attractions: Site of Teton Dam disaster; Kelly Canyon Ski Area; Heise Hot Springs; Yellowstone National Park; Harriman State Park; world-class fly fishing on the Henrys Fork River.

The Drive

The northeastern section of Idaho is a sparsely populated agricultural region. This drive begins at Rexburg, one of its earliest settlements, visits some of the nation's largest sand dunes, and travels across the volcanic plain before turning north through a pair of wildlife preserves. The drive concludes with a hunt for gem-quality opals and a drive along the Nez Perce Trail into the Island Park area west of Yellowstone Park.

Rexburg, a quiet town of about 15,000 people, is located in a lush, agricultural setting in eastern Idaho. After Pocatello and Idaho Falls, it is the largest town in eastern Idaho. Potatoes and sugar beets are the area's predominant crops. Rexburg is the home of Ricks College, a two-year college affiliated with the Church of Jesus Christ of Latter-day Saints. The college was established by Thomas Ricks, one of the town's founders and the inspiration for the town's name, a Latinized version of his last name. From US 20, exit onto Main Street, which is also ID 33, and head east into town. Turn left (north) on Center Street and proceed to the Teton Flood Museum, housed in the basement of the old Fremont Stake Tabernacle.

Just north of the museum, in front of the library, is a memorial of green stones. The stones are all that is left of the old library, which was destroyed, along with many other buildings in the Rexburg area, when Teton Dam collapsed on the morning of June 5, 1976.

The museum is open weekdays during the summer. It contains a collection of pioneer artifacts and photographs, as well as a detailed chronology of the events surrounding the dam break. Vials of mud, news photos of the damage and geological cross-sections tell the tale quite clearly. Notice the water marks on the wall as you enter the museum. They provide an idea of the depth of the flood at its peak.

Teton Dam, built of earth fill, was a project of the U.S. Army Corps of Engineers. When the dam failed, the reservoir behind it was, for the first time, nearly full. Early on the morning of the disaster, engineers noticed erosion around a small pipe set into the dam, and frantically began work to repair the small breach. As the morning wore on, the water leaking through the dam got the upper hand, swallowing earth-moving equipment brought up to patch the dam. When the dam finally broke, the 280-foot-deep reservoir emptied rapidly, and the floodwaters headed for Sugar City and Rexburg, 10 miles downstream. Houses washed away; roads, croplands, and livestock were destroyed; and 14 lives were lost. The floodwaters flowed into the Henrys Fork and then into the Snake River; they were finally contained by American Falls Reservoir, 100 miles away.

From the museum head east to East Second North and turn left onto ID 33. After 2 miles you will come to Sugar City, an agricultural center of less than 1,300 people. A historic marker describes the site of Fort Henry, which was 6 miles west of here.

For a short side trip to Teton Dam, follow ID 33 east 10 miles from Sugar City. At milepost 110, turn left at the sign for the dam. Continue north 1.5 miles to a parking lot and overlook. The center section of the dam remains intact. The flood broke through the left side. Notice the spillway structure that remains. The dam's right side was excavated in an attempt to determine the cause of the failure.

Return to ID 33 and turn right (west). Turn right on US 20, which is four-lane divided highway from here into St. Anthony. Pass the first St.

Drive 4: Rexburg to Island Park

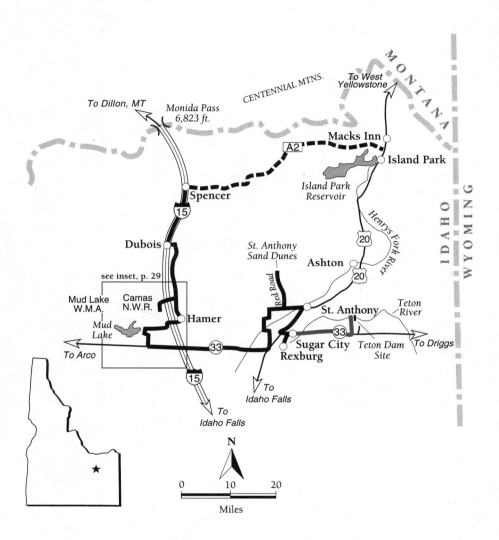

Anthony exit and leave the highway at milepost 345 on the north end of St. Anthony. Turn left and take West Fourth North, following signs to the St. Anthony Sand Dunes. When the road bends left toward the settlement of Parker, bear straight ahead. Turn right on 1900 East, also known as Red Road. You will climb a rise into the dunes. Orange flags on dune buggies and all-terrain vehicles will catch your eye as you continue. The top of the

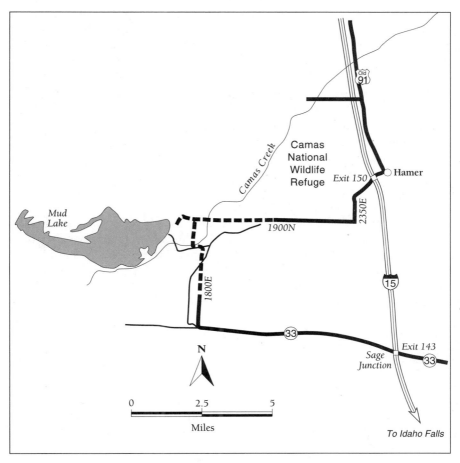

See map on page 28.

ridge is the end of dune access on paved roads, but unimproved roads branch off left and right, providing access to more dunes. Obtain a map locally for any extensive exploration in the dunes.

The Bureau of Land Management administers the area's recreation resources, allowing dune access to all sorts of off-road vehicles. There is no real destination in the dunes, so just explore, climb, slide and roll wherever you'd like.

To continue the main drive, return to Red Road and head south. Continue south past the previous turn, setting your sights on the water tower on the horizon in Rexburg. This section of the road is known as the Salem-Parker Highway. This area was the 1810 winter shelter of the party of Andrew Henry and his trappers. While trapping beaver in Montana, the

Henry party had been attacked several times by Blackfeet warriors. As a result, the party was forced to winter here. It was a harsh winter, and the party was forced to eat their horses to survive. To add insult to injury, they brought just 40 packs of beaver pelts back to St. Louis the following spring—a meager result, considering the hardships they had endured. The Henrys Fork River is named for Andrew Henry.

After crossing a series of canals and the Henrys Fork River, the Salem-Parker Highway intersects US 20. Take US 20 south back to Rexburg and turn right again at ID 33. The two hills ahead and to the south are the Menan Buttes, a pair of volcanic cinder cones. The big letter R on the butte is for both Rexburg and Ricks College. The western tradition of decorating hillsides with giant letters tends to lose its effect when there are no closer hillsides to town than these small buttes!

ID 33 crosses the Henrys Fork again 5 miles west of US 20. Immediately ahead on the left is Beaver Dick Park. This pleasant, grassy picnic area and campground on the west bank of the Henrys Fork honors Richard Leigh, a trapper who lived in this area until 1899. Leigh had come west from England toward the end of the trapping boom. After the market for beaver hats declined, he made his living as an outfitter and guide. He accompanied the Hayden Party that surveyed Yellowstone in 1871. Leigh Lake in Grand Teton National Park is named for him, and Jenny Lake in the Tetons is named for his first wife.

As the drive continues west, it appears that civilization has been left behind. A slow climb onto a broad plateau reveals nothing but silvery green sagebrush and stark, black lava. The scenery in the 19 miles from the bank of the Henrys Fork to the town of Terreton consists of raw lava and sagebrush, broken only by a set of railroad tracks, a power line, and the intersection of I-15.

At milepost 52 turn right on 1800 East. Go north for 2 miles. Continue straight ahead, following signs to Mud Lake Wildlife Management Area. Do not turn where there is a chance to bend to the right. Instead, cross Camas Creek where the pavement ends and then turn left at 1800 North, right onto 1775 East and left again at a T intersection at 1900 North. This is the east entrance to the wildlife management area.

Mud Lake Wildlife Management Area consists of 8,853 acres of wetlands managed to preserve and improve nesting habitat for waterfowl. The lake averages only 5 feet deep and is surrounded by a mix of marshy habitats and drier sagebrush areas. Duck, geese, and the rare trumpeter swan all inhabit the refuge, and cormorants, great blue herons, and cattle egrets all nest in the trees of the refuge. Shorebirds and raptors add to the mix, and deer, elk, pronghorn antelope, and moose are frequent visitors.

Leaving Mud Lake from the east entrance, take 1900 North due east.

Island Park Reservoir.

After 3 miles the pavement resumes. At 2350 East, turn left (north), cross I-15 into the town of Hamer, and turn left onto the Old Butte Highway (formerly U.S. Highway 91) which parallels the interstate for about 3 miles before crossing it and heading west. Follow the signs for 2 miles to the Camas National Wildlife Refuge.

Camas National Wildlife Refuge is a 10,000-acre mix of lakes, ponds, marshes, sagebrush, meadows, and farm fields. As many as 100,000 ducks and 3,000 geese visit the refuge as they pass through to their summer and winter ranges. Grain grown in the surrounding fields is left to provide feed for the large numbers of migratory residents. A portion of refuge land was once used in a commercial venture to raise muskrats for their fur. Rat Farm Pond, on the refuge's east side, is a legacy of that venture.

Enter the refuge and wander the small, single-lane roads south and west of the refuge headquarters. In a single pass visitors are likely to see deer, herons, and a variety of ducks. Lucky wanderers might also see an owl or a family of foxes. Return to the I-15 crossing the way you came, and then turn left on the frontage road heading north 14 miles to Dubois, or turn right and return to Hamer, entering I-15 northbound to Dubois (17 miles). All of the land in this territory is either sage-covered lava flows or agricultural acreage. In either case, the land does not support a thriving population.

Clark County, which comprises the towns of Dubois, Spencer, and Kilgore, is home to only 800 people. It has the distinction of being the wealthiest county in Idaho when measured on a per capita basis. This shows how misleading statistics can be, since local residents will tell you that most of the county's wealth resides with just one family, the one whose name is spelled out on their grain silos on the side of the highway, and on countless other signs along I-15.

Dubois is the last good chance for fuel and food before the drive continues north to Spencer and the 50 unpopulated miles east to Island Park.

The little town of Spencer lies 13 miles north of Dubois. Spencer got its start as a railroad station on the Utah and Northern Line in 1897. The station was moved here from Beaver Canyon, a few miles farther north. Spencer today is little more than a collection of gem shops and the staging area for adventurers in search of rare opals. Just 8 miles east is an opal mine, high on a ridge formed of volcanic rhyolite rock.

The opal found at Spencer is deposited in thin layers and is usually referred to as "triplet" opal. Very thin and fragile, this opal generally is layered on a base of black stone, typically basalt, and covered with a dome of quartz.

Between Memorial Day and Labor Day visitors are welcome to try their hand at mining the beautiful gem-quality opal for a fee of about $20 per day. Insurance requirements may eventually close the open-pit mines to the public, but for now they are still open. Inquire at any shop in town for directions and information. Opal mining is dirty, wet work, so dress accordingly. Be sure to bring safety glasses and shoes, rock picks and hammers, a spray bottle, and your lunch and drinking water.

At Spencer, the drive leaves the interstate heading east, though travelers passing through on their way to Dillon or Missoula, Montana, may prefer to part company here. For those who choose to continue north, I-15 north of Spencer begins a gradual climb to the summit of Monida Pass at an elevation of 6,823 feet. The summit is 18 miles north, at the Montana border and the Continental Divide. The Bitterroot and Beaverhead mountain ranges dominate the view to the west as you approach the pass over rolling sage and grazing land. You can catch glimpses of old highway bridges spanning the stream bed and railroad tracks that cut through the lava flows near the summit.

For those who wish to continue to the end of the drive, leave I-15 at Exit 180 and enter Spencer. Turn right immediately and then left (east) across the railroad tracks onto Idmon Road. You are now heading for Kilgore on a good gravel road. The road crests a small hill in the first mile. If the weather is clear, the summits of the Tetons may be visible south and east. After 5 miles, the scars of 50 years of opal mining are visible near the top of the hillside to the north. The mines are clustered in a small area high on the south-facing slope.

East of Spencer, the terrain is dominated by sagebrush, but as the road approaches Idmon and Kilgore, pastureland takes over. Much of the plain south of here is dedicated to research conducted by the U.S. Sheep Experiment Station. Research focuses improving production of wool and lamb meat. A large herd of research animals grazes here and in the surrounding forests, and is herded to feedlots near Mud Lake in the winter.

Turn left (north) onto pavement at Clark County Road A2, 15 miles from Spencer. The settlement at this junction is called Idmon, which takes its name from the states of Idaho and Montana, as does Monida Pass. Just southeast of here, the Nez Perce fought two engagements with the U.S. Cavalry during the protracted Nez Perce War of 1877.

On the night of August 19, 1877, Chief Looking Glass, along with chiefs Toohoolhoolzote and Ollokot, led a small group of warriors on a raid of General Oliver Howard's camp. The Nez Perce were intent on stealing Howard's horses, but at first light they realized that they had come away with nothing but mules. Howard's troops pursued them as they retreated to the northeast, engaging them in another battle the next afternoon.

After 2 miles, follow the big right-hand curve, and continue east. The hamlet of Kilgore lies 1 mile to the north. A mile after the curve, the road becomes gravel again. Continue straight ahead. The road turns to the northeast and dips in and out of a forest of aspen, lodgepole pine, and ponderosa pine for the next 15 miles, passing the small Sheridan Reservoir on the right, 10 miles past Kilgore. This route is part of the Nez Perce Trail, followed by Chief Joseph, his warriors, and hundreds of women and children as they fled General Howard and the U.S. Cavalry. From here the Nez Perce passed through Yellowstone before heading north through Montana, where they ultimately surrendered two months later.

The road surface changes from gravel to pavement 45 miles from Spencer. Above and left, the white dome of the weather station on top of 9,866-foot Sawtell Peak is visible. A road climbs to the summit from Island Park.

This drive crosses the Henrys Fork River again, 3 miles after reaching the pavement, and in another 2 miles it intersects Highway 20, just north of Island Park Reservoir. The drive's starting point at Rexburg is 57 miles south of here, on US 20.

5

Idaho Falls to Craters of the Moon

General description: A 102-mile drive across lava plains on two-lane paved roads between Idaho Falls, the largest city in eastern Idaho, and Craters of the Moon National Monument on the northern edge of the Snake River plain.

Special attractions: Idaho Falls; Hell's Half Acre, a highway rest area set in an otherworldly landscape; the World Potato Expo in Blackfoot; Experimental Breeder Reactor-1 (EBR-1), the first commercially feasible nuclear reactor, located at Idaho National Engineering Laboratory (INEL); and Craters of the Moon National Monument.

Location: East-central Idaho, along the northern edge of the vast Snake River plain.

Drive route numbers: Interstate Highway 15 and Business Route 15 at Blackfoot, U.S. Highways 91, 26, 20, and 93.

Travel season: The entire drive is on all-weather U.S. highways, and is generally accessible, except during winter storms. Travel on the lava plains can be quite hot in mid-summer. Wildflower blooms peak in mid-June at Craters of the Moon.

Camping: There are private camping and RV parks at Idaho Falls, and campsites at Craters of the Moon National Monument.

Services: Idaho Falls, Blackfoot, and Arco all have motels and restaurants. There are no other services along the route.

Nearby attractions: Heise Hot Springs; Tautphaus Park Zoo in Idaho Falls; St. Anthony Sand Dunes; Kelly Canyon Ski Area; Natural Bridge located near Arco.

 The Drive

This drive starts in the heart of Idaho's potato country and ends in an eerie landscape of lava flows at the edge of the Snake River plain, the broad, flat expanse that dominates the landscape of southern Idaho. In between, the drive visits a museum dedicated to the potato and the world's first commercially operated nuclear reactor.

Begin in Idaho Falls, at the intersection of River Parkway and Broadway, on the west bank of the Snake River. The Eastern Idaho Visitor Information Center is located here, operated by knowledgeable, enthusiastic volunteers, as well as Bureau of Land Management and USDA Forest

Drive 5: Idaho Falls to Craters of the Moon

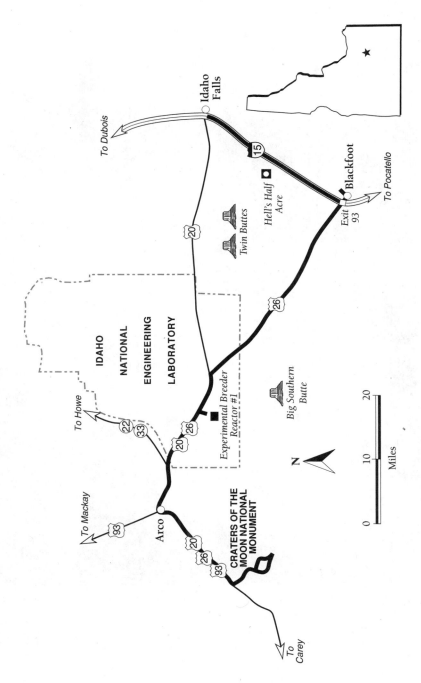

High water and spring runoff in Idaho Falls, the Idaho Falls LDS temple in background.

Service staff. The visitor center also has an extensive selection of informative brochures covering the entire state of Idaho.

Just outside, the low falls that give the city its name are visible. The cascades have been augmented by a low concrete dam, built in 1911 to generate electricity. The original falls were little more than a ledge of volcanic rock that the river spilled over diagonally. The town of Idaho Falls was originally named Taylor's Crossing, but by 1872 it had been renamed Eagle Rock, a name believed to have a more prosperous sound. By 1891, the town was given its present name. In the Bonneville Museum (across town at the east end of Broadway), a basement exhibit recreates some storefronts typical of those early days.

Idaho Falls boasts a population of 45,000. Other than Pocatello, 50 miles to the south, it is the only large city in eastern Idaho. In fact, residents of western Wyoming often travel to Idaho Falls to shop. Like many a Western city, Idaho Falls began as a stop on the way to somewhere else. In this case the "somewhere else" was the mining camps of western Montana and northern Idaho. Irrigation projects began in 1880, and by the time the economy turned to agriculture, the city had grown into a permanent settlement.

From River Parkway in Idaho Falls, travel west on Broadway and take I-15 south, heading for Blackfoot, 25 miles away. Stop at the rest area at milepost 102 for a visit to Hell's Half Acre. The rest area itself is clean and pleasant, with covered picnic pads. The main attraction here, however, is the lava. Two interpretive trails loop through these recent (in geological terms) lava flows. The lower trail is about 400 yards, and the other, steeper trail is about half a mile in length.

This area is just the tip of an enormous flow that covered 220 square miles just 4,100 years ago. The vent, or fissure, from which the lava issued, is located about 17 miles northwest. Look for the smooth, ropy flows called pahoehoe, which have the look of licorice taffy. The trees growing out of the lava are junipers.

Remember the old Burma-Shave ads? Look closely after you leave the rest area. The World Potato Expo in Blackfoot, just ahead, has planted a series of rhyming signboards along the highways approaching the town. Here's an example:

> It's not potatoes
> That put on fat
> But toppings
> Put on after that!

Take the Blackfoot exit from I-15, turn left on Business Route 15 and follow the signs for US 91 about a mile through town. Turn left (north) on US 91 to the World Potato Expo. Housed in an old Oregon Short Line railroad depot, this offbeat museum will enlighten you with more potato-related information than you ever knew existed. A nominal admission fee allows visitors to view a video about the potato's history, and to take a walk through a replica of a modern potato storage facility, complete with the musty, cool smell of potatoes and earth. From former Vice President Dan Quayle's misspelling of the word "potato" as "potatoe," to the world's largest potato chip, it's all here. As a special bonus, the Expo offers "Free Taters to Out-of Staters" in the snack bar next door. There's nothing better than a fresh-baked Idaho potato with butter and sour cream, especially when it's free!

Afterward, retrace your route through town and continue west on US 26, heading for Arco. Near the intersection of US 26 and I-15, and along the next 25 miles of the drive, you may notice some yellow busses. These commuter busses carry workers the 25 miles from Blackfoot to the Idaho National Engineering Laboratory (INEL), one of the region's largest employers.

This section of US 26 follows the route of Goodale's Cutoff, a branch of the Oregon Trail which crossed the Snake River at Blackfoot. Rather than staying on the south bank of the Snake, Tim Goodale forged this short cut, which rejoins the main Oregon Trail more than 200 miles to the west. The cutoff traded a savings in miles for the uncertainty of water for livestock and the pioneers as they headed directly through some of the West's most inhospitable terrain. Goodale's Cutoff was used extensively by eager miners in the 1860s, after the rich strikes in the mountains of central Idaho.

Just a few miles outside of Blackfoot, the road crosses another lobe of the same great lava flow that the drive explored earlier at Hell's Half Acre. The landmarks visible along this route are the same ones the pioneers used to measure their progress 150 years ago. To the right are the Twin Buttes, and far in the distance is Big Southern Butte, rising almost 3,000 feet above the surrounding plain. The starkness of the sagebrush plain makes the buttes stand out all the more.

One mile south of US 26, and 25 miles west of Blackfoot, is Atomic City. Formerly known as Midway, because it sits halfway between Blackfoot and Arco, the town changed its name in 1950 when the Atomic Energy Commission began to develop engineering laboratories nearby. The small town's dreams of growth obviously never came to pass, and today Atomic City is nothing more than the proverbial "wide spot in the road."

Soon after the turn to Atomic City, US 26 enters the grounds of INEL, run by the U.S. Department of Energy. The facilities cover an area as large as the state of Rhode Island. (Many things in Idaho are measured in terms of the size of small Eastern states!) The 890-square-mile facility contains the largest concentration of nuclear reactors in the world.

Just ahead, US 26 joins US 20. Turn left and continue across this arid

Potato Crossing at the Idaho World Potato Expo.

expanse of sage and lava rock. In sight now are a series of mountain ranges. The names are as follows, from left to right: the Pioneer Mountains extend southward to Craters of the Moon; the White Knobs are tucked behind the Lost River Range, home of Borah Peak (Idaho's highest at 12,662 feet). The Lost River Range extends to Howe Peak in the foreground. To the right is the Lemhi Range. The water that flows from all of these ranges is channeled into the Big and Little Lost rivers and carried down onto the Snake River plain. Here, it slowly disappears underground, swallowed up by the highly porous layers of lava and basalt that make up the plain's surface. The water works its way south and west, joined by groundwater from rain and snow, as well as water from other river drainages. It finally bursts forth from the walls of the Snake River Canyon far to the west, near Hagerman.

A few miles past the junction of US 20 and US 26, turn left at the sign for EBR-1. This National Historic Landmark sits 2 miles south of the highway. Almost in the shadow of Big Southern Butte, this is Experimental Breeder Reactor Number 1, which first came on-line in 1951. It was the first nuclear reactor to generate electricity commercially, lighting up the town of Arco. Allow 1 hour for a free and informative guided tour of the simple reactor, available during the summer. The guides do a wonderful job of making a complex subject understandable. The elementary construction of the reactor belies the intricacies of physics that made it possible.

Return to the highway and turn left, crossing the Big Lost River as it heads for its rendezvous with the Snake River Aquifer. Catch glimpses of an abandoned railroad bed to the right during the next 9 miles to the junction with ID 22/33. Take the sweeping right-hand turn into Arco.

This little town is famous for two things. The first has already been mentioned—this was the first town lighted by nuclear energy. The second claim to fame is on the hillside overlooking the town. Every high school class since 1920 has painted its graduation year somewhere on the hillside. The position and size of each set of numerals probably says something about the energy and ambition of that year's senior class, and the state of repair seems to be tied to the cycle of class reunions.

At Arco, US 93 joins US 20/26. From Arco, follow the combined US 20/26/93 another 20 miles west, skirting lava flows to the left and low foothills to the right until you come to Craters of the Moon National Monument, the end of the drive. This collection of cinder cones and lava flows is one of the most alien pieces of real estate in the world—so strange, in fact, that U.S. astronauts trained here before their lunar missions. Some of the flows are less than 3,000 years old, and little vegetation is able to grow on the harsh, parched rock surfaces.

6

The Oregon Trail

General description: This 115-mile drive follows the broad Snake River west of Pocatello, visiting historical sites along the Oregon Trail. The route passes through rich agricultural lands before finishing at the city of Twin Falls after a stop at powerful Shoshone Falls.

Special attractions: Massacre Rocks State Park, with a stretch of Oregon Trail ruts preserved in the hillside; Register Rock, where emigrants stopped to carve their names; Walcott Reservoir; Minidoka County Museum; Hansen Bridge; Shoshone Falls and Twin Falls; the city of Twin Falls; and the Perrine Bridge.

Location: South-central Idaho.

Drive route numbers: Interstate Highways 86 and 84, Register Road, Idaho Highways 25, 24 and 50, and local roads around Shoshone Falls and Twin Falls.

Travel season: Year-round. Winter storms can be harsh on the plains, and summer temperatures can exceed 100 degrees Fahrenheit.

Camping: Camping and RV sites are available at Massacre Rocks State Park and in Twin Falls.

Services: Heyburn, Burley, and Twin Falls offer all tourist services. The stretch of I-86 from Massacre Rocks to the junction with I-84, and the next 10 miles of I-84 westbound, offer no services.

Nearby attractions: Pomerelle and Magic Mountain ski areas; boating and fishing on American Falls Reservoir; Nat-Soo-Pah Warm Springs; gambling at Jackpot, Nevada.

 The Drive

This drive begins on I-86, 13 miles west of American Falls, at the Massacre Rocks Rest Area (milepost 30). Park at the far west end of the rest area and follow the path for a scenic view of the Snake River Canyon. This paved trail leads underneath the highway to a set of preserved ruts from the Oregon Trail. The round-trip walk from the rest area takes about 20 minutes, so keep an eye on the weather. This part of Idaho can get very hot in the summertime, so be sure to take precautions—carry water, wear sunscreen and perhaps a hat, and watch for rattlesnakes. Note: If you are following this drive in reverse, you can access the trail ruts mentioned above from a

Drive 6: The Oregon Trail

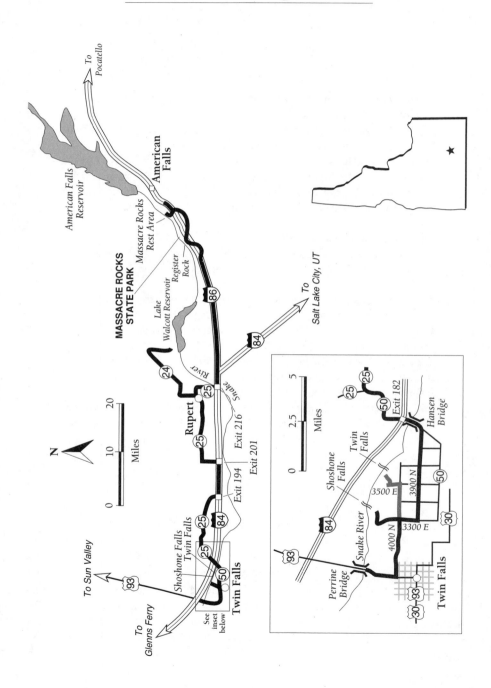

parking area at the east end of Massacre Rocks State Park. It is a 1.5-mile walk. There is no access to the wagon ruts from eastbound I-86.

The Oregon Trail traversed Idaho from east to west, for much of the way following the course of the Snake River, which presented a formidable obstacle to the pioneers and their wagons. Most early pioneers followed this main branch of the trail along the south bank of the river. Starting out early in the spring, bands of settlers hurried across the plains from Missouri in hopes of reaching the Willamette Valley of Oregon before the weather turned bad in the autumn. This meant that most parties were in Idaho from late July through August and into September—a time when the southern Idaho climate is at its driest and hottest. Temperatures in the high 90s were not uncommon, as the travelers fought to make 12 to 18 miles per day.

After you have finished your walk, leave the rest area and continue west on the interstate for 2 miles to the entrance to Massacre Rocks State Park. This state park offers camping, boating, and fishing. Check out the small, but interesting, Oregon Trail exhibit in the visitor center. Consider the purchase of an annual state park pass for $30 if you plan to visit a significant number of Idaho's 30 state parks.

Massacre Rocks was so named because, in 1862, a small contingent of Oregon Trail travelers was ambushed east of here by Shoshone warriors. The place had an ominous feel to emigrants even before the attacks, and had been known as the Gates of Death or Hell's Gate, referring to the narrow defile that the trail passed through.

Also visible from the state park is evidence of the great flood that drained Lake Bonneville, some 25,000 years ago. Southeast of here, near McCammon, was the only outlet of Lake Bonneville, an immense inland lake that once covered all of northern Utah and a large portion of southeastern Idaho. The water flowing out of the lake eventually wore away a hard basalt rock layer at the lake's low point. When the outlet stream began to carve the softer rock layers below, the stream's velocity increased, allowing more water to flow over the lip. The increased flow eroded the rock layers even faster, until finally a catastrophic flood drained the vast lake of more than 200 feet of water. The flood lasted six weeks, scientists estimate, and carved many of the features visible today along the Snake River.

Here, you can see giant basalt boulders that the flood moved down the river. These boulders are called melon gravel, since their polished shapes make them resemble nothing so much as a well-tended melon patch.

After you leave Massacre Rocks, cross the highway bridge and follow Register Road, which turns right and parallels I-86. After 2 miles, turn left into the Register Rock picnic area. This landmark was one of the many places Oregon Trail emigrants stopped and carved their names into the rock. The rock itself is fenced and under a protective shelter. Nearby are other smaller rocks that also were carved by pioneers. According to an interpretative marker at the site, the profile of a tribal chief on one rock was carved by a young lad who passed this way again as an old man, stopping in the 1920s to admire his artwork. The picnic area is very pleasant, with shade trees and grass. Unfortunately, modern man has decided that he, too, needs an outlet for his communication skills, and the area's unprotected rocks also bear the scars of these modern "pioneers."

Continue west on Register Road until it rejoins the interstate at milepost 21. Follow I-86 west. In another 21 miles, I-86 merges into I-84. Follow I-84 another 6 miles to the intersection with Idaho 25. Turn right on ID 25 and go north about 4 miles to Baseline Road. Turn left and go another mile to the Minidoka County Museum, on the left in a large, square, concrete building. If the museum is open, be sure to stop. Housed here is a genuine marble soda fountain, including original wrapped candy bars and other everyday items. The fountain was seized for non-payment of a loan when the business failed in 1926, and the fixtures and inventory were put into storage in a local barn, where they sat for many years before being donated to the museum.

Continue west a short distance into Rupert, and make a sharp right onto ID 24, which strikes out northeast along the railroad tracks. Pass through the small town of Acequia and then turn right again past milepost 11. Follow the Minidoka Dam Road (400N) about 5 miles to Minidoka Dam.

This section of south-central Idaho was much different in the days before the Snake River plain benefited from the irrigation dams along the river. Early settlers fought the bitter winter cold, the blazing summer heat, the plagues of insects and jackrabbits, and the endless dust. One pioneer woman who fought the elements in this area said, "Rather than dust, I just wait three or four days and then use a shovel!"

Minidoka Dam was built in 1906 to pump water up 86 feet from the Snake River to irrigate the vast, surrounding plains. The dam and its life-giving water completely changed the complexion of the land in this part of Idaho. From a dry, desolate, sage-and-basalt desert, the area quickly became an agricultural oasis. The dam also generated electricity. Rupert High School was the first all-electric public building in the United States.

Walcott Park is located near the dam. With its vast expanses of cool, green grass and towering shade trees, it offers a wonderful place for a picnic. Back when the dam was being built, worker housing was constructed here. All of the marvelous trees in the park were planted at that time, and have grown to splendid maturity in the past 90 years.

Retrace your route back on the Minidoka Dam Road and go left on ID 24 to Rupert, a busy agricultural center, where dry beans, sugar beets, and other major crops grown in the area are processed. On some fields, the local farm association has posted signs that identify the crops being grown. While

Shoshone Falls on the Snake River at Twin Falls.

most city dwellers can identify a field of corn, the signs quickly teach those not born on a farm how to identify a number of other crops.

Follow ID 25 out of Rupert, heading west. This stretch of road provides a good feel for the quality of life on the many farms in southern Idaho. The rest of the drive explores this rural lifestyle, as it wanders through the farmlands irrigated by the Minidoka water project. A few miles west of Rupert the road bends south and rejoins I-84 at milepost 201. The interstate is the only road available, so follow it west 7 miles to the next exit (Exit 194) and turn right to ID 25 which makes a long left turn and heads west once again.

Pass through Hazelton, a quiet community of 500, and 4 miles later, enter Eden, population 300. Turn left onto ID 50, 3 miles west of Eden, and take a pair of sweeping turns, right and left. Notice the large farm estate at milepost 6, just before the road turns to cross I-84. Continue on ID 50 across the Snake at Hansen Bridge, and take the first right after the bridge, which is 3900 North Road. If you only have time to visit one of the two waterfalls in the area, head for Shoshone Falls. To reach Shoshone Falls, turn right after traveling west 5 miles on 3900 North, and head north on 3300 East, also known as Champlin Road, for 3 more miles to Shoshone Falls Park.

The park is operated by the city of Twin Falls, and the entrance gate is part way down the basalt cliff. Entrance fees are a reasonable $2 per car, and include use of the picnic grounds, the spectacular sight of the massive

Shoshone Falls, and an old-fashioned swimming hole called Dierkes Lake. The lake has a grassy section of beach and is studded with basalt cliffs that are just right for a jump into the cool waters. Shoshone Falls' majesty is dependent on water released from upstream dams, so the falls are much more impressive when water levels are high and irrigation demands low. By midsummer, irrigation requirements reduce the flow dramatically, but the falls are a wonder nonetheless.

The area's other falls, Twin Falls, are less impressive, but worth the short drive. To reach Twin Falls from Shoshone Falls, take 3300 East south to 4000 North. Turn left, and head east 2 miles to 3500 East. Turn left again, and the entrance to the falls parking area, maintained by the Idaho Power Company, will be about a half mile ahead, below the canyon's rim.

From either falls, return to 4000 North and turn right. Almost immediately you will be surrounded by some of the lovely homes of Twin Falls, south-central Idaho's major metropolitan area. Continue west 2 miles past Shoshone Falls to Blue Lakes Boulevard (US 93). Turn right on Blue Lakes Boulevard and head north 1.5 miles to view the Snake River Canyon and the graceful arch of the Perrine Bridge. An overlook on the left side of the road, just before it crosses the river canyon, offers an appealing vista. Also located here is a well-staffed visitor center, loaded with helpful information. This bridge, and the Hansen Bridge east of the waterfalls, are the only crossings of the Snake River in the area. Residents of Twin Falls are connected to the interstate highway system and to the rest of Idaho north of here by these two bridges.

7

Thousand Springs

General description: This is an easy 61-mile drive on two-lane roads through a rich agricultural landscape, beginning at a historic stage stop, and ending at a pocket-sized canyon. Side trips to Balanced Rock, Hagerman National Fish Hatchery, and The Nature Conservancy's Thousand Springs property can add another 56 miles to the tour. The route follows the Snake River to a series of natural springs that burst from the basalt cliffs along the Snake River Canyon's rim.

Special attractions: The historic Stricker Store and stage stop; the city of Twin Falls; Twin Falls County Historical Museum; Thousand Springs, with its myriad of springs gushing from the cliffs; Hagerman Fossil Beds National Monument; and Malad Gorge State Park.

Location: South-central Idaho.

Drive route numbers: U.S. Highway 30, Rock Creek Road, 3200 North Road, 3600 North Road, Castleford Road and other local roads leading to Balanced Rock, Bell Rapids Road and other local roads in the vicinity of Hagerman, the Justice Grade, and Ritchie Road.

Travel season: All-season drive, although agricultural regions are more appealing during growing season.

Camping: Commercial campgrounds are available at Twin Falls and near Hagerman.

Services: Twin Falls offers all services, and there are motels and restaurants at Buhl and Hagerman.

Nearby attractions: Magic Mountain Ski Area; Nat-Soo-Pah Warm Springs; gambling at Jackpot, Nevada; the Herrett Museum; Shoshone Falls.

 The Drive

Begin at the historic Rock Creek Station site, a stage stop on the line operated across southern Idaho in the 1860s by Ben Holladay. The stage carried passengers to and from the gold-mining operations then springing up in the Boise Basin and elsewhere in the Idaho territory. Also known as the Stricker Store, the station site is southeast of Twin Falls. Take US 30 east from Twin Falls to 3800 East Road, which is also known as Rock Creek Road. Head south to 3200 North Road and turn right to the stage stop site. Also here are the remains of a jail, several other buildings, and a house that belonged to Herman Stricker, who ran the store for many years. The house has been restored to its 1901 condition and is occasionally open to visitors. The rest of the site is open for self-guided tours.

After visiting the site, continue west to 3600 East Road. Turn right and head north for 6 miles to US 30 (this stretch of US 30 is also called 3700 North Road or Sugar Factory Road). Turn left on US 30 and follow the highway westbound through Twin Falls.

Twin Falls grew up as a result of the Carey Act, which encouraged the development of western lands through irrigation projects. A group of businessmen led by I. B. Perrine spearheaded the project that built the Milner Dam, several miles east of the site of Twin Falls. By 1909, the town was named the seat of Twin Falls County.

Today Twin Falls is the economic and cultural hub of south-central Idaho. With a population of more than 30,000, it is the largest city between Pocatello and Boise. It is also home to the College of South Idaho and to the Herrett Museum, with its outstanding anthropological collections.

Leaving Twin Falls on US 30 westbound (which is also US 93 southbound), pick up the Thousand Springs Scenic Byway, one of the many designated scenic routes in the state. This is also the Oregon Trail Auto Tour route.

Housed in an old school building on the south side of the road between mileposts 214 and 213 is the Twin Falls County Historical Museum. True to the area's heritage, the museum displays an assortment of agricultural implements, as well as other regional memorabilia. Try to imagine working this harsh land using the simple tools housed in this museum.

Ahead, US 30 leaves US 93, which heads for Nevada after leaving the central Idaho mountains and coming south across the Snake River plain.

Traveling westbound on US 30 along the Snake River canyon's southern rim it may be possible to glimpse some of the peaks of the Sawtooth National Forest far off to the north.

At Buhl, about 20 miles west of Twin Falls, a well-marked side trip to the south takes you 17 miles to Balanced Rock, a precariously perched pillar of basalt in the small canyon of parapets and spires that gave the nearby town of Castleford its name. For this side trip, leave Buhl heading south on Main Street. Turn right on Burley, and then left (south) on Castleford Road (1400 East), following this road for 5 miles. Turn right (west) on 3600 North, and after 2 miles, turn left (south) on 1200 East. After one mile, turn right (west) on 3500 North, through the town of Castleford. After 6 miles, turn right (north) on 600 East and then left (west) on 3700 North. Travel 2 miles on 3700 North into the little canyon that is home to Balanced Rock. If you take this excursion, retrace your route to Buhl, rejoining the main drive on US 30 in the middle of town.

From Buhl, continue west on US 30, catching occasional glimpses of Snake River Canyon to the right. The roads sweeps north, makes a wide

Stricker Store was a welcome sight to Oregon Trail travelers.

turn west and then north again as it drops below the rim of the canyon into an outer gorge, eroded at the time of the Bonneville Flood. On the river a short distance upstream from here is a series of cascades known as Fishing Falls. The famed explorer John C. Frémont described these falls in 1843. He watched the natives spearing salmon here, as the fish made their way upstream over the series of cascades.

Also near here was Payne's Ferry, an oar-powered ferry that operated from 1852 until 1910. Some Oregon Trail emigrants crossed here to the north bank of the Snake, rather than risk the treacherous Three Island Crossing downstream near Glenns Ferry, even though the overland stretch from here to Glenns Ferry was somewhat more difficult.

At milepost 185 on US 30 turn left at the sign for Bell Rapids. Follow Bell Rapids Road 2.8 miles to the Snake River Overlook site in Hagerman Fossil Beds National Monument. Continue up the hill to see some well-preserved ruts on the Oregon Trail. A short walking trail near the top of the hill may also tempt you to get out and stretch your legs. Look for golden eagles and other raptors soaring on summer thermal currents above the hills. To resume the drive, turn back at the top of the hill and return, turning left at the one-lane Ousley Bridge across the Snake and rejoining US 30.

Immediately after the return to the highway, there is a decision to make. In short succession, a right turn and a left turn both offer short, interesting side trips.

Drive 7: Thousand Springs

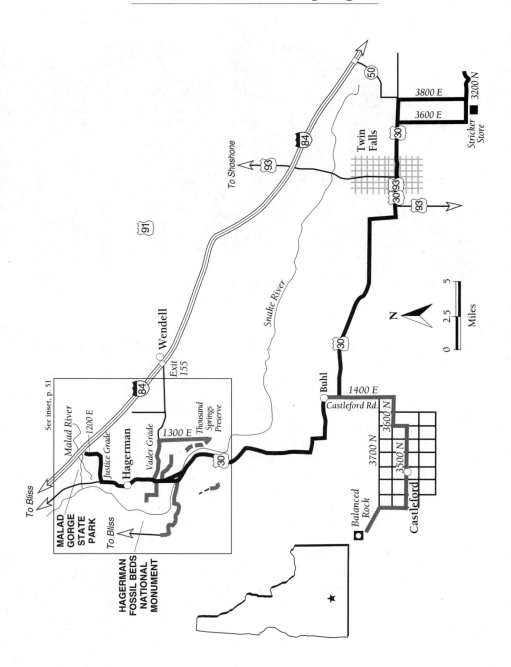

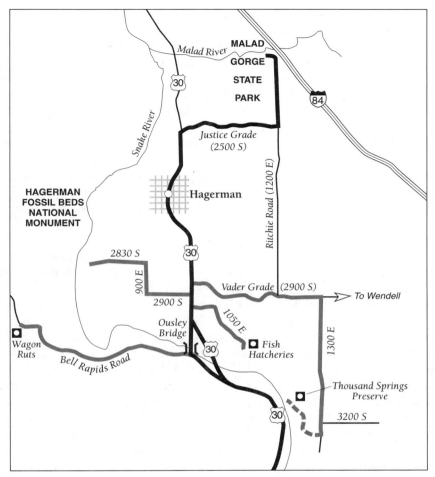

See map on page 50.

The right turn leads 2 miles down Fish Hatch Road to the Hagerman National Fish Hatchery, which nurtures steelhead trout. The fish have already been reared and transplanted by summer, so viewing is best in the spring. A small pond on the grounds holds several white sturgeon, large fish with a prehistoric appearance which have inhabited the Snake River for thousands of years. Sturgeon wighing as much as 1,500 pounds have been pulled from the river, but the construction of numerous dams has since restricted the number and size of these bottom-feeding fish. It is still possible to cast a line for the giant fish, but your catch must be returned to the water unharmed. Check current fishing regulations for more information about sturgeon fishing.

Also along the same road is a state hatchery, as well as numerous commercial hatcheries raising catfish, rainbow trout, and tilapia, a South American fish that is growing in commercial importance. The abundance of hatcheries in this stretch results from the most significant feature of the area—the Thousand Springs. The fresh water, constantly flowing at a steady temperature, is ideal for rearing large quantities of fish. Most of the nation's commercial production of rainbow trout is concentrated along this stretch of the Snake River Canyon.

The left turn from US 30 heads 3 miles down to the river on narrow roads. Turn onto 2900 South Road, then right (north) on 900 East Road, which passes through a large field of melon gravel deposited here by the Bonneville Flood. The route then turns west again on 2830 South Road to the river's edge and a close view of a series of landslides across the river that have been quite active in the past ten years. Return to US 30 and continue north (left).

The Thousand Springs name is, like many such, an approximation, although certainly not an exaggeration. All along the north wall of this strecth of the canyon, small and large springs gush from the basalt. The water comes from all across the northern half of the Snake River plain, which is covered in hundreds, even thousands, of feet of basalt—a hard rock of volcanic origin. Water that falls as rain on the plain, water that flows down from the central Idaho mountains, and some of the water from the myriad irrigation projects simply soaks in and percolates down through the basalt layers until it hits an impermeable rock layer. Since the plain tilts slightly from north to south and from east to west, all of the water in this aquifer eventually bursts forth in the vicinity of Hagerman.

The steady flows at a constant temperature have stimulated other economic activity in the area as well. The most notable enterprise was electric power generation. An early project ran a ditch across the face of the cliff to collect spring water before it fell to the river. Using the water to produce hydroelectric power, the power plant across the river at one time contributed more than 10 percent of Idaho's total electric power.

Another early attempt to profit from the water was more unusual. In 1890 William Priestly built a pneumatic pump—a series of water pipes as large as two feet in diameter. The pump used the air pressure created by falling water to pump spring water from another pipe 75 feet up the cliff, in order to irrigate the fields above. No motors of any sort were involved in the design, which skeptical engineers grudgingly pronounced 70 percent efficient.

Before heading into the town of Hagerman, a pleasant side trip visits The Nature Conservancy's Thousand Springs Preserve. Turn east on the Vader Grade heading for Wendell. After 3 miles turn right (south) on 1300 East Road, and right again (west) after another 3 miles on 3200 South Road.

At Thousand Springs, fresh, cool water emerges from its long journey across the Snake River plain.

Follow the signs down the rough, gravel Thousand Springs Grade to the preserve. Trailers are not recommended on the steep, narrow grade.

The Thousand Springs Preserve combines tranquil bottomland, marshes and meadows with dramatic basalt cliffs, three spring-fed creeks and the last free-flowing cascade on the Thousand Springs stretch of the Snake, Minnie Miller Falls. The pristine, 58-degree Fahrenheit water flows year-round, supporting plant and animal life in the creeks of the preserve.

The rock farmhouse that is the center of the preserve is open to tours with advance notice. The self-guided nature walk to the old dairy barn and the falls overlook is a pleasant walk of about a quarter mile. Return to US 30 by retracing your route. Turn right (north) on US 30.

After the side trips to the river's edge, the hatcheries, and the Thousand Springs Preserve, head north on US 30 into the small town of Hagerman. Here is the headquarters of Hagerman Fossil Beds National Monument, where you will find a small interpretative exhibit showcasing a complete skeleton of the Hagerman horse, whose fossilized remains are found in great numbers in the monument itself, across the river. The fossils are laid down here in such great abundance because of a geological event that occurred here more than 3.4 million years ago.

You may have noticed how strikingly different the two walls of the canyon are near Hagerman. Lava flows from the north and east dammed water flowing from the south and west here, and the accumulated sediments from the flowing water covered the remains of the abundant animal life of the time, including some well-preserved, intact specimens of the small, zebra-like Hagerman horse. The Snake River cut through the basalt cliffs and the accumulated sediments, leaving behind two distinctly different banks.

North of Hagerman the highway passes a small winery at Billingsley Creek. If you are running short of time, a quick end to the drive can be made by continuing across the Malad Gorge Bridge on US 30. The road begins to climb the side of the canyon, topping out at the small town of Bliss, on the canyon rim. On your left as you climb the rim are glimpses of the Old Bliss Road, which emerged from the canyon along an earlier grade. The Old Bliss Road is home to the only structure in Idaho designed by famed architect Frank Lloyd Wright. Surrounded by chain-link fence, the home is a private residence and is not open to the public. If you take this shorter option, the drive ends at the junction with I-84 at the top of the grade in Bliss.

The main drive leaves US 30 and turns right just north of the Billingsley Creek crossing on a road known as the Justice Grade. After climbing to the canyon rim, turn left (north) on Ritchie Road and continue 2 miles to Malad Gorge State Park, where the waters of the Malad River have carved a small, but spectacular gorge in the solid basalt. Footpaths along the rim and across the gorge on a metal footbridge provide dramatic views of the pocket-sized gorge. Grassy picnic areas make this a pleasant end to your drive.

8

Shoshone to the Sawtooths

General description: This 116-mile excursion starts in an arid, desolate portion of the Snake River plain, passes lava fields and ice caves, and winds through the lovely Wood River Valley to Sun Valley. From there, it continues over dramatic Galena Summit along the face of the aptly-named Sawtooth Range and past some of Idaho's prettiest lakes before coming to an end in Stanley, whose 75 year-round residents enjoy access to some of the wildest country left in the lower 48 states.

Special attractions: Idaho's Mammoth Cave; Shoshone Ice Caves; Ketchum and Sun Valley; Hemingway Memorial; the Sawtooth National Recreation Area and views of the Sawtooth Range.

Location: South-central Idaho.

Drive route numbers: Idaho Highway 75.

Travel season: The entire highway is maintained year-round, but north of the section from Shoshone through Ketchum severe winter weather may result in the closure of Galena Summit for extended periods.

Camping: Commercial campgrounds are available in Hailey, Ketchum, and Stanley. There are numerous campgrounds in the Sawtooth National Forest north of Ketchum, and at Alturas, Redfish, and Stanley lakes.

Services: Hotel rooms, food, and gas are available in Shoshone, Hailey, Ketchum, Sun Valley, and Stanley.

Nearby attractions: Skiing at Sun Valley; white-water rafting on the Middle Fork of the Salmon River; cross-country skiing, backpacking, and hiking in the Sawtooth Wilderness.

 The Drive

Begin on ID 75 in Shoshone, at its intersection with US Highway 26. Shoshone got its start as a mining supply town during the silver boom in the mountains to the north. Miners and camp followers would step off the train in Shoshone and spend the night in the hotels lining the tracks before setting off in wagons for the mining camps. The town then had a well-deserved reputation for wildness, but today it is a quiet town of 1,200, supporting the agricultural interests of the area.

Shoshone has some architectural gems, including the little ivy-covered train station and a number of old hotel buildings from its earlier days. Just north of the tracks on ID 75 is the Doncaster, a unique structure built in

1905 of basalt blocks. The ubiquitous basalt was rarely used as a building stone because of the difficulty of shaping it. Masons who worked with basalt had to inspect large piles of the stone in order to find blocks already in exactly the shapes they needed. The Doncaster was apparently never used as a boarding house, though the National Register of Historic Places lists it as such. It is known to have been a speakeasy during the days of Prohibition.

About 8 miles north of Shoshone is Idaho's Mammoth Cave, located about half a mile west of the highway along a bumpy dirt road. Turn left at the second sign, about one quarter mile north of the large sign and A-frame structure. The cave is a lava tube, created when flowing lava cooled more quickly on the outer edges of the flow. The lava inside the flow retained its heat longer and continued to flow through the cooled tube, eventually draining and leaving behind a hollow tube.

This tube, as well as the one at Shoshone Ice Caves 10 miles farther north, has the unusual property of remaining cold year-round, having a floor of ice. Cold air, heavier than the surrounding air, falls into the cave's single entrance. With no natural ventilation, warm air never enters the cave. As the years pass, the buildup of cold air freezes any water that seeps into the cave, perpetuating the cold. If you visit, be sure to bring a jacket and wear sturdy shoes, as the floors of these ice caves are slick and often muddy.

Mammoth Cave is privately owned. The small admission fee allows access to the cave and the museum at the cave entrance. An eclectic collection, the museum contains dusty skulls and stuffed animals, as well as a complete bison skeleton. All the taxidermy, interpretative signs, and just about everything else were done by the cave's owner. The structures are built of wood scraps, and the menagerie of turkeys, peacocks, and pigs running loose in the parking lot adds to the quirky ambiance of the cave.

Head north on ID 75. In places, the remains of former U.S. Highway 93 can be seen to the right of the road. US 93 was relocated many years ago and now follows the path of US 26 from Shoshone to Arco. After passing the small cone of Kinzie Butte, off to the right, the route crosses a younger lava flow that extends 16 miles, stretching almost as far south as Shoshone. Collapsed lava domes are evident as the road traverses the flow. Lava domes are created by a skin of lava enclosing volcanic gasses. Once the lava cools, these relatively thin skins remain. Over time, some have broken and collapsed, leaving a depression. The cone, or vent, from which the flow issued is visible to the west. It is in this flow that the Shoshone Ice Caves are located.

In short order, ID 75 crosses the Big Wood River, the Blaine County line, and the Richfield Canal, which carries irrigation water from Magic Reservoir southeast to the fields around Richfield. Thanks to this infusion of water, these irrigated areas are islands of green surrounded by the flow of

Drive 8: Shoshone to the Sawtooths

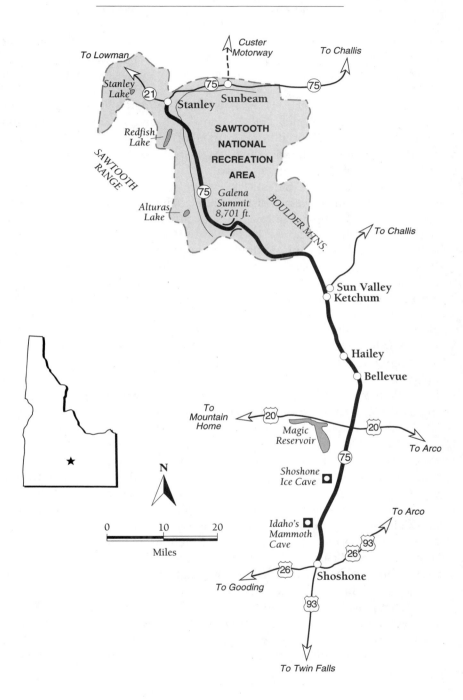

To Lowman

Custer Motorway

To Challis

Stanley Lake

21 75 Sunbeam

Stanley

Redfish Lake

SAWTOOTH NATIONAL RECREATION AREA

SAWTOOTH RANGE

75 Galena Summit 8,701 ft.

Alturas Lake

BOULDER MTNS.

To Challis

Sun Valley
Ketchum

Hailey

Bellevue

To Mountain Home

20 20

Magic Reservoir

To Arco

75

Shoshone Ice Cave

To Arco

Idaho's Mammoth Cave

93

26

26 Shoshone

To Gooding

93

To Twin Falls

N

0   10   20

Miles

inhospitable lava. Over the next 10 miles, the road gradually leaves the sage hills, crossing US 20 and entering the charming Wood River Valley. Towering cottonwood trees along wet river bottoms dominate the landscape here, and more and more lovely, little farms and ranches come into view. The flanking hills grow closer together until ID 75 reaches the small town of Bellevue, in the shadow of Lookout Mountain, which rises 2,500 feet above the valley floor.

Bellevue once served as the gateway to the Wood River mining district. Names like Croesus Gulch and Bullion Gulch give an inkling of the fortunes that were made, or at least dreamed of, in this region. Between 1881 and the 1893 crash of the silver market, the region produced more than $60 million worth of gold, silver, and lead.

North of Bellevue 5 miles is Hailey, a community of 4,500 people, many of whom work in the resort of Sun Valley, some 12 miles north of Hailey. Hailey was the birthplace of one of the twentieth century's most influential poets, Ezra Pound. Although he moved to Pennsylvania at the age of two due to his mother's health, Idaho has long claimed him as one of its own. Pound was controversial throughout his life. His poetry is thought by many to be nearly incomprehensible, but his influence extended to poets and writers, including T. S. Eliot, William Butler Yeats, e. e. cummings, and Marianne Moore. He worked with Ernest Hemingway, Robert Frost, and James Joyce. No wonder he shows up on everyone's list of important Idahoans.

North of Hailey, the old railroad bed has been converted to a biking and hiking trail. On a sunny afternoon, the trail bustles with bicyclists, in-line skaters, and walkers. The old railroad bridges across the Big Wood River have taken on a new life carrying their load of recreational traffic. The rail line's first incarnation supported the region's silver, lead, and gold mines in the 1880s. Transport of sheep to market from the surrounding high mountain pasture land was an important secondary use of the line. Each fall, sheep were driven down along the Big Wood River from the Boulder Mountains north of Ketchum into pens in town at the railhead. Traces of the old sheep trail are still visible on the sage hills north of town.

The road follows the river into Ketchum. The homes become larger, more elegant, and definitely more expensive as the road approaches the resort town. On the left, looming over Ketchum, is Bald Mountain, affectionately called Baldy by the valley's residents. After the excitement of the mining boom, which had ended by 1890, Ketchum became a sleepy village, served by train from Shoshone twice a week, until 1936.

That year, Averell Harriman, chairman of the board of the Union Pacific Railroad, directed Austrian Count Felix Schaffgotsch to find a site for a ski resort. Harriman's interest was purely profit-oriented. He was looking for a way to fill trains with paying passengers. He gambled that skiing, popularized by the 1932 Lake Placid Winter Olympics, would attract them. Schaffgotsch searched the West for the ideal mountain. After touring the western states, he contacted Harriman from Ketchum. He had found the ideal location. Bright sunshine, a mountain with the perfect slope, lots of dry powder snow, and a location at the end of a spur line all combined to create the perfect resort package. Harriman acted fast and the Sun Valley Lodge was built in less than a year. Steve Hannagan, a public relations genius who had developed Miami Beach, was hired to attract skiers. With Hannagan's flair for promotion, the resort quickly became the only place for Hollywood's elite and the social set from the East Coast to be seen.

The original Sun Valley Lodge is still in operation, and is a wonderful place for visitors to wander about. From Ketchum, turn right on Trail Creek Road/Sun Valley Road and go 1 mile to Sun Valley, where you will notice the construction of the lodge itself. It was built of concrete poured into rough-sawn frames and then treated with acid to look like wood. This was the only way to build the lodge in the short time that was allowed for its construction.

Walk inside and inspect the hundreds of publicity photos taken at the resort over the years. If you can believe the pictures, the sun never hid behind a cloud at Sun Valley. Celebrities from John Wayne to the Kennedy family

Train station at Shoshone.

are all shown outdoors, with crisp snow and bright sunshine in every photo. Behind the lodge there is a large ice rink, used year round. Each summer there is a spectacular ice show daily, showcasing some of the world's best skaters.

The chairlift was invented here by a Union Pacific mechanical engineer who had worked in Panama. He had developed a cable system for loading bunches of bananas onto steamships. The chairlift design simply replaced the banana hooks with chairs. Lifts were built on Dollar Mountain and Proctor Mountain. The ski area on Bald Mountain, across the valley at Ketchum, was not developed until later. The steep terrain was too challenging for the skills—and the equipment—of skiers in the 1930s.

No visit to Ketchum and Sun Valley would be complete without paying respects to its most famous resident, Ernest Hemingway. "Papa" Hemingway lived in the valley for short stretches between his adventures around the world. It was in Ketchum that he took his life in 1961, depressed over his failing health. He is buried next to his wife Mary in the Ketchum Cemetery north of town, under two towering spruces. A memorial to Ernest Hemingway sits along Trail Creek Road about 1.5 miles northeast of the Sun Valley Lodge. The bust sits on a simple stone base topped by a concrete pillar. Hidden in a grove of cottonwoods alongside a narrow irrigation channel overlooking the sage-covered hillsides of Sun Valley, the monument is a peaceful spot to rest. The inscription on the brass plaque, from an epitaph Hemingway had written about a friend, certainly characterizes the author and his love of the outdoors.

> Best of all he loved the fall. The leaves yellow on the cottonwoods, leaves floating on the trout streams and above the hills. The high blue windless skies . . . now he will be a part of them forever.

During the 1880s, ores from the mines of the Yankee Fork district were brought to Ketchum for smelting. Wagons traveled up and over Trail Creek summit northeast of town on their 160-mile round-trip journey between the mines and smelters. The wagons used to haul the ore were imposing vehicles. Standing more than 12 feet tall, with massive wheels and long, narrow freight boxes, the wagons shook the earth as they rumbled into town.

Ketchum celebrates its early history as a mining town during its Pioneer Days celebration each year on Labor Day weekend. The highlight of the celebration is the parade of rebuilt and restored freight wagons through the streets of Ketchum. The wagons can be heard, and even felt, long before they come into view. Visitors who aren't fortunate enough to be in town during the celebration can see the wagons on display at the Ore Wagon

Pettit Lake outlet in the Sawtooth National Recreation Area.

Museum located two blocks east of Main Street on Fifth Street.

There is enough to do in Ketchum to occupy a pleasant weekend, including such outdoor pursuits as hiking, river rafting, and, of course, shopping. Don't be surprised if you spot a famous face from the evening news or Hollywood as you wander about town. Be cool, though. Ketchum prides itself on the fact that it treats the rich and famous just like everyone else. In the grocery store or on the street, celebrity watching here is much more low-key than it would be in Aspen.

Ketchum is a logical place to break the scenic drive from Shoshone with an overnight stay. A night at the Sun Valley Lodge or any of the other comfortable motels and lodges in the valley allows you time to sample some of the area's wonderful restaurants. From a practical standpoint, there are not many places to stop once you leave Ketchum for Stanley. If you are camping, either in a tent or a motorhome, you will find splendid spots to stop for the night as the drive continues north from Ketchum.

After you leave Ketchum on ID 75 northbound, the landscape gradually takes on more of an alpine character as the road enters the Sawtooth National Recreation Area. The SNRA Headquarters Visitor Center offers something a bit unique—audio tapes you can take with you on your drive from here to Stanley. The tapes are free, and you can return them to the ranger station outside of Stanley. They offer an entertaining and personal guide to the SNRA. The narrators will tell you when to start and stop the tapes, and will provide you with detailed information that will enhance your drive.

The road follows the Big Wood River to its source at the crest of the Boulder Mountains. At first it climbs gently, but once you've passed the tiny settlement of Galena, it ascends steadily and sharply to Galena Summit. In winter this pass is often closed because of severe weather, so check with local authorities if the weather is doubtful. Stop at the first switchback and enjoy the view back down the valley. Don't use all your film here, though, as more spectacular vistas await over the summit.

Stop again at the scenic overlook on the first curve descending the north slope. This is the Sawtooth Valley, enclosed on the west by the jagged spires of the Sawtooth Range. Similar to the more famous Tetons, with stark, bare granite spires and a string of glacial lakes at its feet, this range is very young by geologic standards. At your feet are the headwaters of the Salmon River, one of America's treasures, unchecked by dams for its entire length of more than 420 miles.

As you continue down into the valley, the highway soon crosses the Salmon. Make note of the modest size of the river here, and then, as you continue, marvel at how quickly the river picks up volume. Fed by snowmelt and the runoff of summer storms, the Salmon soon grows into a formidable torrent. In these upper reaches, look for adventurous individuals in wetsuits floating the chilly river in inner tubes.

West of here, but not worth the trip, is the site of Sawtooth City, a mining camp that had a brief but rowdy existence in the 1880s supporting the nearby Silver King mine. When the mine's facilities burned in 1892, the town was doomed. Today nothing remains of the town's former glory.

Along the base of the Sawtooth Range lies a string of lakes, their basins carved by the same glacial activity that shaped these toothy peaks. As the glaciers, with their great weight of ice and rock, slowly moved off the mountains' slopes, they pushed stones and soil out of their way, leaving behind long ridges, called lateral moraines. They also pushed debris before them—debris that remained when the ice melted. These mounds, or terminal moraines, in combination with the lateral moraines, acted as large natural dams to hold back the melted glacial ice and snowmelt. These moraines are now visible as long, flat ridges, often covered with lodgepole pine. Exposed portions often reveal a mixture of gravels, finely ground dirt and assorted sizes of rounded stones, all shaped by the moving ice.

The lakes created by the moraines all eventually carved outlets through their moraine, allowing some of their waters to join the Salmon River. From south to north, the major lakes accessible to automobile traffic are Alturas, Pettit, Yellowbelly, Redfish and Little Redfish, and Stanley. Except for Stanley Lake, all of these are reached by well-marked roads leaving from the west side of ID 75. On ID 75, it is 17 miles from the turn to Alturas Lake to the turn to the Redfish lakes. None of the lakes is more than a 2- to 3-mile detour from the highway, and each offers its own interpretation of the classic alpine landscape of water, pine, rock, and snow. Stanley Lake is reached by taking ID 21 northwest from the town of Stanley 4 miles to the lake's access well-marked road, and then 3.5 miles west on the access road.

9

Stanley to Lost Trail Pass

General description: Leaving Stanley on Idaho Highway 75, the route covers 161 miles, following the Salmon River north through Challis to Salmon before leaving the river at North Fork and continuing to the top of Lost Trail Pass on the Montana border. The river itself is the main attraction of this route, but the steep hillsides that drop right to the water's edge sometimes steal the show.

Special attractions: Sawtooth National Recreation Area; Sunbeam Hot Springs; old mining camps of Bonanza and Custer on the Yankee Fork; the Yankee Fork gold dredge; the stark beauty of the Salmon River and canyon; Land of the Yankee Fork Visitor Center at Challis; Lemhi County Museum in Salmon.

Location: The central Idaho mountains.

Drive route numbers: Idaho Highway 75 and U.S. Highway 93.

Travel season: Best driven during late spring, summer, and fall. Snow and ice in the shadowed canyons can create severe driving hazards in winter.

Camping: Commercial campgrounds are available at Stanley, Challis, and Salmon, and there is a Challis National Forest campground at Twin Creek, below Lost Trail Pass.

Services: Motels and restaurants are available in Stanley, Challis, and Salmon. Limited services are available at Sunbeam Hot Springs.

Nearby attractions: Whitewater rafting on the Middle Fork of the Salmon River and on the Salmon's main stem; site of Borah Peak earthquake south of Challis; skiing at the summit of Lost Trail Pass.

 The Drive

Stanley is the staging area for wilderness adventurers of all stripes. From here, hikers can explore the Idaho State Centennial Trail and the wild areas of the Sawtooth Wilderness, which straddles the jagged spine of the Sawtooth Range. Fishermen pursue their prey in the region's many lakes and streams. Photographers and painters find inspiration in the postcard-quality views that are present at every turn. The main draw, however, is the free-flowing Salmon River. The Middle Fork of the Salmon, in particular, has a reputation as the premiere stretch of whitewater in the nation.

On any summer afternoon in Stanley, you will find river guides repairing rafts and testing equipment, eager river runners laying out their gear for

Drive 9: Stanley to Lost Trail Pass

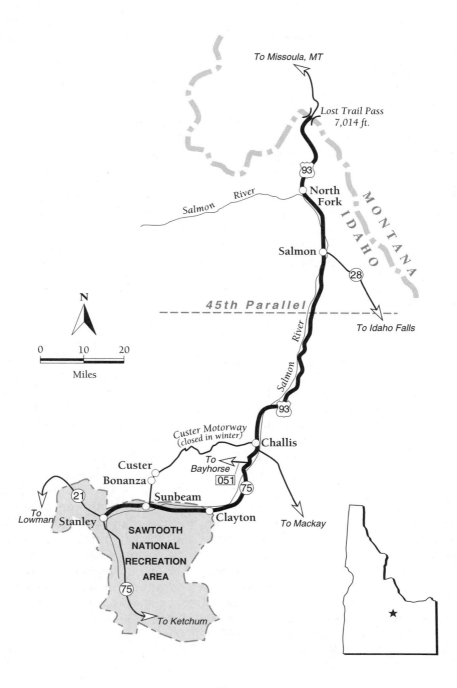

To Missoula, MT

Lost Trail Pass
7,014 ft.

93

North
Fork

Salmon River

Salmon

M O N T A N A

I D A H O

28

45th Parallel

To Idaho Falls

N

0   10   20
Miles

Salmon River

93

Custer Motorway
(closed in winter)

Challis

Custer

To
Bayhorse

051

75

Bonanza

Sunbeam

21

To
Lowman Stanley

Clayton

To Mackay

**SAWTOOTH
NATIONAL
RECREATION
AREA**

75

To Ketchum

★

a final inventory before departure, and returning rafters spreading sleeping bags and tents to dry, looking for the luxury of a bit of junk food at the only market in town.

Small as it is, with only about 75 year-round residents, Stanley is divided into upper Stanley and lower Stanley. The upper town sits astride the junction of ID 75 and ID 21, while the lower town is strung out along ID 75 just north of the junction.

The junction also marks the only spot in the state where three designated scenic byways come together. The Sawtooth Scenic Byway heads south to Sun Valley and beyond; the Ponderosa Pine Scenic Byway travels to Boise on ID 21; and the Salmon River Scenic Byway follows the main stem of the Salmon downstream to North Fork.

Leave Stanley on ID 75 heading north.

The Salmon River came by its name quite naturally. It was named for the prodigious runs of salmon that returned each year from the ocean to their birthplaces in the streams and lakes high in the Sawtooths. Redfish Lake, above Stanley, was named for the crimson color of the spawning salmon. They were said to be so thick that the water appeared to run red. Dam building along the Columbia River has reduced the migration of salmon to a mere trickle. The number of returning fish is now counted in the tens or hundreds, rather than the thousands and millions that once traveled this river.

The earliest recorded explorer to pass through was Alexander Ross. In 1824, he described bears rooting in the fields across the river. The fertile lowlands were a smorgasbord for the bears, with crops of camas lily, onions, and wild celery. The meadows were so thoroughly turned over that they reminded Ross of cultivated fields.

Just north of town is the small Stanley Museum, housed in the old Valley Creek ranger station (built in 1934), and run by the Sawtooth Interpretative and Historical Association.

At the site of Sunbeam Hot Springs, 10 miles beyond Stanley, stands one of the many lasting contributions of Franklin Roosevelt's Civilian Conservation Corps (CCC). In order to create gainful employment in the dark days of the Great Depression, the CCC was charged with implementing improvement projects throughout the country. The projects ranged from trail- and road-building to erosion control and forestry. The stone bathhouse here was built in the 1930s as part of a CCC camp. Water from the hot springs on the hill was piped to the bathhouse, and the pipes were shunted through cooler river water to give the CCC workers the luxury of a hot shower after their hard work. Today, the hot water from the spring runs down the hill and into the river. On days that are a bit chilly, river runners stop here to warm their feet by standing in the spring's outflow.

The CCC camp was not the first settlement here. The presence of warm water made this an ideal location to raise chickens year-round, since the water could be used to keep the chickens comfortable through the long, cold winters this area experiences. Barzilla Clark, who later became governor of Idaho (1937–1939) operated a chicken ranch in this vicinity.

Ahead is the site of the only dam that ever stretched across the Salmon River. Built in 1910 to supply electric power to a mill on Jordan Creek, the dam takes advantage of the hot springs to keep the turbines spinning through the winter. The mines on Jordan Creek were not profitable, however, and by 1934 the dam was dynamited and the river again ran free.

At Sunbeam, a side trip up the Yankee Fork River on good gravel road (24 miles round-trip) is a worthwhile option. Turn left at Sunbeam, onto Forest Service Road 013. The road follows the river and traverses mounds of dredged gravel up to the historic Yankee Fork gold dredge, then ascends a narrow valley, coming to two ghost towns that only whisper their glorious past. Scan the slopes above Bonanza for elusive mountain goats. The museum at Custer provides an excellent collection of mining equipment and restored buildings that bring the old mining camp to life. See Drive 10 in this book, the Custer Motorway, for a more complete description of the towns of Bonanza and Custer and of the historic Custer Motorway, which linked these mining settlements with Challis, on the other side of Mill Creek Summit.

After returning to ID 75 from Custer and Bonanza, turn left (east) and continue down the Salmon River from Sunbeam, following the road as it winds gradually between steep hillsides. The incredible power of the river is evident near milepost 207, where rounded boulders of up to 3 feet in diameter are exposed in a roadcut. The river deposited these rocks during some long-past flood. Notice how much the boulders look like the bed of a stream. Imagine the forces necessary to move and polish so much stone.

Side streams enter the Salmon at regular intervals here. Creeks named Peach, Gardner, Burnt, Slate, and Holman all enter the river in a short span. Thompson Creek, joining the Salmon from the north, is the site of an active molybdenum mine. Lead and silver were mined in the region for many years. Clayton, 20 miles downstream from Sunbeam, was the site of a smelter operated from the 1880s until after the turn of the century. The mines have made this area southern Idaho's primary silver-producing district since 1935, when prices rose. The barren piles of gravel littering the hillsides are the old mines' tailings piles. The larger the pile of tailings, the more successful the mine—or at least, the farther into the hillside the miners went before giving up.

The East Fork of the Salmon joins the river's main stem at a broad clearing known as Poverty Flats, 5 miles past Clayton. Even though the river brings its abundant moisture through the flats, the sage and cottonwoods here are sparse and scrawny. The closer you get to Challis, the drier the hillsides appear. The occasional irrigated plots in relatively flat patches on the valley floor make the dry and dusty slopes look even more barren by comparison. Below the confluence, the valley has occasional wide spots, but steep slopes still predominate.

Another 8 miles downstream from Poverty Flats, a broad open meadow opens up near the mouth of Bayhorse Creek. Bayhorse Creek Road (Forest Road 051) travels up the creek to the mining camp of Bayhorse. Old charcoal kilns and other evidence of early mining are visible here. This area is private, though, so observe signs and ask permission before exploring. If you take this side trip, be sure to look for bighorn sheep on the inhospitable slopes. Return to ID 75 and turn left (east).

Below Bayhorse Creek on ID 75, you will see increasing signs of settlement as you approach Challis. Just before milepost 244, a historical marker points out the site of a Shoshone bison jump. Native American hunters would herd bison along the upper reaches of the hill until they reached this cliff. Here the bison would be herded over the cliff, where their carcasses could be easily butchered. Artifacts found here make this a valuable archaeological site. Researchers have determined that bison were still present until the 1860s or 1870s, much later than earlier research indicated. The jump is on the National Register of Historic Places.

Just ahead on the left is the Land of the Yankee Fork Visitor Center. This modern facility, designed to evoke the area's mining heritage, contains informative exhibits as well as friendly, knowledgeable staff to answer questions. This is a good place to inquire about the accessibility of the Custer Motorway, which is usually closed through the winter and spring. The visitor center is located at the end of ID 75, where it meets US 93.

The Salmon River is more than a mile east of Challis, at the foot of the low hills across Round Valley. Nestled at the base of the cliffs across the river is Challis Hot Springs, with a pool and campground. For a short side trip to the pool, turn right (south) on US 93, cross the bridge that spans the river on US 93 before turning left again, and follow the signs to Challis Hot Springs, about 4 miles from US 93 across the cultivated valley floor.

Back on the main drive, head north on US 93 toward Challis. Challis is a quiet town of 1,100 people. It supports nearby cattle ranches and mining operations, and serves as a base for Challis National Forest operations.

When the Borah Peak earthquake hit in October 1983, Challis bore the brunt of the damage. Had the magnitude 7.3 earthquake struck a more heavily populated area, the devastation would have been significantly worse. As it was, two children were killed on their way to school when a storefront collapsed on them.

As you leave Challis heading north, the landscape is much the same as

The Salmon River between Stanley and Sunbeam offers a calm float.

it was south of the town. Dry, steep hillsides drop to a narrow river bottom spotted with cottonwoods. The road cruises along with the river to the right for several miles before crossing to the other side. Glimpses of the Pahsimeroi Mountains are visible to the right until the canyon walls close in and hide them from view. Soon the river narrows again, despite small streams entering from both sides of the canyon.

At Ellis, nothing more than a post office 15 miles north of Challis, there is no longer room in the canyon for anything more than the river and the road. The hillsides are covered with chunks of flaky, crumbly metamorphic rocks, broken down by the endless freeze-and-thaw cycle of nature. The jagged nature of the fractured rock has helped to create the precipitous walls of the canyon, since it piles up at a steep angle. Rounded rocks would never create such a steep canyon wall, as they would continue to roll, and come to rest at a much flatter angle.

The rock doesn't hold much moisture; thus, little soil is created, allowing only the most tenacious vegetation to take hold. In places you can see tracks, like avalanche chutes, where fresh rockfalls still shape the canyon. Of course, it is the river that has performed the lion's share of the carving here, digging the floor of the canyon ever deeper.

Ahead is a geographical curiosity. The road crosses the 45th Parallel— the imaginary line that circles the earth halfway between the equator and the North Pole.

At this point, it becomes quite easy to tell just how far it is to the town of Salmon: a series of creeks enter the river at fairly regular intervals, beginning with Twelve Mile Creek, Eleven Mile Creek, and so on, counting down the distance to the town. Soon the canyon spreads out, becoming a broad, open valley with lush meadows and tall, stately cottonwoods in the moist river bottoms. Looming beyond the valley is the Continental Divide, following the crest of the Bitterroot Mountains. The divide marks Idaho's border with Montana.

Follow US 93 through Salmon, crossing the river at the far end of the town's central business district. Just before the bridge, on the right side of the street, is the Lemhi County Museum, which houses artifacts and memorabilia from the region's early mining days, as well as exhibits of Native American artifacts. The museum also features a compelling display of Chinese lacquerware, bronze, and pewter pieces encrusted with jade and carnelian. There is also a Tibetan altar set. All were brought back from the Orient in 1920 by a local resident.

From Salmon, continue north on US 93. This stretch has historic significance as well as scenic beauty. The Lewis and Clark Expedition first crossed the divide at Lemhi Pass to the south, and followed the Lemhi River here, to its confluence with the Salmon. The party then traveled along the

Salmon River, hoping that they could ride it downstream to the Columbia River and the Pacific Ocean. Just as they had been told by the Nez Perce tribes, however, this was truly the "River of No Return." In search of an easier crossing, the expedition followed roughly the same path as US 93, heading back across the divide at Lost Trail Pass.

This section of highway is also designated part of the Nez Perce Trail—the path that Chief Joseph and his followers took in 1877 in their flight from government pursuit.

At milepost 326 sits the town of North Fork. Here, the North Fork of the Salmon joins the main river as it turns to the west. Some 30 miles downstream, the small road following the river abruptly ends, and river runners part company with civilization.

Back on US 93, we slowly climb toward the Continental Divide, more than 3,000 vertical feet above North Fork and some 25 miles away. Gibbonsville, a flourishing gold camp from 1880 to 1889, is 11 miles north of North Fork. Dahlonega Creek, which trickles down to the North Fork at Gibbonsville, is a reminder that the prospectors here were always on the move, and eternally optimistic: the creek is named for the Georgia location of the first major United States gold strike, back in 1828.

Shortly, the steep climb to the top of Lost Trail Pass begins in earnest. Through 1996 and 1997 this road was under heavy construction, with closures of up to 12 hours at a stretch. The construction has resulted in a much safer roadway, but the long delays associated with the construction have required some advance planning by motorists. Be sure to ask locally for any road closure information related to ongoing construction.

The drive ends at the summit of Lost Trail Pass, on the Continental Divide at the Montana border. From here Missoula, Montana, is 92 miles north on US 93.

10

Custer Motorway

General description: This 46-mile drive is a backcountry adventure on gravel and unimproved dirt roads, following a historic wagon road from Challis to the gold mining towns of Custer and Bonanza over an 8,800-foot mountain pass. The road is rough and narrow, with no services available along its entire length.

Special attractions: The Custer Motorway itself; backcountry forest scenery; ghost towns of Custer and Bonanza; historical exhibits at Custer; the Yankee Fork Gold Dredge; and the possibility of sighting mountain goats on the slopes above Bonanza.

Location: Custer is the geographic center of Idaho.

Drive route numbers: Garden Creek Road and Challis National Forest Road 070 (Custer Motorway).

Travel season: The Custer Motorway is open only when it is free from snow, from sometime in May or June until snows cover the road again, usually in October. Call the Land of the Yankee Fork State Park office or the Challis National Forest office in Challis for road information.

Camping: There are commercial campgrounds in Challis, with RV and tent sites. Six national forest campgrounds are located along the route— Mill Creek Campground on the east side of Mill Creek Summit, Eightmile and Custer campgrounds between the summit and Custer, and Pole Flat, Flat Rock, and Blind Creek campgrounds between Bonanza and Sunbeam.

Services: Challis has motels, restaurants, and fuel. Limited food service can be found at Sunbeam. There are no other services along the 46-mile route.

Nearby attractions: Challis Hot Springs; Borah Peak; whitewater rafting on the Salmon River; the scenic beauty of the Sawtooth National Recreation Area.

 The Drive

The Custer Motorway is a bit different from most of the other drives in this book. It is a 46-mile exploration of the Yankee Fork mining district, almost entirely on gravel or unimproved forest roads. The drive is accessible only from sometime in May or June (depending on the previous winter's snow depths and the warmth of the spring) until the snow flies again in the fall. It is a rough, narrow road with steep sections, ruts, and the possibility

Drive 10: Custer Motorway

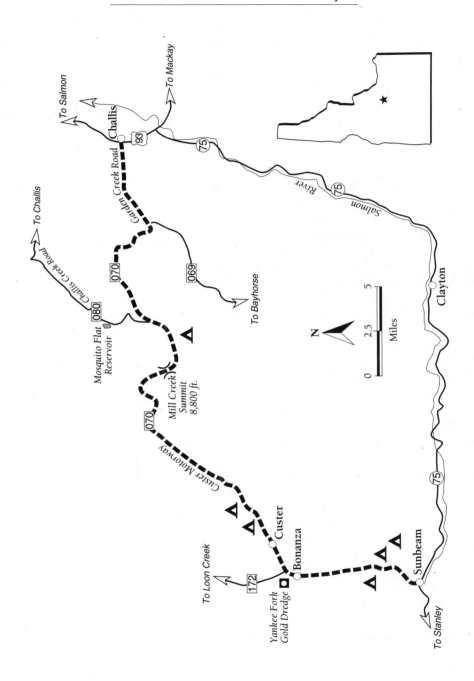

of exposed rocks which could cause damage to the undercarriage of a passenger car.

The official description of the road, from a brochure partially funded by the Idaho Travel Council, describes the road:

> Forest Road 070 from Challis to Custer is a narrow, dirt road suitable for pickups and other high-clearance vehicles. Not recommended for low-clearance autos, large motorhomes, and travel trailers. Watch for other vehicles and please drive safely. The road is usually closed from late October through May due to winter snow conditions.

Be certain that your vehicle is in good working order. Pack fuel, water, and a working spare tire before taking this journey. It is a long walk from Mill Creek Summit to either Challis or Custer, and there will be little traffic on the road, particularly on weekdays.

Now that you have been properly warned, this is a wonderful drive through forests and over a low pass (almost 8,800 feet above sea level). The scenery along the route and the opportunity of sighting mountain goats are enough to make this a pleasant drive. Add the route's historical significance, the wonderful museum at Custer, and the Yankee Fork dredge at the mouth of Jordan Creek, and this is one of the premiere short excursions in all of Idaho.

The Custer Motorway follows the route of the main road that supplied the mining camps of Custer and Bonanza in the 1880s, the region's heyday. Freighters and stagecoaches plied the route for 10 years, paying a steep toll for the privilege. The passenger fare for the nine-hour stagecoach trip was $8—a fortune in 1880!

Before you start the drive, a stop at the Land of the Yankee Fork Visitor Center south of Challis at the junction of Idaho Highway 75 and U.S. Highway 93 will provide you with up-to-the-minute road conditions as well as an orientation to the entire Yankee Fork Mining District. The friendly staff will answer your questions and make your visit more enjoyable.

The route begins at the west end of Main Street in Challis. Note your odometer reading here, or set the trip odometer in your vehicle to zero, and proceed west on Garden Creek Road. The road passes the small Challis golf course and a number of homes and ranches before giving way to the dry, steep hillsides so typical of this part of Idaho. The pavement ends in 4.8 miles, just after the junction with FR 069, which continues up Garden Creek. Turn right and head uphill on Forest Road 070, the official designation of the Custer Motorway. Down the valley to the right, you can see back to Challis and across the valley to the cliffs cut by the Salmon River on its journey north.

The Yankee Fork Gold Dredge chewed up miles of creek bed in search of gold.

Visible from the top of the hill, behind the ranch in the distance, is the slope known as the Corkscrew Grade. The steep grade required additional draft animals to pull the heavy freight wagons up the hill, and extra teams were available here to be pressed into service. The road drops back down Big Hill (as it is known locally), crosses Mill Creek, and begins a slow climb. At 13.5 miles, you will pass a junction with FR 080, which crosses a low saddle to Mosquito Flat Reservoir, in a quiet valley 2 miles north.

This junction was the site of Greenwood Station, one of the stops along the mining camp route. The horses, mules, and oxen could rest and get water here. Greenwood Station also provided passengers with a temporary respite from the constant bouncing and jarring of the wagons on the rough roads. The station was operated by Fannie Clark, who later moved her business farther up the road.

Mill Creek Campground is another mile up FR 070; it offers the only improved campsites on this side of the Mill Creek Summit. There are two more campgrounds located ahead on the downhill run into Custer, and there are several others between Custer and Sunbeam.

Above Mill Creek Campground, the road seems no wider or better maintained than it was 120 years ago. If there is snow remaining, here is where you will find it. I made a trip here at the end of June 1996, and the road was blocked by six-foot drifts.

The remains of Tollgate Station are still visible 2.5 miles past Mill Creek Campground. Strategically located, the toll station was far enough from either end of the road that non-payment of the toll was not an option—no one would invest the time and effort it took to make it this far without shelling out the cash needed to get through. As is quite obvious, there would have been no way to slip around the tollgate, either. The heavily forested, steep, rocky slopes were quite effective at preventing gate crashers.

Mill Creek Summit itself is a non-event. No dramatic change in the forests or surrounding mountain vistas marks the apex. Instead, the summit is a gentle saddle. The run down from the summit passes the sites of Homestead Station, Twelve-Mile Station, and Eleven-Mile Barn. Almost no traces remain of these once lively stops along the toll road. At just under 36 miles from Challis, the road arrives at Custer. This well-preserved ghost town once had a population of more than 600 people. The larger of the 2 towns in the Yankee Fork basin, Bonanza, lies another mile ahead.

Today Custer is home to many historic displays of old mining equipment, including a stamp mill. These machines used hydraulic or steam power to pound ore into a fine powder from which the heavier gold could be washed more easily. The walking tour of the town and the exhibits in the old schoolhouse are both worth your time. A model of the entire town of Custer, painstakingly carved of polished stone, sits inside the old schoolhouse museum.

A deserted cabin at Bonanza.

Below Custer is the confluence of Jordan Creek and the Yankee Fork. Jordan Creek, named for early prospector Sylvester Jordan, was the site of the first gold finds in the Yankee Fork district, in 1870. A pond here is the final resting place of the Yankee Fork Gold Dredge. Built between 1939 and 1940, the dredge weighed around 1,000 tons. It had 72 buckets, each of which could scoop up 8 cubic feet of creek bed at a time. The gravel was dredged from depths of up to 35 feet. As the dredge slowly moved forward into the pond it continuously excavated, the gravel was processed through filter screens on the main deck of the dredge. Successivly smaller filter screens trapped the fine, heavy, gold-bearing sediments, while the larger, lighter stones and gravel were deposited onto a conveyor belt that ran out the back end of the dredge.

As the dredge moved forward, the gantry swung from side to side while the conveyor carried away the debris. The gantry's back-and-forth motion formed the patterns of the gravel deposits seen along the Yankee Fork for almost 6 miles downstream from here, tracing the dredge's entire active lifespan. Driving across the tailings, you get a good feel for the impact this awesome machine had on the Yankee Fork drainage. It is estimated that the dredge moved more than 6 million cubic yards of stream gravel (enough to fill a football stadium several times over), and recovered more than one million dollars in gold and silver.

The last owner of the dredge was J. R. Simplot, who had his finger in many Idaho pies, from potatoes, fertilizers, and frozen foods to real estate and mining. Simplot is said to have gotten his start when, as a young man, he salvaged a truckload of seed potatoes that had been left inadvertently on the side of a road. From that first crop, he went on to supply dehydrated potatoes to the troops in World War II, and then frozen potatoes to McDonald's, amassing a fortune in the process.

Simplot donated the dredge to the USDA Forest Service after it ran out of accessible ground to chew up. The Yankee Fork Gold Dredge Association conducts tours of the dredge on summer weekends.

About a half mile below the dredge is the old Bonanza City townsite. There's not much left to see here, and what remains is private property. Across the stream, on the cliffs that tower above the townsite, visitors may spot mountain goats perched on the steep slopes.

In 1878, Bonanza was the setting for a story of romance and murder. That year, Richard and Lizzie King came to Bonanza from California. They were befriended by Charles Franklin, who had laid out the town and operated its hotel. Lizzie ran a saloon and dance hall while her husband prospected—until he was shot and killed in an argument over a piece of land. After Lizzie buried Richard, Franklin took upon himself the task of consoling her. He did a fine job of it and by the summer of 1880 the citizens of Bonanza were convinced that they would soon be invited to a wedding. They were, but not the wedding of Charles and Lizzie. Instead, Lizzie married Robert Hawthorne, who very recently had arrived in town.

Just a week later, the young couple was found shot to death in a little cabin at the north end of Bonanza. No weapon was ever found, and no one was ever convicted of the crime. Charles Franklin himself, now grief-stricken as well as heart-broken, laid them out in their burial plot in the Bonanza Cemetery, with Lizzie lying forever between Richard and Robert. Franklin refused to put Lizzie's new married name on her headstone.

Franklin eventually left town. He worked a placer claim on a nearby creek, becoming increasingly reclusive over the next ten years. In 1892, his body was found in his cabin, a locket with Lizzie's picture clutched in his cold, dead hand. He was buried in an unmarked grave behind his cabin. The plot that holds Lizzie and her two husbands is located in the Bonanza Cemetery on FR 074, about 1 mile from the Custer Motorway.

Below Bonanza, the road travels over and through the dredge tailings before reaching the first of several pleasant Forest Service campgrounds in the last few miles above the small resort of Sunbeam, which sits on ID 75 at the mouth of the Yankee Fork. The Land of the Yankee Fork State Park maintains an interpretative overlook on the Salmon River, just across ID 75 from Sunbeam. Here are the remains of the last dam on the Salmon River, dynamited in 1934 to allow salmon to return to the lakes of the Sawtooth range. The dam was originally built to supply electrical power to the mining operation up the Yankee Fork. The site was chosen to take advantage of the hot springs just upstream, which allowed the project to generate electricity all year long. The dam was in operation for only a short time before the mine was abandoned.

This ends your backcountry drive. From here, it is 10 miles upstream on ID 75 to Stanley, or 45 miles downstream to Challis on the same road.

11

Trail Creek Road

General description: An 80-mile drive on gravel and paved roads from Sun Valley up a pleasant valley and over Trail Creek Summit, east to the base of Borah Peak, Idaho's highest point, through Grand View Canyon, and into Challis.

Special attractions: The ski resort communities of Ketchum and Sun Valley; the Hemingway Memorial; scenic vistas along Trail Creek, and views of the Pioneer, White Knob and Lost River mountains, including two of Idaho's three highest peaks; the Earthquake Visitor Information Center at the base of Borah Peak.

Location: The central Idaho mountains.

Drive route numbers: Sun Valley Road/Trail Creek Road and U.S. Highway 93.

Travel season: The road over Trail Creek Summit is closed by snow from October until sometime in May or June. Check in Ketchum for road conditions.

Camping: There is a Sawtooth National Forest campground east of Sun Valley and two Challis National Forest campgrounds just over Trail Creek Summit.

Services: Full services, including resort hotels, motels, restaurants, and shopping are available at Ketchum and Sun Valley. Food and lodging is also available at Challis.

Nearby attractions: Sawtooth National Recreation Area, with scenic views, fishing, hiking, and cross-country skiing; Land of the Yankee Fork—historic region of gold mines and ghost towns; Challis Hot Springs.

 ## The Drive

This pleasant mountain drive takes you up the valley of Trail Creek, with a climb over the top of the Boulder Mountains and down into the drainage of Big Lost River. The drive offers scenic views of Idaho's highest summit, Borah Peak, in the Lost River Range.

Trail Creek Road is usually closed by snows from October through May. Most of its length is unpaved, but it is an improved road and is easily negotiable with a passenger vehicle. Be sure to inquire in Ketchum or Sun Valley before taking this route.

Drive 11: Trail Creek Road

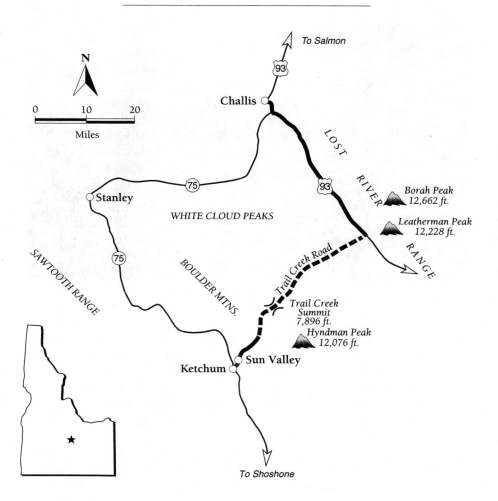

Begin the drive on Sun Valley Road/Trail Creek Road in the center of Ketchum. Head east, into the resort of Sun Valley. This "twin cities" community rivals Aspen or Santa Fe for its popularity with trendsetters and celebrities, even though residents pride themselves on treating them as if they were "just folks." Sun Valley is also a popular spot for those who appreciate the area's plentiful opportunities for year-round outdoor recreation.

The valley has had its fair share of characters. Some years ago, the story was told of a man who hiked out to a secluded hot springs pool. So entranced was he with the pool that he jumped right in to soak his tired

The valley of Trail Creek, east of Sun Valley.

bones. After he had been in the warm water for some time, he realized that he had neglected to remove his clothes. Since it was mid-February, deep in the heart of winter, all he could do was remove the wet garments and wait in the warm water until they dried. Unfortunately, the cold weather froze his gear before it could dry, and he was trapped in the pool. By the time he was discovered and rescued 28 days later, moss was growing on his body and he had lost more than 60 pounds.

Sun Valley was developed by Averell Harriman, former director of the Union Pacific Railroad, to fill seats on railroad cars. In 1936, Harriman sent a young Austrian count who knew something about ski terrain, Felix Schaffgotsch, out across the American West to find the perfect winter resort. After visiting sites in Washington, Oregon, Colorado, Utah, and Wyoming, the count found what he was looking for in Idaho. With a railhead a mile away in Ketchum, blankets of powder snow on gentle mountain slopes, and incredible winter sunshine, Schaffgotsch knew that Sun Valley was perfect.

He contacted Harriman, who immediately came to inspect the site. Construction began quickly, and the Sun Valley Lodge was open for guests by the beginning of the 1936–1937 ski season. Ski runs on Dollar Mountain and Proctor Mountain also opened that year with chair lifts that Union Pacific engineers modeled after banana conveyors used to load ships in the tropics.

Visit the lodge and walk the halls on either side of the main lobby.

Borah Peak is the highest point in Idaho.

There you will find publicity photos of the many celebrities who have enjoyed the Sun Valley experience. From the photos it would seem that it really is sunny all the time. If that were the case, though, there wouldn't be any of the glistening crystal snow that makes this a skier's dream. Beyond the lobby is an ice rink, where world-renowned skaters perform in a show that's a summer tradition. Hot summer days are a challenge for an outdoor ice rink, and a thin sheen of meltwater often sits on the ice's surface, the sheltering canopies notwithstanding.

Back on Sun Valley Road (also known as Trail Creek Road), about a mile beyond the lodge, sits the peaceful Hemingway Memorial. In a wooded bend on a 3-foot-wide canal, a simple bust of the famous author sits on a pedestal of sandstone and concrete. The inscription is taken from an epitaph Ernest Hemingway wrote about a friend. On a crisp autumn day, sitting on the secluded stone bench and watching cottonwood leaves drift by in the canal, it's easy to understand his love of the outdoors.

Beyond the memorial, the road narrows and follows Trail Creek between sage-covered hills until it angles upward. Trail Creek quickly shrinks as the road climbs over the crest of the hills that forms the Blaine and Custer county line. The road now heads gradually downhill. After you cross Big Fall Creek, look for a parking area on the left. A short walk upstream leads to the 30-foot Big Falls. As the road crosses Kane Creek 3 miles farther on, the peaks visible to the right are Phi Kappa (10,516 feet) and the jumbled cliffs known as the Devil's Bedstead (10,750 feet). Behind them is 12,078-foot Hyndman Peak, the highest point in the Pioneer Mountains, and the third highest point in Idaho.

Ahead lies the Lost River Range, named for the river that drains this valley and heads south into the Snake River plain, where it vanishes into the ground. The waters eventually resurface in the vicinity of Hagerman, on the rim of the Snake River canyon more than 100 miles away. The main peaks of the Lost River Range, Leatherman Peak (12,228 feet) and Borah Peak (12,662 feet), are the highest summits in the state. Borah Peak is named for the "Lion of Idaho," Senator William Borah, who served Idaho in the U.S. Senate from 1907 until his death in 1940. Borah's career included a law practice in Kansas, after which he headed toward Seattle. When he stopped enroute in Boise, he watched a drunken lawyer try a case and decided that a sober attorney could do very well in Idaho. He stayed, and made a name for himself trying the case against "Big Bill" Haywood for the assassination of former governor Frank Steunenberg.

The Pioneer Mountains to the rear, the White Knobs to the east, and the Lost River Range across the valley are all part of the Basin and Range, a series of mountain ranges and intervening valleys that generally tends northwest to southeast. The mountains are continually being formed by movement along thrust faults, which is slowly raising the peaks and dropping the valley floors across broad sections of Nevada, Idaho, and Utah.

The last major movement along the fault line that defines the Lost River Range came in 1983. A 7.3-magnitude earthquake resulted from a 5-foot movement along the fault, visible across the lower slopes of Borah Peak. The valley floor dropped 4 feet, and the peaks gained 1 foot in elevation. Scientists have estimated that an earthquake of this magnitude would have to occur every 3,300 years over a 5-million-year span to explain the displacement between the identical rock formations at the top of Borah Peak and below the valley floor on the other side of the fault line. That's 1,500 earthquakes along this fault alone.

The damage done by an earthquake of that magnitude can be devastating. If the Borah Peak quake had occurred in a heavily populated area, hundreds or thousands of lives might have been lost, and property damage would have been catastrophic. As it was, two lives were lost in the 1983 quake. In Challis, just 30 miles north, two schoolchildren were killed by falling brickwork as they walked to school. The quake catapulted a 50-ton boulder down a hill into Challis, chimneys cracked here and clear into Montana, and groundwater began to behave differently. In Yellowstone, Old Faithful became less faithful; in the valleys, new fountains spouted and springs flowed furiously. A silver mine flooded near Clayton. The Big Lost River flowed at nearly double its normal flow for six months afterward.

Trail Creek Road deadends at US 93, 41 miles from Sun Valley. Turn left (north) onto US 93. There are two turnoffs ahead for visitors to Borah Peak. About half a mile past milepost 129, Birch Springs Road (FR 279) leads to the base of the foot trail that winds 6 miles to the summit, a climb of more than 5,000 feet. About a mile and a half farther, at milepost 131, turn right onto Doublespring Pass Road (FR 116) for a short drive to see the fault line and the self-guided exhibits at the Earthquake Visitors Information Center.

Continuing north on US 93, the road tops Willow Creek Summit at 7,160 feet and follows Warm Springs Creek. After 10 miles, it cuts through Grand View Canyon, a surprisingly rugged, and somewhat unexpected, defile. The canyon was formed by the waters of the creek cutting through softer deposits. Then, fully entrenched, the stream encountered harder rocks and had no choice but to continue carving through the harder layers. The softer sediments around the canyon have since eroded away, but the stream's course was already "set in stone."

US 93 arrives in Challis 14 miles after leaving Grand View Canyon. Here the drive ends. From Challis, US 93 continues 60 miles north to Salmon, while Idaho 75 heads south and west 55 miles to Stanley.

12

Lemhi Pass

General description: The 39-mile drive is a backcountry loop on gravel roads that are, in places, narrow, steep, and rough. Climbing from the Lemhi Valley to a saddle on the crest of the Beaverhead Mountains, the route visits the location where Lewis and Clark's party first viewed the western slope of the Rocky Mountains.

Special attractions: The tranquil Lemhi Valley; the chance to spot deer in a backcountry setting; mountain vistas across the Bitterroots to the northeast and the Lemhi Range to the west; Lemhi Pass, where Meriwether Lewis first tasted the waters of the mighty Columbia River.

Location: The east-central portion of Idaho, south of Salmon.

Drive route numbers: Old Highway 28, Salmon National Forest Road 185 (Warm Springs Road), and Salmon National Forest Road 13 (Lewis and Clark Highway).

Travel season: This is a fair-weather drive on dirt and gravel roads. It is inaccessible until winter snows melt, usually sometime in June. Do not attempt the drive in extremely wet weather at any time of year. September provides an opportunity to view the changing colors of aspen trees on the higher slopes.

Camping: There are no established campgrounds on the route. Commercial campgrounds are available in Salmon.

Services: Other than a small general store in Tendoy there are no services of any sort on the route. All tourist services are available in Salmon, north on Idaho Highway 28. There are almost no services south on ID 28 until Rexburg, more than 110 miles away.

Nearby attractions: Lemhi County Historical Museum in Salmon; downhill skiing at Lost Trail Powder Mountain; whitewater adventures on the Salmon River; the Birch Creek charcoal kilns.

 # The Drive

This is a 39-mile backcountry loop on gravel roads in the Salmon National Forest. From the tiny town of Tendoy on ID 28, it scales the steep hills of the Beaverhead Mountains to the summit of Lemhi Pass on the Idaho-Montana border. From this point, the Lewis and Clark Expedition first viewed the west side of the Continental Divide. The rugged terrain that stretched to the west dashed their dreams of finding a water passage between the Atlantic and the Pacific oceans.

Drive 12: Lemhi Pass

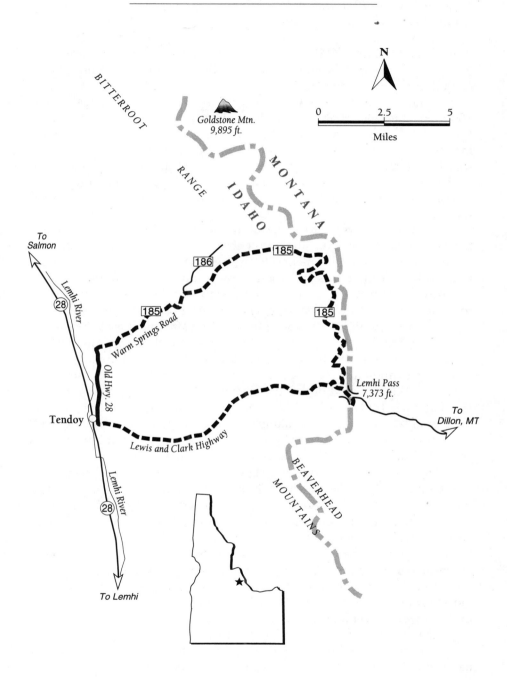

Begin at Tendoy, little more than a post office and a few farmhouses located on ID 28, 20 miles south of Salmon. Tendoy sits in the valley of the Lemhi River, whose drainage includes the eastern flank of the Lemhi Range and the western slope of the Beaverhead Mountains. The crest of the Beaverheads defines the Montana-Idaho border and the Continental Divide. Neither range overwhelms the landscape, although individual summits rise 6,000 feet or more above the valley floor.

Coming from Salmon, turn left (east) at Tendoy, and left again after 100 yards onto Old Highway 28. Signs direct motorists to the Lewis and Clark Back Country Byway, which consists of three different roads, including Old 28, Warm Springs Road (FR 185), and the Lewis and Clark Highway. The byway is one of 14 Idaho scenic and historic tourist routes identified by the Bureau of Land Management and the USDA Forest Service. Brochures at visitor centers and Forest Service offices identify all of the designated routes.

The road follows the east edge of the valley for almost 3 miles. Follow the signs for the byway, turning uphill on FR 185 (Warm Springs Road). A small covered pavilion at milepost 3 displays a map of the route, as well as information on the Lewis and Clark Expedition. (As this route's brown-and-white mile markers are the best indicators of distance on this gravel road, descriptions throughout this drive will refer to the mileposts.)

From the pavilion continue uphill to a fork after milepost 9. Be sure to stay to the right here and avoid FR 186 (Kenney Creek Road). After climbing through grassy hills the road soon enters a lodgepole pine forest as it continues to approach the divide. At milepost 16 the route turns south as the road crests just west of the Idaho-Montana state line. The Continental Divide Scenic Trail, a footpath that closely follows the divide, crosses the route at milepost 20. The road along the crest here generally is smooth and wide, although wet weather or logging trucks can make conditions treacherous. Forest clearcuts are visible occasionally along this stretch.

The practice of clearcutting a stand of timber means just that. An entire stand of timber is felled, and the remaining branches and debris, called slash, are burned off. The forest is then replanted with new seedlings, which will grow to a uniform age and size. Clearcutting has long been a contentious issue. Loggers look at the lower short-term costs of removing all trees from a section of forest, and conservationists complain that the method removes habitat for forest fauna, some of which may be endangered. They also argue that the replanting of a forest at a uniform age and size is not the most beneficial strategy for either the forest, which may become susceptible to disease and insect infestation, or for the loggers, who must wait 25 years or more to re-harvest the same plot of timber.

The more enlightened, and more expensive, approach to timber harvesting is called selective cutting. Only a predetermined percentage of the trees in a plot are cut at any one time, leaving behind a forest that can

Along the Lewis and Clark Back Country Byway.

still sustain wildlife. The entire forest is healthier when it is made up of trees of different species and ages.

At milepost 24 the road begins a gradual descent along the divide to a ridge with gravel roads leading to the east and the west. Here, at milepost 26, is the summit of Lemhi Pass. A fence marks the border of Montana and Idaho.

In August 1805, Meriwether Lewis, with a small party, left William Clark and the main body of their party near present-day Dillon, Montana, to search out Shoshone tribesmen with whom they might trade for horses. The Shoshone woman, Sacagawea, who accompanied the expedition, knew there should be Shoshone nearby, since she recognized the country. The party ascended the eastern flank of the Bitterroots, arriving at the summit of Lemhi Pass on August 12. From this point Meriwether Lewis first glimpsed the ranges of mountains that still lay before his expedition as they searched for the fabled Northwest Passage. As Lewis stood here, his spirits must certainly have flagged a little, for the sight of range after range of imposing mountains would have told him that the hoped-for short portage across the divide, and an all-water passage from the Missouri River to the Columbia River, was not to be.

At the summit, turn left through the fence and then immediately head south 0.2 miles on a rough, rocky road to a peaceful campground with a short wildflower trail. This grove, called the Sacagawea Memorial Camp, was dedicated in 1935 to the Indian woman who accompanied Lewis and Clark from Montana on into Idaho. From the grove, return to the saddle at the Lemhi Pass summit, and head west, down the steep valley. FR 13, heading down the valley, is called the Lewis and Clark Highway, although this rocky, steep, and narrow track is about as far from being a highway as Tendoy is from needing a stoplight.

Just before milepost 28, a marker indicates the site of Meriwether Lewis's first campsite in Idaho. At this point, the trail taken by the expedition separates from the road, heading up a short draw north to the next valley, on Pattee Creek. As Lewis headed down this valley, he dipped his cup into the waters of the little stream and declared that he now had tasted, for the first time, the waters of the mighty Columbia River. After working their way down to the Lemhi River, his party found the Shoshone camped in the Lemhi valley, and began the process of negotiating for the horses they would need to continue their expedition. He convinced the Shoshone, including their chief, Cameahwait, to accompany him back across Lemhi Pass, and to meet there with Captain Clark and the rest of the party, to help carry the expedition's supplies over the divide.

When Lewis, Cameahwait, and other Shoshone tribesmen found Clark, Sacagawea recognized one of the Shoshone women as a friend from her youth, prior to her capture by the Mandan tribe, and before she had been taken east across the mountains into what is now Montana. Sacagawea and her friend, named Jumping Fish, screamed, shouted, and cried in their excitement.

The spirit of reunion enveloped the entire party when Sacagawea then recognized the Shoshone chief as her brother Cameahwait. Their relationship cemented the deal between Lewis and Cameahwait, and the Shoshone shared their horses, food, and information with Lewis's party.

The road continues to drop down this steep-walled valley paralleling Agency Creek, eventually reaching private lands and pastures before dropping back to the floor of the Lemhi valley. In a private cemetery near here is the grave of Chief Tendoy. Tendoy was a great orator and spokesman for the combined tribe of Shoshone, Bannock, and Sheepeaters that came to be known simply as Tendoy's Band. He successfully protected his band from the Indian Wars of the late 1870s. He had the respect of white leaders, who negotiated with him in 1880 to persuade his tribe to move onto the Fort Hall Reservation. He insisted on a clause that allowed his people to move to the reservation only when they were ready to go. They finally moved onto the reservation 25 years later, in 1905. Tendoy's grave marker is not accessible to the public.

At milepost 38, turn right onto Old 28 to complete the loop. FR 13 deadends in Tendoy. Turn left again in 200 yards to return to ID 28.

13

Glenns Ferry to Nampa

General description: The 120-mile drive explores Oregon Trail history in the town of Glenns Ferry before striking out across an arid portion of southwestern Idaho. The route parallels the south bank of the Snake River on two-lane paved roads through a sparsely populated region of desert and occasional irrigated fields.

Special attractions: Three Island Crossing State Park, site of a dreaded Snake River ford used by Oregon Trail emigrants; the Bruneau Dunes, a small set of 400-foot-high sand dunes; C. J. Strike Reservoir; the stark beauty of high desert landscapes.

Location: The southwest corner of Idaho.

Drive route numbers: First Avenue, Commercial Avenue and Madison Streets in Glenns Ferry, Interstate Highway 84, and Idaho Highways 78 and 45.

Travel season: Route is available for year-round travel, although the remoteness of the drive calls for extra caution in winter. Best times to travel are spring and fall, to avoid the severe heat of midsummer travel in the desert. The best chance to spot raptors along the Snake River is between mid-March and June.

Camping: Camping is available at Three Island Crossing and Bruneau Dunes state parks, and at C. J. Strike Reservoir.

Services: There are motels, restaurants, and service stations in Glenns Ferry and at Nampa, and limited services are available at Bruneau and Grandview.

Nearby attractions: Glenns Ferry Museum, housed in a 1909 schoolhouse; Bruneau Canyon; the 145-mile Owyhee Uplands Back Country Byway; the historic town of Silver City; Givens Hot Springs; World Center for Birds of Prey; Deer Flat National Wildlife Refuge; Old Fort Boise at Parma.

 The Drive

The Oregon Trail stretched from Missouri to the Willamette Valley of Oregon, luring emigrants west to settle the lush Oregon valleys and find for themselves a new life of bounty and self-sufficiency. There was a steep price to be paid for their elusive goal, however, and several installment payments came due as they traveled across the Snake River plain.

Drive 13: Glenns Ferry to Nampa

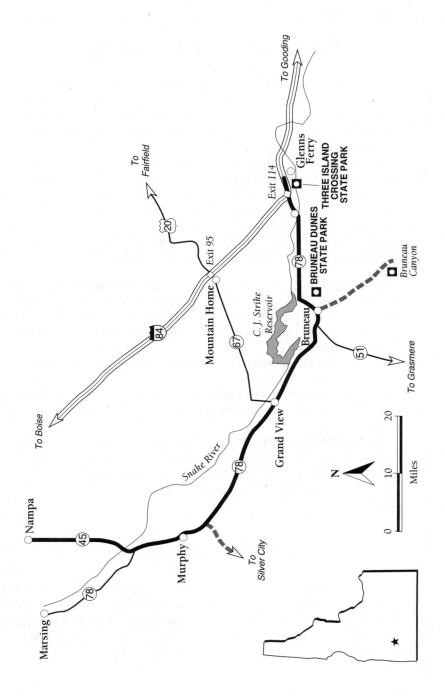

To Gooding

To Fairfield

Glenns Ferry

Exit 114

THREE ISLAND CROSSING STATE PARK

To Boise

84

Exit 95

20

To Fairfield

Mountain Home

67

C. J. Strike Reservoir

BRUNEAU DUNES STATE PARK

78

Bruneau

Bruneau Canyon

51

To Grasmere

Grand View

78

Snake River

N

0   10   20
Miles

Nampa

45

Murphy

To Silver City

78

Marsing

This Oregon Trail drive begins at one of the critical sites on the path of the westward migration that took place in the 1840s and 1850s. Glenns Ferry was named for Gustavus Glenn, who built the ferry here about 1870 to accommodate stagecoach traffic to Boise from railheads in Utah and Nevada. Unfortunately, the ferry came too late to benefit the many pioneers who passed this way prior to its establishment.

Oregon Trail emigrants had been on the trail for four months or more before reaching this point, and were now experiencing the worst of the dry, hot summer months as they progressed at a rate of 8 to 13 miles per day across the basalt flows and sagebrush plains. They had been following the southern bank of the Snake since they had first encountered it near Pocatello, more than 150 miles to the east, and still they were looking for a safe crossing and the promise of better going on the other side. This crossing was no bargain, but the alternative—staying on the south side to Fort Boise—was an even worse prospect. Parties that tried the Three Island Crossing, as this one was known, faced a ford of 6 to 8 feet in depth and a width of 350 yards or more.

Occasionally, a group of wagons would be turned back by high water or a deficiency of equipment. These parties then had no choice but to continue on the south bank of the Snake through some of the harshest terrain encountered anywhere on their journey.

This drive will parallel that hellish southern route almost to the Oregon border, but will cover in just a few hours what took early settlers ten or more days to accomplish. Starting from Exit 121 on I-84, head into Glenns Ferry on First Avenue (Business Route 84). Turn left onto Commercial Avenue and drive 8 blocks to Madison Street. Turn right on Madison. You will pass through a 50-acre cultivated vineyard and golf course. Try a sample of the wines being produced here, or shoot a round of golf! The winery produces several grape varieties, including chardonnay, riesling, and merlot. After the vineyard, you will approach Three Island Crossing State Park, situated inside the river bend that contains the crossing.

The park has a small visitor center with displays of life on the Oregon Trail and some cool, grassy areas with tall cottonwoods for picnics and camping. Take the short walk to the river's edge and imagine the sounds of pioneer wagons creaking down the clearly visible trail across the river, and the shouts of pioneers struggling to get their families, animals, and possessions safely across. If you want a more tangible image, a reenactment of the crossing is held each summer, during the second weekend of August. This park and others in the state system tend to be heavily used in summer, so be sure to inquire about reservations if you plan to spend the night.

Backtrack to I-84 westbound at Glenns Ferry and head west to Hammett at Exit 114. Turn left on ID 78 here, passing through this small settlement which seems to rely heavily on the hay business. Watch for deer if you pass through near sunrise or sunset. The road soon begins to wind as it enters a small canyon alongside the Snake River. Cross the river in an area of basalt cliffs and rockfalls. The river here marks the boundary of Owyhee County, which encompasses the entire southwest corner of the state.

In another mile the road leaves the river, eventually climbing to a dry bench. In the distance you can see the river disappearing into another stretch of canyon as it curves around Flatiron Butte. The view from this elevated stretch includes the ridges that enclose the Bruneau Dunes, which come into sight on the left as the road drops back to the level of the plain. Turn left at the sign for Bruneau Dunes State Park. A 1-mile drive takes you to the park's visitor center, with aerial photos of the dunes and exhibits of wildlife found in the park.

An aerial view clearly shows that the dunes are stellate, or star-shaped. The prevailing winds here blow from opposite directions, holding the sand in place, and have created this unusual shape, complete with a crater in the center of the dunes, which rise to more than 470 feet in height. The sand was deposited here some 15,000 years ago as a consequence of the great Bonneville Flood, which scoured the entire Snake River drainage. The receding floodwaters left this pocket of sand trapped by the surrounding hills.

Visitor center personnel can give you information on camping in the park, and can recommend activities, including fishing for trophy bass. The dunes themselves are 2.5 miles beyond the visitor center. There are picnic tables and campsites in the park, as well as swimming and hiking opportunities.

Leaving the dunes, return to ID 78, and turn left (west). The marshlands visible across the highway along the Snake River are a valuable wild bird habitat, part of the C. J. Strike Wildlife Management Area. As many as 100,000 ducks and geese winter on this wildlife area's 12,500 acres, and pheasants, partridge, quail, and chukar are found in the drier portions of the refuge.

After two miles, ID 78 meets ID 51, which comes in from Mountain Home, 20 miles north. Turn left here on the combined highways, and climb to the plateau that protects the dunes. The wind seems to blow constantly here, hot and dry in summer, cold and biting in winter—another ingredient in the mix that has built the Bruneau dunes. Quickly the road drops off the plateau, arriving in the little community of Bruneau. A sign proclaims that Bruneau is the only home of the federally listed endangered Bruneau hot spring snail.

A side trip from here heads 18 miles up the unsurfaced Hot Springs Road to an overlook of dramatic Bruneau Canyon. The 60-mile-long canyon engulfs its infrequent visitors with 800- to 1,200-foot high cliffs which cut into ancient rhyolite rock, older than the Snake River plain to the north. Turn left at the only intersection in Bruneau for this side trip.

Continue west on ID 78, being sure to bear right on ID 78 where ID 51 splits off to the left. On the right is C. J. Strike Reservoir, a hydroelectric power producer and 7,500-acre warm-water fishery. The reservoir holds back the waters of the Snake River below a big turn in the river, and backs up the Bruneau River's confluence with the Snake as well, forming a U-shaped impoundment. The road follows the upper part of the reservoir for a short distance. Some 10 miles after ID 78's junction with ID 51, the power plant and dam are a short drive off to the right, at a marked turn.

ID 78 roughly follows the Oregon Trail alternate southern route through this stretch. You can imagine the magnitude of the challenges that faced the westward emigrants before this harsh landscape was tamed. Even now, it's obvious that it takes a special kind of person to make a living in this territory. As you proceed, a clear example of the beauty and desolation of the high desert is nearby. The Owyhee Uplands National Back Country Byway begins a few miles below the C. J. Strike dam. This 145-mile drive on lightly traveled, mostly gravel roads is a challenge for motorists, even those who possess both a sense of adventure and a trustworthy vehicle. No services of any sort are available along this drive. Weather conditions can change rapidly, so be sure to inquire in Grand View or Bruneau before setting out on this all-day backcountry drive.

Beyond Grand View, ID 78 begins to move away from the river. The surrounding countryside becomes even more severe, and fewer acres are under cultivation. The land across the Snake River north and east of here is protected by the Bureau of Land Management as the Snake River Birds of Prey National Conservation Area. The cliffs and plateaus of this area are home to one of the world's largest concentration of raptors. Eagles, hawks, falcons, owls, and other airborne hunters find the terrain and climate ideal— it provides wonderful habitat for their primary food sources, mostly prairie dogs, rabbits, and other small rodents. More than 800 pairs of raptors mate and raise their young on these Snake River cliffs. The Conservation Area should not be confused with the World Center for Birds of Prey, located south of Boise, which houses exhibits and captive raptors, and is dedicated to protecting and rearing endangered raptor species.

At milepost 34, a gravel road strikes off southwest. This is the Silver City Road, leading to the historic town of Silver City, a well-preserved mining camp at the base of 8,065-foot War Eagle Mountain, 23 miles off the highway. If the weather is good and you have the time, this is an interesting side trip. The road is rough, narrow, and dusty. Some of it is improved gravel, but much of it is unimproved dirt—treacherous when wet, and impassable in snowy conditions. There are steep drops and climbs, sharp turns, and

The mountains around Silver City are a formidable obstacle.

blind corners. In short, it's a treat for drivers seeking adventure. Think twice before towing a trailer or driving an RV over these roads, and, as always, inquire locally if you are at all unsure of the conditions ahead.

The Silver City Road dives and climbs, bucks and pitches, rising to 3,000 feet at New York Summit (18 miles from ID 78) before dropping into the neat little valley that cradles Silver City. Even on a summer weekend, it is quite possible to make the entire side trip without encountering another vehicle. Much more likely is an encounter with some of the hundreds of cattle enjoying the open range along this route.

Silver City itself has been designated a National Historic District. Dubbed a ghost town even though a few hardy souls still live there, Silver City is one of the West's best-preserved historic towns, with more than 40 historic structures still standing. Almost all of the property is private, but the 1892 schoolhouse museum is open occasionally, and the Idaho Hotel, built in 1866, still rents rooms (furnished much as they were 130 years ago!) and houses a small café. Please respect the privacy of the people who still call the town home.

If you've taken the side trip to Silver City, return to ID 78 and head left (north) to Murphy, the Owyhee county seat, population 75. The Owyhee County Historical Museum at Murphy reflects the town's former glory days as the largest livestock shipping terminal in the Pacific Northwest. Continue down to the river, 11 miles north of the Silver City road. Take ID 45 across the river at Walters Ferry. From here civilization slowly returns. Fifteen miles later the city of Nampa signals the end of this scenic drive. ID 45 becomes 12th Avenue in Nampa.

Nampa's economy is based on agriculture, with sizable seed crops of alfalfa, sweet corn, onions, carrots, radish, and lettuce, as well as beans, sugar beets, apples, cherries, peaches, and wine grapes. The Nampa Chamber of Commerce offers "Farm to Market Agricultural Tours"—self-guided tours of local farms, most of which have signs identifying the crops being grown, so that city dwellers can get a look at the vegetables and crops they normally see only in the supermarket. The tours also take you by fruit and produce stands, allowing you to purchase some of the locally grown treasures. Brochures describing the tour routes are available from the Nampa Chamber of Commerce's offices at the corner of 3rd Street South and 13th Avenue.

14

Boise to Stanley

General description: This 135-mile drive begins with a tour of a penitentiary in Boise and follows mountain roads to Idaho City, the early center of mining activity in the Boise Basin. From there, it continues to Lowman, nestled deep in a protected valley, and then to Stanley, the center of Idaho's wilderness activity. Along the way are reminders of some of Idaho's early history, spectacular natural scenery and a pair of placid mountain reservoirs, the scene of a disastrous forest fire, a majestic ponderosa pine forest, and two high mountain passes.

Special attractions: Idaho's state capitol; stately mansions in a historic Boise neighborhood; the Old Idaho Penitentiary; Lucky Peak Dam and Lucky Peak Lake; historic Idaho City, with its collection of well-preserved frontier structures; thick forests and evidence of past forest fires around Lowman; the beauty of Stanley Lake and the Sawtooth Range.

Location: The west-central part of the state, north and east of Boise.

Drive route numbers: Boise city streets, including Warm Springs Avenue, Idaho Highway 21.

Travel season: Best times to travel this route are between April and October. Winter snow and cold weather can create hazardous driving conditions. The section from Lowman to Stanley may be closed altogether in winter, although the route provides access to cross-country ski trails in the Boise National Forest.

Camping: More than a dozen Boise National Forest and Challis National Forest campgrounds are located along the route, mostly between Idaho City and Stanley. There are commercial RV campgrounds at Lowman and near Stanley.

Services: Boise is a big city, with all big city services. Idaho City has limited services, as does Lowman. Stanley offers motels, restaurants, a grocery store, and fuel.

Nearby attractions: Julia Davis Park and Zoo, Boise; the Basque Museum and Cultural Center in Boise; World Center for Birds of Prey and Snake River Birds of Prey National Conservation Area, both located southwest of Boise; and the ghost towns of Atlanta and Rocky Bar.

Drive 14: Boise to Stanley

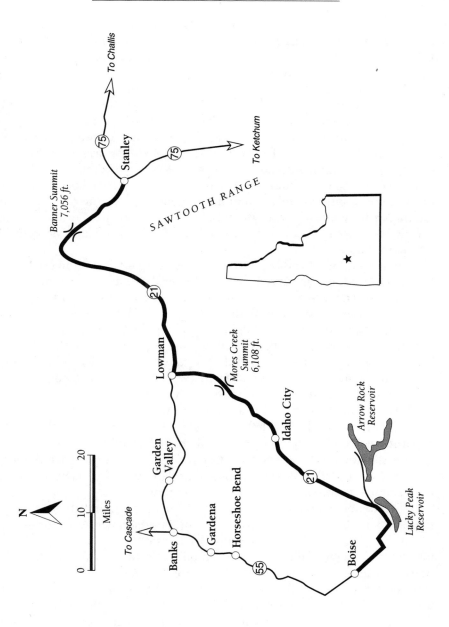

 # The Drive

This drive begins in Boise and follows mountain roads to Idaho City, the early center of mining activity in the Boise Basin, and then continues to Lowman, nestled deep in a protected valley, and on to Stanley, the center of Idaho's wilderness activity.

Begin in the center of Boise, in front of the Idaho State Capitol. This is a smaller version of the U.S. Capitol, topped with a statue of an eagle. Inside are interesting exhibits that represent the state's diversity of natural resources, including salmon, timber, and mining, as well as potatoes and other agricultural crops. Look up 208 feet to the field of 43 stars inside the capitol's dome, representing Idaho's admission as the 43rd state of the union. Notice also the pillars in the rotunda. They are not marble, like the floors and walls of the capitol, but *scagliola,* a mixture of gypsum, glue, marble dust, and granite, artfully assembled to resemble marble. Crafted by an Italian who traveled to Boise to create them, the pillars give the rotunda a distinctively bright appearance.

In the rotunda stands a gilded statue of George Washington astride his horse. The statue was carved in 1869 by an Austrian immigrant named Charles Ostner, who labored as a miner in the fields of the Florence basin north of McCall. Inspired by Washington's image on a postage stamp, and working by lantern light each night after a hard day's work, Ostner carved the statue from a single piece of yellow pine. He gave the statue to Idaho Territory upon its completion, and was granted $2,500 by the territorial legislature in gratitude for his efforts. In 1934, the statue was moved inside from the capitol grounds. It was refinished in 1966.

Across from the capitol is a statue of Frank Steunenberg, killed by a bomb in 1905, after he had left his post as Idaho's governor. Although he was a staunch union supporter, Steunenberg had been forced to quell a violent uprising of union miners in the Coeur d'Alene mining district of northern Idaho. He called in federal troops and declared a state of martial law that lasted almost two years, seriously weakening the unions.

Steunenberg's assassination shocked the country, and the capture of the bomber, Harry Orchard, led to his life imprisonment and the subsequent arrest of "Big Bill" Haywood, on charges of union conspiracy in the murder plot. Haywood's arrest in Colorado, and his illegal extradition to Boise, made national headlines. The famed Clarence Darrow defended Haywood, and William Borah, who would go on to serve in the U.S. Senate until 1940, helped to prosecuted the case. After a trial that lasted almost two months, Haywood was found innocent, since there were no witnesses who would corroborate Orchard's claim of Haywood's involvement in the conspiracy.

From the capitol, the drive heads southeast on State Street to 1st Street. Turn right on 1st Street, passing under a portion of a hospital parking garage, then left onto Warm Springs Avenue. This neighborhood boasts some of the most beautiful homes of turn-of-the-century Boise. At that time a trolley line led down the avenue to a natatorium (swimming pool) at the far end of the avenue. The pool was 125 feet long, and protected by a huge building constructed with wooden arches that spanned the pool's 80-foot width. The water was naturally heated—pumped from a geothermal well at 172 degrees F. The hot water was also used to heat hundreds of homes in the Warm Springs district, as well as the state capitol. To this day, many of the homes and government buildings in downtown Boise are dependent on geothermal energy for their heat.

About 2 miles from the start of Warm Springs Avenue, turn left to the Old Idaho Penitentiary. Nestled against the foothills, the prison was built of sandstone (quarried from the nearby hills) by convict labor. It operated for more than 100 years, and saw more than 13,000 inmates pass through its portals. After it was closed in 1973, the buildings were added to the National Register of Historic Places. Today, the prison museum offers an excellent tour, either with a guide or on your own. Included are looks at cell blocks, death row, and a gallows, last used in 1957. Most bizarre is an exhibit of inmate tattoos, most of which were inked with crude equipment by prisoners with plenty of time on their hands.

Also on the site are small museums devoted to transportation in Idaho, the generation of electricity, and mining and geology, as well as a botanical garden with nine different theme gardens. The Basque and Chinese gardens honor the heritage of two of the most significant cultures in Idaho history.

The Bishop's House, relocated to the site from its original location in the center of Boise, was the home of Idaho's first Episcopal bishop. In 1903, Bishop Tuttle was named presiding bishop of the Episcopal Church of America. The house was moved to this site in the 1970s, and is now used for weddings and other private and public functions.

Leaving the penitentiary, turn left on Warm Springs Road and continue southeast. The road ahead becomes ID 21, and for its entire 130-mile length to Stanley, it is known as the Ponderosa Pine Scenic Byway.

This short stretch from Boise into the foothills parallels the path of the Oregon Trail into the valley of the Boise River. Sections of wagon ruts may be visible coming off the rim on the opposite side of the river. Above the rim, and inaccessible from here, is Bonneville Point, where the members of Captain Bonneville's party first saw the Boise River valley in 1833. In their excitement, his French soldiers cried out, *"Les bois!, Les bois!"* at the sight of tall, shady trees after their long, hot trek across the desert. The Boise Diversion Dam diverts Boise River water into the New York Canal, which carries water across the lower valley into Lake Lowell west of Nampa, allowing cultivation of up to 300,000 acres of land.

Above the diversion dam, the road follows the river through the canyon it cut into the volcanic basalt rock. The Lucky Peak Dam, with a public service message displayed across its 2,340-foot-wide, 340-foot-high face, serves to control flooding, as well as to release irrigation water as needed. The road climbs alongside the dam to its top and then detours from the water's edge, passing through low hills covered with grass and brush. Trees sprout in low pockets where moisture collects. The road passes through a saddle at Highland Valley Summit, elevation 3,782 feet—1,000 feet higher than Boise.

Just after crossing a bridge over the Mores Creek Inlet to Lucky Peak Lake, 6 miles from Lucky Peak Dam, a right turn onto a graveled road leads the curious on a 6-mile side trip to the base of Arrow Rock Dam, on the Boise River above Lucky Peak Lake. At 351 feet high, Arrow Rock was the world's highest dam when it was built in 1912. (The Dworshak Dam, in north-central Idaho, rises to 717 feet, so Arrow Rock is now not even the highest in Idaho!)

From here, the road drops back down to river level, following Mores Creek. It winds between the basalt parapets slowly carved by the river. Grimes Creek, which empties into Mores Creek near milepost 29, was the site of the first gold discovery in the Boise Basin. A party led by George Grimes and Moses Splawn found gold above here on August 2, 1862. Grimes was shot and killed a few days later, and the miners returned to Walla Walla with the news of their strike. The rush was immediately on, and soon miners were crawling over the entire Boise Basin. Both Grimes Creek and Grimes Pass into the Payette River drainage to the north were named for George Grimes.

Above Grimes Creek, the terrain becomes more gentle, and Mores Creek has a more gradual gradient. The flows here weren't powerful enough to wash the fine gold downstream, and it settled into the crevices and cracks in the rocks and under the creek bed. As a result, miners found rich deposits of the placer gold in the creek bottom. Dredges eventually chewed up the flood plain and spit back the worthless stones in neat ridges and hummocks. Even today the devastation caused by the dredges remains.

Another mining technique that was efficient, but equally devastating, was hydraulic mining. A powerful stream of water would be played along a sand-and-gravel bank, disintegrating it and leaving the heavier gold dust to be washed through a sluice box. Not only did this method erode banks, it also deposited the fine silt, sand, and gravel father downstream, changing the character of every stream it touched.

After the gold strike, prospectors and adventurers of all sorts hurried to the mining camps. Placerville, Centerville, New Centerville, Pioneerville, and—most successful of all—Idaho City, sprung up overnight. Within two months, Idaho City was the largest settlement in the Northwest, bustling with more than 6,000 inhabitants. Today, the community has only about 300 residents and is a pleasant spot to wander and explore. Here you'll find the primitive Idaho Territorial Penitentiary, the International Order of Odd Fellows Pioneer Lodge No. 1, the oldest Masonic Temple in use west of the Mississippi, the state's longest-published newspaper, *The Idaho World*, a museum, and a general store that has operated from the same building for more than 130 years.

Above Idaho City, ID 21 travels through forests of ponderosa as it makes its way to Mores Creek Summit, 14 miles past Idaho City. From there, the road drops more than 2,000 feet in the 20 miles to Lowman. This isolated town, which did not even have telephone service until 1976, was the scene of devastating forest fires in 1989. The extent of the fires is evident from the road, which passes both through burned stretches and areas untouched by the fire. Interpretive signs along the road explain the chronology of the fire and describe some typical fire behaviors.

Lowman sits on the South Fork of the Payette River, another one of Idaho's premiere whitewater rivers. The South Fork is popular with kayakers and rafters. Depending on the time of year and the amount of spring runoff, the South Fork can have from Class III to Class VI whitewater, though it is generally rated Class III to Class IV.

Above Lowman, ID 21 is usually closed from late fall until Memorial Day because of snow. In spring and fall, check road conditions with local authorities before attempting to proceed above Lowman.

If conditions permit, stay on ID 21, headed for Stanley. About 4 miles past Lowman is a national forest campground, at Kirkham Hot Springs, located on a hillside that has borne the brunt of nature's wrath. In 1986, a microburst, or intensely localized windstorm, downed timber and generally wreaked havoc here. Then, in August of 1989, a forest fire, feeding upon the downed timber from the earlier storm, swept through the area. The scars will be visible for many years. The campground, originally on a wooded slope, is now laid bare, though the hot springs were always the campground's best feature and they remain undamaged. The springs have been channeled into several tubs in the campground, as well as natural pools along the banks of the river. As of this writing, the pools can be bathed in free of charge, but national forest budgets being what they are, a small fee may someday be assessed for their use.

Farther up the road, the patchy, almost random nature of the fire damage is still quite visible. The pattern of burned areas and untouched stands of timber is called a fire mosaic. Ten miles on, the fire damage is no longer evident, and the forest begins to change from predominantly ponderosa pine

The canyon of the South Fork of the Payette River.

to species which are more hardy, such as the lodgepole pine, with its slender, straight trunks. The change in the forest accompanies the change in elevation.

Having climbed steadily since Lowman, ID 21 now turns north and leaves the South Fork of the Payette River. Here, a graveled side road leads 6.5 miles to the little community of Grandjean. Grandjean was named for a Danish immigrant who settled here and became supervisor of the Boise National Forest. The Sawtooth Wilderness is accessible from the town, and hikers use the campground there as a staging area for their forays into the dramatic Sawtooth Mountains. The Idaho State Centennial Trail, which runs all the way from Nevada to the Canadian border, leaves the crest of the Sawtooths just to the east of Grandjean.

Our road heads north, up the drainage of Canyon Creek. After 12 miles, it reaches the crest at Banner Summit, near the turnoff for Bull Trout Lake. The summit marks the divide between Boise County and Custer County, as well as the boundary between Boise National Forest and Challis National Forest. The summit also is the entrance to the Sawtooth National Recreation Area. The 756,000-acre SNRA is part of the Sawtooth National Forest. With more than 1,000 high-mountain lakes, four mountain ranges, and the headwaters of four major Idaho rivers, it is the hub for recreational activities in central Idaho.

ID 21 follows Cape Horn Creek downstream, and makes a broad turn from the northeast to the southeast as it crosses the creek. From here, it heads up Marsh Creek along a wide, flat meadow. Cape Horn Creek, Marsh Creek, and Beaver Creek all come together just north of the apex of the turn to form the Middle Fork of the Salmon River, renowned as the queen of whitewater rivers.

At milepost 126, a 3.5-mile gravel road leads west to Stanley Lake. This glacial lake sits at the base of the northern end of the Sawtooth Range. The backdrop of rough granite spires, combined with the serene blue water and the dark green of the lodgepole pine forest on the glacial moraines, is worth the often dusty, bumpy drive to the lake.

Just 4 miles past the turnoff to Stanley Lake, the road enters Stanley proper. This small town has an energy all its own. Perhaps it's the contagious enthusiasm of the many visitors who come here to climb, hike, float, fish, and hunt that gives the place an aura of excitement. Or, it may just be that few places exist—anywhere—that are set in the midst of so much natural splendor. Whatever the reason, this is a place that feels alive.

15
Payette Lake and Long Valley Loop

General description: A 124-mile drive, mostly on paved roads, with short stretches of good gravel road. The route follows closely the forested shores of Payette Lake before heading south through pastoral Long Valley, past Cascade Reservoir, and over Big Creek Summit to Warm Lake. The return to McCall takes visitors through another portion of Long Valley, past a number of historic buildings, including a pair of old churches.

Special attractions: McCall, a pleasant tourist town on the shore of Payette Lake; scenic views of the lake from the shoreline drive; a short interpretive walk through a marsh popular with wildlife; a visit to Ponderosa State Park; the rare opportunity to spot a sea serpent; the small town of Cascade and Cascade Reservoir; ospreys nesting on power poles along the road; the possibility of seeing moose in the wild; the serene beauty of Warm Lake, with its trophy mackinaw trout; the museum and historic buildings at Roseberry; the Finnish Church and cemetery.

Location: West-central Idaho.

Drive route numbers: Idaho Highway 55, Warren Wagon Road, Eastside/Lake Drive, Lick Creek Road, local roads in McCall, Warm Lake Road, Farm to Market Road, and Finn Road.

Travel season: This loop is best traveled in late spring through fall. Heavy snow and cold winter weather combine to make winter access difficult or impossible.

Camping: Commercial RV parks are available south of McCall at Cascade and Donnelly, and camping is available at the Main Unit of Ponderosa State Park and at Warm Lake.

Services: McCall and Cascade both offer all necessary tourist services, including food, lodging and fuel. The lodges at Warm Lake offer meals, rooms, boat rentals, and fuel.

Nearby attractions: Brundage Mountain Ski Area; ghost towns of Burgdorf, Warren, Yellow Pine, and Stibnite; Zim's Hot Springs; South Fork Salmon River Interpretive Site and South Fork Salmon River Fish Trap.

The Drive

McCall sits at the edge of one of the loveliest lakes in Idaho. This is a bold claim, with stiff competition from such contenders as Coeur d'Alene, Pend Oreille, and Redfish lakes. But Payette Lake is up to the challenge.

Drive 15: Payette Lake and Long Valley Loop

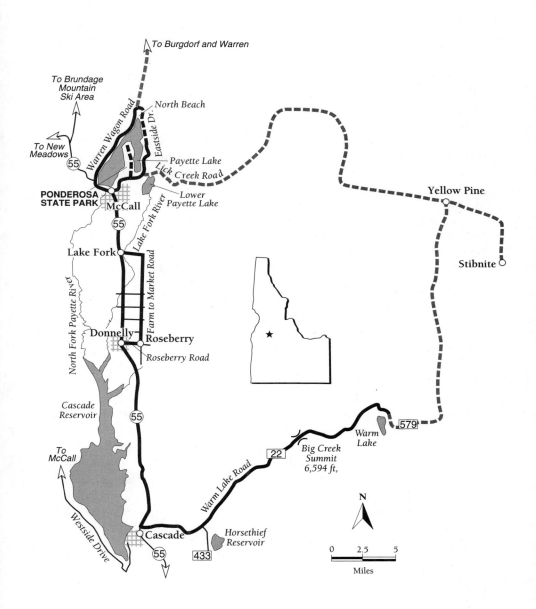

To Burgdorf and Warren

To Brundage
Mountain
Ski Area

North Beach

To New
Meadows

Warren Wagon Road

Eastside Dr.

55

Payette Lake

Lick Creek Road

PONDEROSA
STATE PARK

Lower
Payette Lake

McCall

Lake Fork River

55

Lake Fork

Farm to Market Road

North Fork Payette River

Donnelly

Roseberry

Roseberry Road

Cascade
Reservoir

55

To
McCall

Warm
Lake

579

Big Creek
Summit
6,594 ft,

22

Warm Lake Road

Westside Drive

Cascade

Horsethief
Reservoir

55

433

Yellow Pine

Stibnite

N

0   2.5   5

Miles

Scenic vistas will enchant you all the way around its forested shores, and it has something all those other lakes only wish they had—a genuine sea serpent!

Beginning in the center of McCall, follow ID 55 west where it makes a sharp left at the lake. After a mile through town, the road crosses the Payette River at the lake's outlet. Take an immediate right onto Warren Wagon Road (Forest Road 21). The woods on both sides of the road are sprinkled with vacation homes, ranging from humble to huge. Glimpses of the 6-mile lake's shore are visible to the right. Keep an eye on the road, though, since logging trucks are active along this stretch.

Some 4 miles up Warren Wagon Road is a small group of homes tucked into a sheltered cove on the lake, protected by the high cliffs behind them. Across the lake from them is the peninsula of Ponderosa State Park's main unit, which the drive will be visiting later. For now, notice the high cliffs and the promontory visible at the north end of the peninsula.

Another 2 miles brings you to the North Beach unit of Ponderosa State Park. Turn right after another mile on FR 451 into flat, wetland terrain as the road crosses the inlet to Payette Lake.

If you have several hours, you can make a side trip from here by continuing north on Warren Wagon Road, past Upper Payette Lake, and over 6,434 foot Secesh Summit to the ghost towns of Burgdorf and Warren, 37 miles from McCall. An auto tour on audio cassette is available at the ranger station in McCall for the trip up to the ghost towns.

Warren was the home of Lalu Nathoy, who came to Idaho as a Chinese slave. Known by the derogatory name of "China Polly," by which the miners referred to all Oriental women, she worked as a dance-hall girl in the mining camp. She met a gambler named Charlie Bemis and nursed him back to health after he was involved in a fight and left nearly dead. Charlie and Lalu Nathoy fell in love, and she followed him to his homestead cabin in the Salmon River canyon north of Warren. They lived there together for 50 years, growing their own food, until their deaths in the 1930s. Their story is told by Ruthanne Lum McCunn in the biographical novel *Thousand Pieces of Gold,* and in a film of the same name made in 1990.

If you've taken the side trip, return to the main drive by turning left from Warren Wagon Road onto FR 451, following signs to the North Beach unit of Ponderosa State Park.

FR 451 changes from asphalt to improved gravel for the next 5 miles—indicative of the lesser number of vacation homes at this end of the lake. The road crosses the Payette River on a narrow, one-lane bridge within sight of a long, low granite cliff. The granite here has been smoothed by glacial activity. The same glaciers that polished the stone deposited their sediments in the long valley that runs between Cascade and McCall. They also carved out the basin that ultimately became Payette Lake.

Turn right after about one more mile for access to the north beach. A short interpretive walk leads 500 feet south to the beach, on a boardwalk over the wetlands. The Payette River meanders through the gap between granite cliffs in an area filled with glacial outwash materials. Waterfowl inhabit the swampy areas, and deer and moose come for an occasional drink from the slow-moving waters. The view from the beach encompasses the main body of the lake and its smaller, shorter east arm.

The broad lake view here may be the best opportunity to spot Payette Lake's resident sea serpent, named Sharlie by the locals. Sightings of the monster are infrequent, but vivid. Sharlie has a long neck and either one or two humps. A flurry of sightings in the early 1950s led to an article in *Life* magazine. Keep a close eye on the water, particularly as the light fades at the end of the day.

Leaving the beach, continue along the lakeshore. Watch for moose if you are traveling early or late in the day. Pass a small waterfall coming off the granite cliff and then return to the pavement. The road here is known as Eastside Drive, or Lake Drive.

Turn right at Lick Creek Road, and right again at the entrance to Ponderosa State Park. A small entrance fee allows access to the 840-acre park, which offers camping, swimming, and fishing. The peninsula is home to a wide variety of wildlife, including deer, smaller mammals, and a wide variety of birds. Even black bear or moose are seen occasionally. Follow the road out to the end of the peninsula and the three overlooks high above the lake. The road becomes narrower and steeper as it climbs to the overlooks. Long RVs, trailers, or vehicles with very low ground clearance should stop short of the final steep loop.

After visiting the park, it's a little more than a mile back to McCall. Turn right (west) at the park exit onto Lake Drive, and then take a right turn onto Hemlock Street. Follow the turns south and west back into town.

The McCall area offers a number of attractions for winter visitors. Snowmobile and cross-country ski trails abound in the forests surrounding the town. Brundage Mountain Ski Area, located just northwest of town offers a full-service winter sports facility. The town's Winter Carnival, featuring a parade, chili cook-off, and dogsled races, relies on the region's abundant snowfall (over 150 inches annually) for raw material for the intricately carved snow sculptures that spring up all through town.

Leave McCall heading south on ID 55. Look on the far side of the McCall Airport for the orange and silver aircraft of the USDA Forest Service's elite forest fire-fighting base. As the road leaves McCall, it enters the valley of the Payette River's North Fork and Lake Fork, which leave Payette Lake and Lower Payette Lake, respectively. The two rivers have smoothed and leveled the Long Valley, which stretches more than 20 miles from here to Cascade.

The meadows are rich with hay crops throughout the short summer in this valley (elevation 4,800 feet). Ospreys and hawks are commonly seen here. Continue south through the towns of Lake Fork and Donnelly, where the two rivers empty into Cascade Reservoir, which stretches south along the east side of the West Mountains to the town of Cascade.

ID 55, which we've been traveling, is as close as you'll come to a major highway in central Idaho, except for U.S. Highway 95, the north-south link which runs parallel some 20 miles to the west. ID 55 is the primary thoroughfare in Cascade, a town of 900 inhabitants that is supported by timber and recreational businesses.

After crossing the Payette River where it exits the reservoir, the road enters Cascade. Turn right onto Old State Highway, which climbs a short hill to the left, just before the highway straightens to enter the town. Just over the hill is a small park and a boat ramp. Across the reservoir are the West Mountains, a low range that separates the drainage of the Weiser River from the Payette drainage. To the left is a small municipal golf course, and, along the lakeshore, a number of picnic and camping facilities. A pleasant, low-key drive winds from the park, around the southern end of the lake, and then on good gravel roads past a number of vacation properties and up the far shoreline, coming back to ID 55 near the town of Donnelly, some 35 miles north.

The drive continues from the lakeshore in Cascade. Return to ID 55, and then go north (left), across the lake's outlet. Turn right 300 yards past the river onto Warm Lake Road (Forest Road 22). The road passes a series of small ranches before climbing into the forested hills. This area is blessed with heavy winter snowfalls that make these hills very popular with cross-country skiers and snowmobilers. Park-and-Ski program is administered by the Idaho Department of Parks and Recreation. Permits for the limited parking spaces are coveted possessions on winter weekends. A season parking permit costs less than $20, and provides access to 18 designated trails throughout the state.

Just more than 6 miles from the beginning of Warm Lake Road is a turn to Horsethief Reservoir, a 275-acre lake stocked with rainbow and cutthroat trout. A boat ramp and camping facilities are available at Horsethief, 2 miles from Warm Lake Road.

The road parallels power lines for several miles. You may see nests of sticks and branches atop some of the towers. These nests house ospreys, raptors that thrive on the fish that are so plentiful in the streams here. Watch carefully—ospreys are frequently seen returning to the nest with a meal for their young. The young birds can then be seen jostling for a position in the

Old barn along the road to Warm Lake.

front of the food line. Adult ospreys are magnificent birds, with black bars on the undersides of their white wings, and snowy white breasts. Occasionally, you can see adults diving into the water to grab fish.

After the road parts company with the power lines, it begins a 4-mile climb to 6,594-foot Big Creek Summit, after which it drops sharply into the Trail Creek drainage. Signs posted here warn motorists of the presence of moose, which frequent the area. Trail Creek appears through thick trees to the right as the road swoops down a steep incline and crosses the South Fork of the Salmon River.

Although the area is heavily forested now, this land was extensively cultivated when the mines at Stibnite, 10 miles east, were first worked in the 1910s. Potatoes and other crops were grown to feed the miners; even today traces of irrigation ditches and old cabins are visible back in the woods. The woods are lodgepole pine, which grows straight and slender. These stands are the result of natural regeneration.

Several small roads branch off from the main road in this vicinity. Follow the main road (now Forest Road 579) as it bends around the northern end of Warm Lake, still hidden from your view at this point. Follow the signs to either of the lodges located along the north and east shores. This is a peaceful place, and it has one of the most civilized rules of any backwoods location anywhere. Powerboats are restricted to operation between the hours of 11 a.m. and 6 p.m., leaving the early morning and sunset hours undisturbed by the sounds of outboard motors.

The adventurous can extend the drive by continuing on FR 579 past the lake and up the hill another 5 miles to Landmark Ranger Station. From there, forest roads lead to the Yellow Pine and Stibnite mining areas, where tungsten, mercury, and gold mines operated from 1910 until the 1950s. It is possible to return to McCall by following FR 413 (Johnson Creek Road) north to Yellow Pine, and then FR 48 (East Fork Road, Lick Creek Road) back into McCall. As always, inquire locally before attempting to drive any of these backcountry routes, and be certain that you have enough fuel, water, and spare parts for your vehicle.

This drive backtracks from Warm Lake to Cascade, and then returns to Donnelly on ID 55. At Donnelly, turn right on Roseberry Road. In just a little more than a mile, at Roseberry Road's intersection with Farm to Market Road, is a pair of original buildings that constitute Roseberry's Long Valley Museum. The buildings, a brilliant white clapboard church and the old general store, date to the early part of this century. The church is still in use, but the store is awaiting renovation funds. Roseberry was the main community in this part of the Long Valley until the railroad arrived at Donnelly, and the settlement moved from Roseberry to be closer to the railroad.

Follow Farm to Market Road north 7 miles to Finn Road. The small church at the intersection here was the center of the region's Finnish community for many years. The cemetery across the road holds the graves of many of Long Valley's early Finnish immigrants. Turn left (west) on Finn Road and return to ID 55 at Lake Fork. McCall, the end of this scenic drive, lies 6 miles ahead. Perhaps Sharlie, the sea serpent, will make an appearance on Payette Lake later in the evening.

16

Hell's Canyon

General description: A 125-mile trip into the depths of Hell's Canyon on a mixture of roads ranging from paved two-lane highway in the canyon to a rough, narrow, unimproved dirt road with steep climbs out of the canyon. A pleasant forest-and-prairie drive on good gravel roads to Council, Idaho, completes the drive.

Special attractions: Brownlee, Oxbow, and Hell's Canyon dams; the Snake River in 8,000-foot-deep Hell's Canyon; a short, steep haul up to the canyon rim on the Kleinschmidt Grade; and an enjoyable cruise through open forest and bucolic pasturelands.

Location: West-central Idaho.

Drive route numbers: Idaho Highway 71, Hell's Canyon Road (Forest Road 454), Kleinschmidt Grade (Forest Road 050), Cuprum-Council Road (Forest Road 002), Hornet Creek Road.

Travel season: The roads in the canyon are accessible year-round, but the climb out on the Kleinschmidt Grade should not be attempted until the road is cleared of snow, sometime in April or early May.

Camping: Idaho Power operates very nice campgrounds at Woodhead Park on Brownlee Reservoir, McCormick Park on Oxbow Reservoir, Hell's Canyon Park on Hell's Canyon Reservoir, all on the Idaho side of the canyon; and at Copperfield Park on the Oregon side, just below Oxbow Reservoir.

Services: The small towns of Cambridge and Council offer limited services. Both offer dining, groceries, and fuel.

Nearby attractions: Jet boat tours of Hell's Canyon from Hell's Canyon Dam; National Old-Time Fiddlers Hall of Fame in Weiser; the Charles Winkler Museum in the Council City Hall; Zim's Hot Springs north of New Meadows.

 The Drive

Forming a portion of Idaho's border with both Oregon and Washington, Hell's Canyon on the Snake River extends from Brownlee Reservoir north to Lewiston, a distance of more than 80 miles. The canyon is the deepest and steepest gorge in the United States, exceeding the Grand Canyon's depth by 2,000 feet, and its width by more than a mile.

Early fur traders explored the canyon, looking for a navigable path to

Drive 16: Hell's Canyon

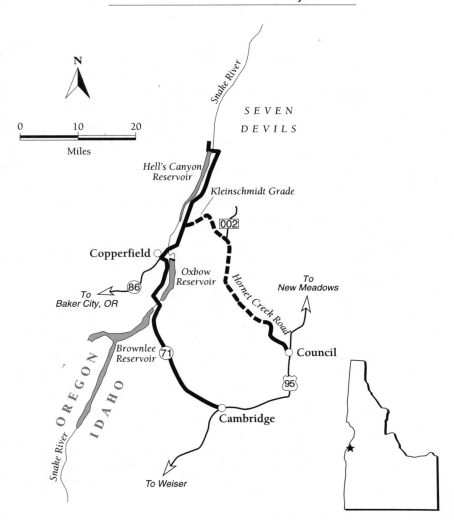

the Pacific Ocean from their trapping territories in Idaho, Wyoming, Utah, and western Colorado. The Bonneville party also investigated the canyon, nearly perishing when they were forced to climb out of a frozen canyon when caught by an untimely thaw.

Travelers on the Oregon Trail gave the entire chasm a wide berth, passing by on the Oregon side after crossing the river near Old Fort Boise at Parma. Emigrants who had not braved the Three Island Crossing at Glenns Ferry rejoined the main trail just west of Parma, in Oregon.

This drive begins in the sleepy town of Cambridge, at the intersection of U.S. Highway 95 and ID 71. After entering Hell's Canyon at Brownlee Dam, the drive passes Oxbow Reservoir and Hell's Canyon Reservoir before it provides glimpses of the wild depths of the canyon below Hell's Canyon Dam. It then backtracks a bit before climbing the Kleinschmidt Grade, passing through the Cuprum-Bear mining district, and ending up in the historic town of Council.

Cambridge got its start when the Pacific and Idaho Northern Railroad pushed its lines north to serve the mines in the Seven Devils region. The original route would have taken the railroad through the nearby town of Salubria, but a profiteering resident of that town tried to rob the railroad, demanding a small ransom for the property the railroad needed. Rather than succumb to blackmail, the Pacific and Idaho Northern accepted a competing offer and realigned its tracks on the other side of the Weiser River, and Cambridge was born.

Cambridge today is an agricultural center, supporting dairy farms and hay operations. It is also the last, best place to stock up on fuel and supplies before entering the gorge. Take ID 71 (Hopper Avenue) west from the north end of Cambridge, one block south of the sharp bend US 95 takes as it leaves town and heads north toward Council and New Meadows. ID 71 mounts a small hill, passes the town's water tower (a landmark visible for miles in either direction along US 95), and soon parallels little Pine Creek, a tributary of the Weiser River. Climbing several hundred feet from Cambridge, the road tops out at an elevation of 4,131 feet halfway between Cambridge and Brownlee Dam on the Snake River. Winding through low dry hills, the road then drops 2,000 feet over the next 10 miles.

Brownlee Dam is the first of three obstructions the river must face before it rushes headlong into the deepest parts of the gorge. After a decade or more of political maneuvering and bickering between the U.S. Army Corps of Engineers and private power company interests, the decision was made to build three dams instead of one high dam in the canyon. All three projects were approved in 1955, and work commenced immediately. Built by Idaho Power Company, and completed in 1959, Brownlee Dam created a 59-mile-long reservoir.

Below Brownlee Dam, the road crosses the river into Oregon, and follows the shore of Oxbow Reservoir, the second impoundment in the chain, for 12 miles. At Oxbow Bend, the river loops sharply, turning 180 degrees around a high, rocky outcrop. Out of sight on the bend, the 205-foot-high Oxbow Dam holds back 10 miles of the Snake River. The road takes a short-cut over the shoulder of the hill and enters Copperfield. Built around the turn of the century, the town housed railroad workers who were running a line to support the copper mines several miles north.

In 1906, while the mining boom was on, a plan was formulated to generate electricity from the river here. While the river travels almost 3 miles around the promontory at Oxbow Bend, it is only a thousand feet or so across the neck of the loop. A tunnel was dug from the upstream to the downstream side of the bend, where a turbine was positioned. Water dropped 20 feet through the tunnel, spinning the turbine and generating power for the mine operations. Unfortunately, the power generated was hardly enough to cover expenses, and the works were soon abandoned.

Copperfield had its moment in the spotlight in 1914. The completion of the railroad and the hydroelectric project had reduced the town's population, as well as its wealth. Left behind, merchants and honest businessmen struggled. Their plight was shared by the gamblers and proprietors of saloons and bawdy houses, who were also struggling to survive. The two factions began feuding, and their squabbles led to an order by Oregon's governor to the local sheriff to "clean up" the town. The sheriff declined to interfere (perhaps wisely), forcing the governor to act. In a calculated move, the governor sent his secretary to deliver an ultimatum.

The young woman, Fern Hobbs, stepped off a train in Copperfield and demanded that city officials resign. When they did not, she ordered the Oregon National Guard to implement martial law. Citizens' guns were confiscated, the mayor and councilmen were arrested, and the town's saloons and gambling halls were closed down. Just an hour later, Hobbs stepped back onto the train and departed. The town never recovered from the trauma, and like a seriously ill patient who doesn't survive surgery, slowly expired. Fires in 1915 burned portions of the town, and very soon Copperfield was a deserted shell.

Idaho Power Company maintains an interpretative kiosk at Copperfield with information about the wildlife commonly seen in the canyon. That wildlife used to include steelhead trout, chinook, and sockeye salmon, but the high dams stretched across the Snake River prevented their return from the ocean to their traditional spawning areas in Idaho's cold mountain rivers and lakes. The fish were eradicated from the drainages of the Boise, Weiser, and Payette rivers by the Snake River dams. Dams downstream on the Columbia also contributed to the decline of the indigenous fish, although those dams were designed with fish ladders, structures that allowed fish to bypass the dams with some degree of success.

Another species of fish, one that calls the deep pools of the reservoirs and the river home, is the white sturgeon. This fish, little changed in millions of years of evolution, can grow to enormous size in the still waters of the Snake River reservoirs. Sturgeon weighing 600 pounds or more were regularly caught in the Snake in earlier days. Today the fish is endangered and fishing for the giant creatures is strictly catch-and-release. Brownlee Reservoir is renowned as a hotspot for white sturgeon.

Idaho Power's own words on the subject of the ancestral fish of the

Classic old barn on Cuprum-Council Road above Hell's Canyon.

Snake bypass somewhat its role in the sturgeon's decline: "Although these fish have been present in the Northwest for millions of years, many human activities have contributed to their decline, including habitat alteration, over-fishing and competition with non-native species."

Cross the river here at Copperfield and return to the Idaho side of the Snake. Downstream 4 miles from Copperfield is Hell's Canyon Park, one of several canyon parks that Idaho Power provides. Just across the road from the park, with its picnic and campground, is the old Kleinschmidt Grade, the last road access on this side of the river until Pittsburg Landing, far to the north. (Pittsburg Landing is inaccessible from here by motor vehicle.) Bypass the Kleinschmidt Grade for now and proceed north.

The canyon narrows as you proceed north on Hell's Canyon Road. There were a number of small homesteads in the canyon, mostly on the long sandbars left by the Bonneville flood and on the flood terraces on the sides of the river. Today, along the sides of the road, a number of "volunteer" fruit trees—peach, apple, plum—have continued to flourish long after the homesteads were abandoned or flooded and their orchards left to survive on their own.

In the middle of the river, 9 miles north of the Kleinschmidt Grade, is Big Bar, a dramatic example of the magnitude of the Bonneville Flood. Big Bar was formed as the rushing waters of ancestral Lake Bonneville scoured the canyon of the Snake River for an estimated six months. The lake had drained through a natural dam south of present-day Pocatello, and as it reshaped channels and carved the canyon walls, it deposited vast quantities of sediment in its slower-moving stretches. At Brownlee Reservoir, estimates are that the water was more than 410 feet high, and that it flowed at a rate of 10 million cubic feet per second. In many places, the canyon has a terraced floor, with the height of the terraces representing the bottom of the river during the flood.

Between the river and the road at Big Bar are the graves of two early settlers. Archaeological evidence also indicates that Big Bar was inhabited by native peoples at least 400 years ago.

Beyond Big Bar is Black Point, one of the few places where the road climbs high above the river, providing an outstanding view of the canyon straits downstream. The road follows the banks of Hell's Canyon Reservoir. The canyon continues to narrow for the next 6 miles to Hell's Canyon Dam, the last of the three Idaho Power impoundments in the canyon. At the foot of the dam the elevation is 1,475 feet. The road crosses the dam, going back into Oregon, and stops a short distance ahead at Hell's Canyon Creek.

This is the end of the road, both literally and figuratively. Here is the put-in for float trips through the gorge, and for jet boat excursions which take visitors down the gorge and back in powerful flat-bottomed boats. A good visitor center here has a small auditorium and natural history exhibits. Be careful if you wander away from the building—trails throughout the canyon generally grow a good crop of poison ivy. From the parking lot, look straight up the side canyon to get an idea of just how narrow and steep the chasm is. From here to the top of He Devil Peak across the river in the Seven Devils Mountains is an elevation gain of almost 8,000 feet in just a few short miles.

Turn around here and head back across the dam on the same (and only) road. Traveling back through the canyon in the opposite direction is as enjoyable as the drive in, since the views of the majestic cliffs and hills are completely different on the return. Enjoy the play of light and shadow as the sun strikes the canyon walls from different angles. Look for birds of prey soaring on the thermal currents generated by the warmth of the sun.

At the base of Kleinschmidt Grade it is decision time. The grade is a steep, narrow, rough, and dusty climb of more than 5 miles before the road levels out in the forests around Cuprum and Bear. The road is not advised for RVs, trailers, or other oversized vehicles. Over the grade, it is 43 miles from here to Council, mostly on gravel road, and then another 20 miles on US 95 back to Cambridge. Returning the way you came—up the canyon to Brownlee Reservoir and then on to Cambridge—is about 45 miles, entirely on paved roads.

If the weather is dry and clear, and you have the time and a suitable vehicle, it is well worth the effort to climb the grade. The views of the canyon are unlike any you've seen so far, and the drive across the plateau into Council makes an enjoyable end to a great day of sightseeing.

The grade itself was carved by Albert Kleinschmidt from 1889–1891 to move copper-bearing ores from the mines in the Seven Devils district to a steamboat and ultimately to a railroad terminus on the Oregon side of the canyon. The road was well engineered, and would have solved Kleinschmidt's problems, but for two small details. First, the steamship he counted on never made a successful voyage, and second, the market collapsed in 1893, leaving him with no buyers for his copper. As it turned out, no ore ever was transported down the grade.

The grade is a fair test of passengers' nerves—after 5 miles of a relentless climb with a sheer drop-off to the left side, the road passes through a patch of forest and over a ridge, and then drops away to the right.

About 8 miles from the river, the road passes a large, beautiful barn on the right, just before a Y intersection. If you were to continue straight ahead at this intersection, it would take you past the quiet ghost town of Cuprum, once a lively mining camp, 13 miles up a slow, rocky road (Sheep Rock Road or FR 106) to Sheep Rock, a National Natural Landmark, and Kinney Point. From there you can be assured of the most dramatic views of the depths of Hell's Canyon.

This drive, however, turns right at the Y intersection onto FR 002, also known as the Cuprum-Council Road. As you travel through the forest, the road improves noticeably mile by mile. From the junction at Cuprum, it is 26 miles until the pavement returns, and with it the signs of civilization. More and more ranches and small farms sprinkle the countryside as the road drifts down Hornet Creek, winding up in the town square at Council after another 12 miles.

17

The Seven Devils

General description: This is a short, steep, rough, rocky 35-mile round-trip drive on poorly maintained dirt and gravel road that climbs from the Salmon River to an overlook high on the flanks of the Seven Devils Mountains. It is suitable for passenger cars with good clearance, but not for RVs or trailers.

Special attractions: The wild river town of Riggins and the Salmon River; scenic vistas that change rapidly as the road climbs more than 6,500 feet; views of Hell's Canyon and central Idaho, Washington, Oregon, Montana, and the rugged mass of the Seven Devils Mountains.

Location: West-central Idaho.

Drive route numbers: U.S. Highway 95, Nez Perce National Forest Road 517.

Travel season: The road to Heaven's Gate Lookout is accessible only when all snow has melted along the route, usually from late May or early June through October. Periods of heavy rain may make the road impassable, and lightning is a definite hazard at the summit. Contact the Hell's Canyon National Recreation Area offices just south of Riggins (phone: 208-628-3196) on US 95 for road information before beginning this drive.

Camping: Commercial RV parks are available at Riggins, and a Nez Perce National Forest campground is located at Heaven's Gate.

Services: Riggins has restaurants, motels, groceries, and fuel. There are no other services along the route.

Nearby attractions: Salmon River float trips; Hell's Canyon wilderness raft trips; the little-known Gospel Hump Wilderness Area; White Bird Battlefield; Winchester Lake State Park; the ghost town of Florence.

 The Drive

Forming the border of Idaho and Oregon from the site of Old Fort Boise north to Lewiston, the Snake River is a formidable barrier to east-west travel. The Snake River has cut a channel through the sedimentary and volcanic rocks over the past 15 million years, carving the deepest, narrowest canyon in North America. Unlikely as it may seem, this entire region is believed to be the remnants of a volcanic island, or islands, that crashed into the western coast of North America 100 million years ago. Without

Drive 17: The Seven Devils

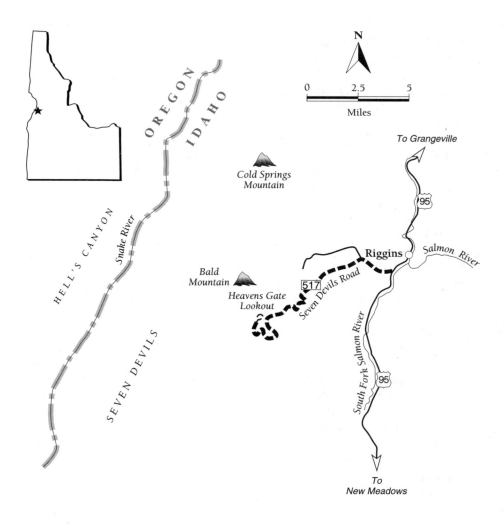

going into a complex geological explanation, suffice it to say that the tectonic plate that makes up North America has been moving slowly west, forcing the floor of the Pacific Ocean beneath it, and fusing all loose continental material it encounters, including this part of Idaho, to itself.

Fortunately for travelers in the West, all this violent movement is happening at the rate of no more than approximately 1 inch every 100 years. It is quite unlikely that continental drift will ruin your scenic drive! But it also makes this one of the most spectacular short automobile ascents that can be made anywhere in the United States.

Start at the Hell's Canyon National Recreation Area offices just south of Riggins on US 95, the main north-south thoroughfare in Idaho. The route climbs from 1,800 feet to 8,428 feet above sea level in just 17 miles, on a surface that stretches the definition of "road." Before you begin the drive, stop into the office and ask for the latest road conditions. This drive follows a narrow, steep, rocky, dirt and gravel surface that will help you pinpoint every squeak in your car's body. In dry weather, it is generally passable in a sturdy passenger automobile, and should present little problem for vehicles with higher ground clearance. Do not attempt to take an RV or trailer up to the top of the Seven Devils Mountains. Seven Devils Road is open only when it is clear of snow, so the season is often no longer than the months of July, August, and September.

Turn right onto FR 517 about a quarter mile south of the ranger station. The road immediately heads up Squaw Creek, between steep slopes covered in low grasses. The patterns on the hillsides are made by grazing animals whose passage causes the underlying loose stones to shift. Since it is easier for cattle to move on level ground, they will tend to find the flatter areas on these very steep hillsides. Over time, the hills take on a web-like texture, softened by the growth of grasses.

Watch for a small sign for the Seven Devils just before milepost 2, and be certain to go left at the fork, staying on FR 517. This is the drainage of Papoose Creek, and the road is still referred to as Papoose Grade by long-time Idaho residents. The road surface here is gravel, and its condition changes as you go. Some stretches seem to be smooth as glass, while others are rough as a washboard. As you progress, the ratio of washboard to glass will increase dramatically. By milepost 4 the change in elevation evidences itself in the differing vegetation, and the road enters the Nez Perce National Forest.

The road continues to narrow, and to grow rougher and steeper. Near milepost 6 the effort earns you a vista to the southeast, across the Rapid River and Little Salmon River. The views become more expansive as the road continues to climb. Past milepost 9, stay to the right. After milepost 11, stay right again. Even though the left-hand fork looks like a smoother and flatter alternative, it leads nowhere. The road grows extremely rocky above here.

Past milepost 15 the road rounds a point, and the Seven Devils appear for the first time. These towers of bare rock, sheer cliffs, and jumbled stone loom ominously to the southwest. The road turns west, passing meadows that become brilliant with wildflowers in July. Ahead is the Hell's Canyon National Recreation Area boundary, and a campground that is the staging

The Seven Devils Range above Hell's Canyon.

area for treks into the Seven Devils Wilderness Area. Turn right here and continue another 1.5 miles to the Heaven's Gate Overlook parking area.

The elevation at the lookout is 8,428 feet, so be aware of the increased toll on your lungs and heart if you exert yourself here. A steep 350-yard hike to the fire tower may be worth the 10-minute effort for those in good condition. The view encompasses four states, the gorges of Hell's Canyon and the Salmon River, and the Seven Devils on the southern skyline. Idaho's state bird, the mountain bluebird, can usually be seen flitting across your field of vision.

From the summit, the ridge line to the north represents the approximate location of an old Native American trail. Many routes used by early Native Americans are found along the ridgetops, rather than in the valleys. The swift waters and steep hillsides were far less appealing for long journeys than the relatively smooth and flat mountaintops.

The Nez Perce believe that Coyote, their clever ancestor, dug Hell's Canyon to protect the traditional Nez Perce homeland in the Wallowa Mountains from the evil of the ominous Seven Devils. The rugged spires retain their evil names, including He Devil and She Devil, Devil's Throne and Devil's Tooth, the Ogre, and Twin Imps.

Return to Riggins along the same route. If you have the time for further exploration, cross US 95 and follow the Salmon River upstream on the narrow road that parallels the river. Each turn of the road and bend of the river brings a new vista of rock, trees, and water before your eyes.

Back in Riggins, look for the large, wooden scow sitting alongside the main street (US 95). Wooden scows like this one were used in the late 1800s to carry goods and ore down the Salmon River. The bulky flat-bottomed boats were able to navigate the rapids, but only on the downstream run. Once they arrived in Riggins, they were torn apart and used for building materials. "The River of No Return" is thus an apt name for the Salmon, for these boats never returned to their origin.

Today's visitors can ride upstream in a shallow-draft jet boat, which skims the river's surface as it powers its way around the river's obstacles.

18

White Bird Battlefield

General description: This is a very short (10-mile) drive with historic significance. It offers broad, expansive views of the hills east of the Salmon River, and takes in both the new and old highway grades while traveling up and down challenging White Bird Hill.

Special attractions: A self-guided tour of the White Bird Battlefield; a drive down the corkscrew turns of the Old White Bird Grade; the views across the valley to the hills along the Salmon River.

Location: North-central Idaho.

Drive route numbers: U.S. Highway 95 and the Old White Bird Grade.

Travel season: Travel on this short excursion is possible year-round, except when the steep, winding White Bird Grade is covered with snow.

Camping: There is a commercial campground at Grangeville north of the site, and at Riggins, 20 miles to the south.

Services: Both Riggins and Grangeville offer restaurants, motels, and fuel.

Nearby attractions: The remote access point at Pittsburg Landing in Hell's Canyon; rafting and jet boating on the Salmon River; the ski area at Snow Haven; the ghost town of Mount Idaho; the rough Elk City Wagon Road through the Nez Perce National Forest.

The Drive

This short loop drive begins on White Bird Hill on US 95, about 10 miles south of Grangeville. Along the route are a series of markers that describe the fighting that occurred here in June 1877, between U.S. troops and a faction of the Nez Perce tribe led by Chief Joseph. The vistas from the summit of White Bird Hill, at 4,245 feet, to the village of White Bird and the canyon of the Salmon River, 2,500 feet below, are impressive.

Begin at the interpretative shelter at milepost 227 on US 95, about halfway up the long grade that hugs the west side of the valley. This road took ten years to construct, being completed in 1975. In places, up to 300 feet of basalt rock were removed, while in others, 300 feet or more of fill were emplaced to smooth out the grade. The new road sliced 5 miles from the trip between Riggins and Grangeville, and replaced the earlier road, visible from the overlook. This scenic drive will follow that earlier route.

Prior to 1921, the parts of the state south of the Salmon River were

Drive 18: White Bird Battlefield

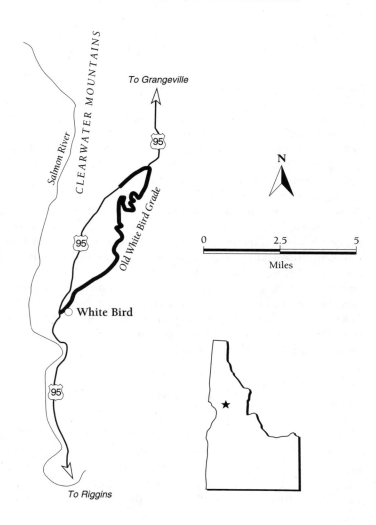

only connected to Idaho's rich Palouse country and the northern counties by roads through eastern Oregon, or by a narrow track over White Bird Hill, which was always either muddy or dusty, depending on the weather. The first highway up the grade was a winding, twisting road, completed in 1921. It was a key stretch of the only link between southern and northern Idaho. This route was not paved until 1938. In 1974, it was added to the National Register of Historic Places.

While the highways along this drive, both new and old, are impressive engineering feats, the heart and soul of the area lies in the historic events that took place here in June 1877. This was the site of the Battle of White Bird Canyon, a victory for the Nez Perce over the U.S. Cavalry. It was also the beginning of the end for the Nez Perce nation.

From the interpretative shelter proceed uphill to milepost 230. Turn right onto the old highway and begin down White Bird Grade. Near the top of the hill is a pullout with a self-serve box with brochures that locate and identify each marked stop along the White Bird Battlefield tour. The pamphlet describes the events of the day of the battle in great detail, using existing landmarks to help you visualize the confrontation. There are generally very few visitors along the roadway, and history buffs will have no trouble bringing the battle to life, imagining the cavalry coming down the hill, or the Nez Perce braves charging around a bluff.

The Nez Perce had a long and peaceful relationship with the white explorers and settlers who developed this portion of Idaho and eastern Oregon. The Nez Perce had provided food and shelter to the Lewis and Clark Expedition in 1805–1806, and were early and eager converts to Christianity. In fact, a contingent of Nez Perce had traveled to St. Louis in 1833 seeking information about the white man's religion. They met with William Clark, then Superintendent of Indian Affairs, and about the only person in St. Louis who understood anything of the Nez Perce language. He had learned it during his short stays in Idaho in 1805 and 1806.

In 1855, a treaty with the Nez Perce was negotiated by the federal government, giving the tribe about 10,000 square miles of territory in eastern Oregon and Idaho. Once gold was discovered at Pierce, and once farming in Oregon's Wallowa Valley began to prosper, the U.S. government began to pressure the Nez Perce to accept a modified agreement that reduced their reservation to little more than one-tenth of its original size. In 1863, the revised treaty was signed by a number of Nez Perce chiefs, although many others refused to sign. Foremost among the "non-treaty" Nez Perce, as they came to be identified, was Old Joseph, whose lands in Oregon were completely lost in the revised treaty.

Over the next dozen years, the two segments of the Nez Perce tribe grew apart, as the treaty Nez Perce practiced Christianity, developed their farms, and grew accustomed to living on their small plots of land near Lapwai, north of Grangeville. Missionaries and developers were concerned about the effect the non-treaty Nez Perce might have on their brothers, and pressed the government to force the non-treaty bands to move onto the reservation.

Old Joseph's son, also called Joseph, had vowed never to give up his people's lands. When the U.S. Army, under the leadership of General Oliver Howard, pressed chiefs Joseph and White Bird, another of the non-treaty

The convoluted hillsides at White Bird, where Chief Joseph's flight began.

Nez Perce, to move onto reservation lands in the spring of 1877, the leaders, sensing the inevitable, reluctantly acquiesced. They began the move, crossing the spring-swollen Snake and Salmon rivers before stopping at Tolo Lake, 5 miles west of Grangeville, before continuing north to Lapwai.

While there, several brash young men of the tribe, perhaps to avenge some earlier incident, or in defiance at the prospect of losing their freedom, rode out and killed three white settlers along the Salmon River. When they returned to Tolo Lake and bragged of their accomplishments, Joseph and White Bird knew that trouble would soon follow. They immediately took about 700 people, including women, children, and the elderly, along with 2,500 horses, to the bottom of White Bird Canyon.

General Howard sent a force of 100 men to bring the Nez Perce back. The soldiers and volunteers set out from Grangeville and began to descend the slopes of White Bird Hill, thinking they had the element of surprise on their side. Joseph's 70 warriors knew precisely how large a force they were facing, however, and the Nez Perce turned the tables on their attackers, killing 34 and sending the rest fleeing back to Grangeville.

Chief Joseph withdrew his soldiers and hundreds of noncombatants across the Salmon River and began a cat-and-mouse game that would last from spring until October. By then Joseph and his people had traveled more

Sheep Lake, Hell's Canyon National Recreation Area (Drive 17).

DAVID JENSEN

Top: Franklin's historic Hatch House, built in 1874 (Drive 1).
Bottom: Sandstone formation in an Owyhee County desert (Drive 13).

Hay field in the Teton Valley (Drive 3).

Sumac along the Snake River in Hell's Canyon (Drive 17).

DAVID JENSEN

SCOTT T. SMITH

Top: *A Salmon River Valley ranch beneath the Sawtooth Mountains (Drive 8).*
Bottom: *Cattails and teasel below the Bear River Range near Franklin (Drive 1).*

DAVID JENSEN

MARK W. LISK

Top: Bruneau Sand Dunes State Park (Drive 13).
Bottom: Lupine and arrowleaf balsamroot in the foothills near Ketchum (Drive 8).

Old plow in the Teton Valley near Felt (Drive 3).

Waterfall on Fall Creek and the South Fork of the Snake River near Swan Valley.

than 1,500 miles and fought more than 20 skirmishes and battles with pursuing cavalry units. When the Nez Perce finally were forced to surrender, at Bear's Paw, Montana, they were just 40 miles from the Canadian border and safety. In fact, Chief White Bird, with a group of his followers, left their Bear's Paw camp in the night, and successfully crossed into Canada. Joseph's speech of surrender stands as a classic:

> I am tired of fighting. Our chiefs are killed. . . . The old men are all dead. . . . It is cold, and we have no blankets. The little children are freezing to death. My people, some of them, have run away to the hills. . . . I want time to look for my children, and to see how many of them I can find; maybe I shall find them among the dead. Hear me, my chiefs: my heart is sick and sad. From where the sun now stands, I will fight no more forever.

Joseph and his people were relocated to reservations in Kansas and Oklahoma, where many died in the unaccustomed surroundings. Joseph himself was ultimately sent to a reservation in eastern Washington, where he died in 1905.

Shortly after the last battlefield tour marker, the road drops into White Bird, a hamlet of 100 people, sheltered by the huge cottonwood trees along White Bird Creek. The town has a pair of simple, elegant, white clapboard churches that set the tone for the architecture of the rest of the buildings. The road climbs the small hill south of town, where it rejoins the new highway, just before it crosses an award-winning modern bridge that spans the creek. This is the end of the drive. From here it is 15 miles north on US 95 to Grangeville, or 29 miles south to Riggins.

19

Lewis and Clark Trail, Eastern Half

General description: Follow free-flowing rivers for 115 miles from the Continental Divide through magnificent forests of towering cedar, pine, and fir trees. The paved two-lane highway was completed as recently as 1962. The drive glides downstream alongside the Lochsa River through a landscape so rugged that it was long avoided by travelers, including Native American tribes and the Lewis and Clark party. The Lochsa then joins the Selway River to form the majestic Clearwater River. The drive skirts vast wilderness areas and visits a Nez Perce legend site.

Special attractions: The USDA Forest Service visitor center at the summit of Lolo Pass; the proximity of the historic Lolo Trail following the ridges to the north; the placid seclusion of the De Voto Memorial Cedar Grove; the wild and untamed whitewater of the Lochsa River; the vastness of the untamed Selway-Bitterroot Wilderness along the length of the route; the Lochsa Historical Ranger Station; Selway Falls; Nez Perce National Historical Park's Heart of the Monster site at Kamiah.

Location: North-central Idaho, east of Lewiston to the Montana border.

Drive route numbers: U.S. Highway 12.

Travel season: This is an all-season highway, well maintained through the winter. Best time to travel the route for its scenic value is late spring, when the river carries heavy loads of snowmelt, and the summer months when activities on the river are at their peak.

Camping: There are a dozen Clearwater National Forest campgrounds sprinkled along the route, and even more along the short stretch to Selway Falls. Commercial camping facilities are located at Lowell and Kamiah.

Services: Limited services are located at Powell and Lowell, with a 60 mile gap between them. Full tourist services can be found on the route at Kamiah and Kooskia, as well as at Missoula, Montana.

Nearby attractions: Horseback riding at Kooskia; backpacking in the vast Selway-Bitterroot Wilderness; the rough Lolo Trail, a 2-day, 100-mile drive on rough roads high above the Clearwater Canyon; whitewater rafting on the Lochsa and Selway rivers.

 The Drive

The drive begins at the top of Lolo Pass on the Montana border, and follows the Lochsa River down to its confluence with the Selway, where it becomes the Clearwater River. From there, the route follows the Clearwater

Drive 19: Lewis and Clark Trail, Eastern Half

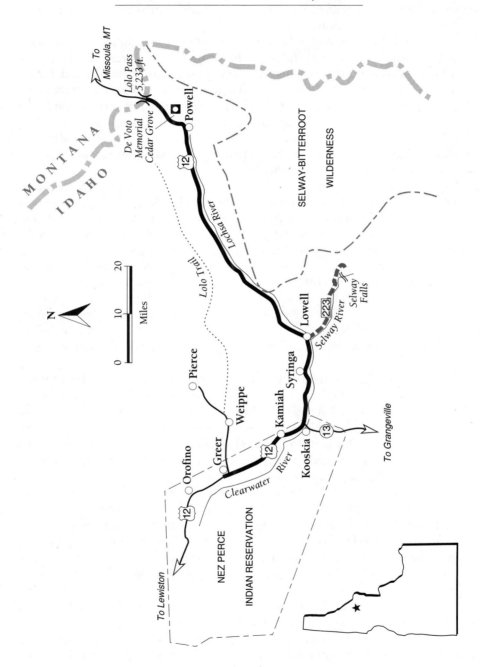

downstream to Greer, 50 miles from Lewiston. This drive can be combined with the western half of the Lewis and Clark Trail (drive 20) to make a complete border-to-border excursion along US 12.

Begin the drive on US 12 at the summit of Lolo Pass, on the Montana-Idaho border. Just west of the 5,233-foot summit is a Forest Service visitor information center that is generally open in the summer months and during the height of the winter season. Federal government budget cuts have had a significant impact on manpower and resources for visitor services throughout the system, and the Clearwater National Forest is no exception. The shortages may mean that the center will be unstaffed. If it is open, be sure to stop and get information on the myriad recreational opportunities that the Clearwater National Forest provides.

The center also features exhibits that trace the journeys of Meriwether Lewis and William Clark, who passed this way in 1805–1806. Although US 12 is called the Lewis and Clark Highway, the explorers' route across Idaho followed the ridges north of the present-day highway, where travel was substantially easier than it would have been along the steep banks of the river.

From the top of Lolo Pass, US 12 drops 1,500 feet in its first 4 miles, and soon joins the Lochsa River on its mad, rocky plunge downstream. A marker located 3 miles from the summit identifies the point where today's highway crosses the route of the Lewis and Clark Expedition's return trip in June 1806. Watch for Stellar's jays along the roadside, their rich blue colors flashing as they swoop out of the tall trees and glide between sunlight and shadow.

A good place to sit quietly and watch for more birds is just ahead at the De Voto Memorial Cedar Grove. This towering stand of western red cedar, with its softly filtered sunlight and carpet of ferns, was a favorite campsite of Pulitzer Prize winner Bernard De Voto, the famed Western historian and conservationist who died in 1955. His ashes were scattered through this grove which was then dedicated to his memory. Paved foot trails loop around and among the fragrant and stately giant trees.

At milepost 162, 3 miles beyond the De Voto grove, the log cabin resort at Powell sits in the woods several hundred yards south of the road. While it looks much like any other hunting and fishing camp, it has a special importance to the traveler who ventures down US 12. This is your only chance to stop for gasoline and potato chips for the next 64 miles; in fact, there are just a handful of buildings of any sort between here and Lowell, at milepost 97.

If it seems that the highway is on the verge of wilderness, it is. The 3-million-acre expanse of the Selway-Bitterroot Wilderness lies just across the river to the south. Occasional footbridges cross the river, providing the only means of reaching the wild country. Parallel to the highway, but following

Cemetery behind Presbyterian church in Kamiah.

the ridge line on the north rim of this canyon, is the Lolo Trail, a four-wheel-drive track. This age-old route was preferred by the native tribes for travel along the river, because it was much easier on both horses and humans than the floor of the canyon, with fewer rocks, rivers, and fallen timber to deal with. When Lewis and Clark came this way, they followed their Shoshone guide along the ridges, descending to the river only when necessary for supplies of fresh salmon. The highway itself was only completed in 1962.

A small parking area and footbridge 11 miles below Powell are the only signs of one of the most popular destinations on the river. The bridge leads to the Jerry Johnson Hot Springs, about a mile into the wilderness area along Warm Springs Creek.

Another thermal seep is located at Colgate Licks near milepost 148. The mineral salts that settle out of the spring's water attract wildlife, which need the minerals to supplement their other food supplies. A short interpretative walk loops around the lick, where it is not uncommon to see deer, elk, or moose, particularly at either end of the day.

George Colgate, for whom the salt lick is named, died near here in unfortunate circumstances. In the fall of 1893, he accompanied a party of hunters to the flats here, working as their camp cook. He had been suffering from prostate and bladder problems for 20 years, which necessitated use of a catheter when his system acted up. He had neglected to pack catheters with him for the trip, and when his old ailments flared up he quickly fell ill with a severe case of uremic poisoning.

His hunting companions, some 30 years his junior, were as unsympathetic to his plight as only young men out for adventure can be. Some of the members of the party were reluctant to escort Colgate back to get medical attention. Colgate did not want the party to split up, and so didn't insist on being helped out of the woods. As his condition worsened, it became obvious that they would have to get Colgate to civilization.

Their first attempt failed when snow made it impossible for them to reach the Lolo Trail at the top of the ridge to the north. They returned to the lick, and began to fashion a raft in an attempt to float out of the canyon. Felling cedar snags with inadequate equipment, they eventually built two rafts and set out in November's cold and inclement weather. After struggling to make just 30 miles in nine days, with the rafts crashing on the rocks and men falling into the frigid waters time and time again, the party reached an infamous decision.

Colgate was by now delirious or unconscious most of the time, and the rest of the party rationalized that it was time to save their own hides: George Colgate was going to meet his Maker. They left him alone and weak on the riverbank and headed for home. It took another ten days of scrambling and scraping along, near death themselves from the exertion, exposure to the elements, and lack of food, before they were found by a search party sent out after them.

As for George Colgate, his death stirred up a storm of controversy. One side bitterly denounced those who had abandoned him, while the other side claimed it was his own fault, and that he had jeopardized the entire party by his actions. The *New York Post* even reported that Colgate eventually stumbled out of the woods on his own. Colgate's own doctor wrote a letter that justified the actions of the hunting party, saying that Colgate could not have survived another 24 hours from the time he was abandoned. George Colgate's body was located the following summer, and his remains were buried near the Colgate Licks.

An extensive exhibit of materials related to the history of the Forest Service is located at the Lochsa Historical Ranger Station, which is open during the heavily traveled summer months. Located 27 miles downstream from Colgate Licks, the museum is housed in the former ranger station, a log structure that dates back to the 1920s. Volunteers, many of whom are retired Forest Service employees, are usually on hand to lend a personal touch to the information contained in the exhibits.

If any point along this route can be considered a center for outdoor activity, the vicinity of the ranger station would be it. Just upstream is the

Wilderness Gateway Campground, the jumping-off point for many wilderness excursions into the Selway-Bitterroot backcountry. The Idaho State Centennial Trail, which runs the length of the state, from the Canadian border to Nevada, splits here into two segments. These segments trace different routes through the mountainous heart of Idaho, coming back together north of Stanley, more than 100 air miles to the south. The entire eastern segment of the trail runs through designated wilderness, while the western route skirts the edge of Gospel Hump Wilderness Area, which is accessible at many points along the trail's length, allowing short forays into the backcountry. There is also four-wheel-drive motor vehicle access to the Lolo Trail, on the ridge a few miles north of the ranger station. Check with the rangers before attempting to explore the Lolo Trail.

The canyon narrows below the Lochsa Ranger Station. The massive exposures of granite faced with dark mosses and lichen give this reach its name, Black Canyon. Near here is the spot where the Colgate hunting party abandoned George Colgate and their rafts before striking out on foot.

At Lowell, milepost 97, civilization, or at least the opportunity to purchase fuel and food, returns. This small collection of cabins and vacation homes is located where the Lochsa and Selway rivers join to form the Middle Fork of the Clearwater River. A side trip up the Selway on Forest Road 223 starts here. A 20-mile drive along the very edge of the smooth-flowing Selway River leads to Selway Falls, a spectacular series of cascades during high water (May through early July), and still an impressive sight the rest of the year. The narrow road is liberally laced with campsites. After visiting the falls, return to US 12 and turn left (west) to rejoin the tour.

From here, more signs of human habitation are evident. Along with the obvious—cars, roads, houses—there are other signs as well. Occasionally a set of cables, with a basket suspended at one end, crosses the river. These are used to ferry both people and supplies to property located on the far bank.

The small town of Syringa, 8 miles below Lowell, is named after the state flower, also known as the mock orange. Between Syringa and Kooskia, 16 miles away, the landscapes changes slowly from a dense, forested canyon with steep walls, to a deep valley with tree-covered stretches of hills broken by open grassy slopes. Several miles outside of Kooskia the road enters the Nez Perce Indian Reservation.

Kooskia, (pronounced KOOS-key) is a contraction of Koos Koos Kia, the Nez Perce words for "meeting of the waters." The town is located where the South and Middle forks of the Clearwater come together to form the Clearwater's main stem. Lewis and Clark mistranslated the Nez Perce words as "clear water," thus giving the river its name. The town that eventually grew up here retained the original Nez Perce name. Kooskia is, at its heart, a lumber town, and the town's 700 residents are struggling, like those of many other similar towns, to accommodate their proud and independent lifestyles to today's changing economic and environmental realities.

Kooskia was one of the first Idaho towns to get telephone service, but it was achieved in a roundabout way. The service was carried on the fence wires enclosing farmland between here and Grangeville, on the plains to the south. The service worked, but breaks in the line caused by cattle rubbing against the wires were a constant frustration.

On the right side of the road 4 miles below Kooskia is the oldest Protestant church in continuous use in Idaho. Built in 1874 by Nez Perce workers, the small clapboard church rests in an open field surrounded by widely spaced ponderosa pines. Behind the church is a small cemetery where Scottish sisters, Kate and Sue McBeth, are buried. Missionaries and teachers, they were for a time the only white women in the Kamiah valley. Also buried in the cemetery is the leader of the treaty faction of the Nez Perce, Chief Lawyer. Given his name by early mountain men because of his powers of persuasion, Lawyer, whose given name was Hallalhotsoot, signed the treaty that gave up the lands of Chief Joseph. Lawyer led his tribe until several years before his death in 1876.

A mile ahead, on the left, is the most important site in the Nez Perce mythology. This is the Heart of the Monster, one of the sites of the Nez Perce National Historical Park. A parking area is available and interpretative signs explain the significance of this volcanic stone mound to the Nez Perce. Since this is a sacred site, it is important that visitors honor its sanctity by observing signs and refraining from climbing on the rocks.

The Nez Perce creation story tells of Coyote, the clever trickster, who, along with other creatures of the forest, was swallowed by a monster. With the flint he carried, Coyote started a fire, and using knives he began to cut the monster's heart. When it came free, the entrapped creatures were released, and Coyote butchered the monster. He scattered chunks of the monster's carcass, and a tribe of native people sprang up where each chunk landed. When he was done, Fox reminded Coyote that there was no tribe in this region. Coyote shook the remaining drops of blood from his hands and, where they fell, the Nez Perce came to life. The heart of the monster remains here, where Coyote left it.

A short distance beyond the Heart of the Monster is another significant site, one that was important in the journey of Lewis and Clark. Anxious to return to civilization, the expedition had hastened out of Oregon early in the spring of 1806. Near this point, at a site they called their "Long Camp," they spent four weeks waiting out the spring snowmelt on the high ridges of the Clearwater country before they were able to continue their eastward journey. Aside from their two winter camps, one at Fort Mandan on the

Great Plains and the other at Fort Clatsop on the Oregon coast, this was their longest camp. It was the middle of June 1806 before they were able to proceed.

At Kamiah, (pronounced CAM-ee-eye) the highway crosses the Clearwater as it enters town. Kamiah, like Kooskia, has prospered in tandem with the fortunes of the lumber industry. After a large mill closed in the 1980s, Kamiah's three-block-long Main Street was polished and scrubbed and its old buildings painted and updated, in hopes of attracting newcomers and passers-by to stop, linger awhile, and leave a few dollars behind. It is worth the short detour through the town to see what these determined folks have accomplished. From Kamiah, continue 15 miles down the river to Greer.

Greer marks the end of the eastern half of the Lewis and Clark Trail scenic drive. The western half (see Drive 20) can be done in conjunction with the eastern half, or as a completely independent excursion.

20

Lewis and Clark Trail, Western Half

General description: This 110-mile drive begins by climbing out of the Clearwater Canyon to visit some of Idaho's earliest mining settlements. After returning to the Clearwater River it heads downstream past towering Dworshak Dam and ends at Lewiston, where the Clearwater River joins the Snake River at the Washington border.

Special attractions: Site of Lewis and Clark's first meeting with the Nez Perce; historic gold-mining community of Pierce; the colorful lumber town of Orofino; massive Dworshak Dam; Nez Perce National Historical Park Visitor Center and Nez Perce legend sites; the port city of Lewiston on the Snake River; the Spiral Grade climbing to the edge of the Palouse prairies high above Lewiston.

Location: North-central Idaho, east of Lewiston.

Drive route numbers: U.S. Highways 12 and 95, Idaho Highway 11, Grangemont Road.

Travel season: This is a year-round route, although winter storms can make travel to Pierce difficult. Lewiston's low elevation helps to moderate the climate on the lower Clearwater. Spring, summer, and fall remain the best times for sightseeing.

Camping: Clearwater National Forest campgrounds are located north of Pierce. Commercial camping facilities are located at Ahsahka, near the base of Dworshak Dam.

Services: Limited services are located at Weippe, Pierce, and Orofino. Lewiston is a large city, offering complete tourist services.

Nearby attractions: Horseback riding at Kooskia; backpacking in the vast Selway-Bitterroot Wilderness; driving the rough Lolo Trail, a two-day, 100-mile drive for four-wheel-drive vehicles on rough roads high above the Clearwater Canyon; whitewater raft trips on the Lochsa or the Selway rivers; Nez Perce National Historical Park's Heart of the Monster site at Kamiah; the site of White Bird Battlefield south of Grangeville; Hell's Canyon on the Snake River.

 The Drive

From Greer, this drive leaves US 12 and climbs the Greer Grade to the Weippe Prairie, where the Lewis and Clark party first encountered the Nez Perce. Scenic vistas of Palouse country and pastoral landscapes will delight

Drive 20: Lewis and Clark Trail, Western Half

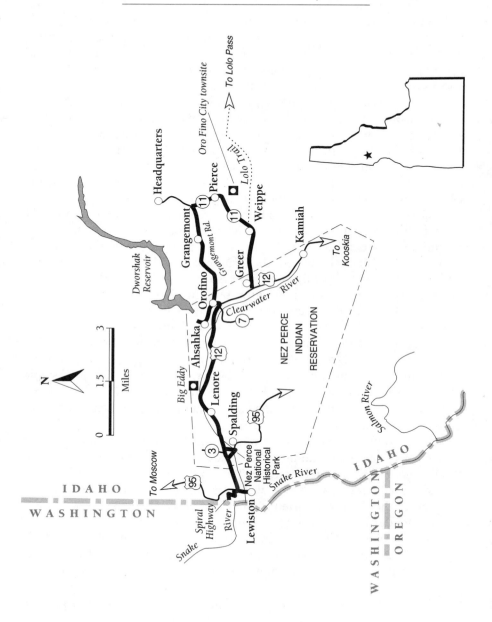

the eye before the drive heads into the heart of Idaho's first gold rush at the town of Pierce. Around Pierce the drive passes the ghost town of Oro Fino City and the site of an infamous hanging. North of Pierce the road winds through low, forested hills before turning back to the Clearwater Canyon at Orofino (not to be confused with the ghost town of Oro Fino City), and continuing on to Lewiston, following the Clearwater River past Big Eddy and a number of Nez Perce historical sites.

Begin this drive by leaving US 12 at Greer. Take ID 11 across the river and immediately begin climbing a series of switchbacks for 7 miles, each sharp turn offering a new angle from which to view the Clearwater Canyon below. The road's gradient becomes less severe as it approaches the prairie above the canyon. The Clearwater carries so much water that it has eroded its canyon faster than have the smaller side streams in this area, leaving the Clearwater Canyon far below the level of the surrounding terrain.

Greer was once the site of a ferry across the Clearwater, built in 1861 to profit from the miners heading up the hill to Pierce. In 1877, when Chief Joseph and his band of 700 Nez Perce passed through here pursued by General O. O. Howard, they cut the ferry loose and burned the supporting buildings in order to slow down their pursuers. Like many early ferries, this one was eventually the site of a bridge, built in 1914.

When the road tops out 9 miles above Greer, it begins to cross the Weippe Prairie. Fringed in ponderosa and planted with wheat, barley, rapeseed, and other dry-land crops, the prairie is a fertile, benign oasis. The Nez Perce harvested camas bulbs here each year, setting up camps after the long winter. The camas plant, of the lily family, was an important food staple of Native Americans, who depended on the starchy roots. The blue flowers of the camas lily are still seen in late spring, although in nowhere near the profusion they once were.

This prairie is also the western end of the Lolo Trail, the ancient path across the Bitterroot Mountains that follows along the ridgetops north of the impassable Clearwater Canyon. Today identified as Forest Road 500, the Lolo Trail winds its way for well over 90 backcountry miles from the east end of the Weippe Prairie to Lolo Pass on the Montana border. It is a rough, two-day outing for four-wheel-drive vehicles.

When William Clark came off the Lolo Trail on September 20, 1805, this prairie is where he first encountered the Nez Perce tribe. He met two young Nez Perce boys, who led him and his men into their village. A marker just east of Weippe (pronounced WE-yipe) commemorates that meeting. The town of Weippe is a small collection of neat yards and houses. The town is dependent on lumber for its economic well-being.

From Weippe, the road turns northeast along Grasshopper Creek. As it approaches Pierce, 12 miles away, it travels deeper into a heavy forest of

Shoshone County Courthouse in Pierce was one of Idaho's first public buildings.

ponderosa pine. Just outside Pierce is a marker that recalls the vigilante hanging of five Chinese mine workers accused in 1885 of hacking to death a Pierce merchant. The outraged white citizens of Pierce, who were outnumbered at least 8 to 1 by the resident Chinese, demanded justice. A hastily convened kangaroo court, unable to definitively pin the crime on any one person, determined that the crime had probably been committed by any or all of the five Chinese. The deputy sheriff gathered up the bunch and headed out with them in his wagon, intending to take them to the new county seat in Murray, far to the north. A mob of angry citizens waylaid the wagon, stringing the accused up from a pole hung between nearby trees. This incident was the most notorious of the many indignities that Chinese immigrants to the West were submitted to in early Idaho mining camps.

Stranded in the West when their jobs on the transcontinental railroad ended, many Chinese took to mining, hard labor and all, as the only way to make a living. Distrusted by white settlers and miners because of their different language, clothing, and culture, the Chinese were frequently the targets of discrimination. By law they were forbidden to stake mining claims, but, being patient and having little choice but to move huge quantities of gravel for very slight rewards, they managed to eke out a living from claims that whites regarded as "played out."

Pierce and its short-lived neighbor, Oro Fino City (not to be confused with Orofino on the Clearwater River), reveled in gold fever from the first find made in 1861 by Wilbur Bassett on Canal Gulch, until the gravel had been picked clean several years later. Oro Fino City burned to the ground in 1866, while Pierce hung on, though just barely. At its peak, Pierce had been an important center of commerce, and the Shoshone County Courthouse here, the oldest surviving government building in Idaho (erected 1862), was its most imposing structure. Today the two-story structure is preserved, frozen in time. It is located a block east of Main Street on Court Street, in the center of Pierce. Nearby is a collection of tools and equipment used by lumberjacks in the nearby forests, housed in covered sheds with open fronts.

Continue north from Pierce on ID 11 past the large lumber mill and plywood plant at Jaype, named for J. P. Weyerhauser, a former president of the Potlatch Corporation. Just past milepost 35, 2 miles north of Jaype, turn left onto Grangemont Road. From here to Orofino the road winds across the plateau, dipping and swooping through forested stretches and open, harvested areas before beginning the long descent down Whiskey Creek to Orofino and the Clearwater River, 26 miles away.

Orofino, despite its golden name, is first and foremost a lumber town. Each September the town's yearly festival, Lumberjack Days, celebrates the hard-working men who characterize the Idaho woods. Just north of the Clearwater River bridge stands a life-sized statue of a classic Orofino

Along with the Snake and the Salmon, the Clearwater River is Idaho's most important.

lumberjack. Turn right here, before crossing the river, onto ID 7, down the north bank of the Clearwater River.

Ahead on the left is the Dworshak National Fish Hatchery, which rears steelhead, an ocean-going trout. Steelhead historically traveled the 500 miles or more from the Pacific Ocean to the North Fork of the Clearwater, as well as to other drainages in Idaho.

When the Dworshak Dam was constructed, it blocked the natural flow of these wild, fighting fish from the sea to their spawning beds farther upstream. In an attempt to mitigate the damage caused by their dam, the Corps of Engineers built this hatchery in 1968. On the grounds is a small church, built in 1900. The first pastor was a Nez Perce who had been trained at Kamiah by Sue McBeth, a Scottish missionary who is buried at Kamiah.

Across a bridge over the North Fork of the Clearwater, which empties into the main river here, turn right and drive about a mile to the base of massive Dworshak Dam. This 717-foot-high dam, begun in the 1960s and finished in 1973, is a monument to the self-serving, over-reaching power of the Corps of Engineers. The dam, one of the world's highest straight-axis (noncurved) concrete gravity dams, and the third-highest dam of any type in the United States, holds back the little North Fork for more than 54 miles. It has destroyed steelhead and elk habitat, and generates just a fraction of the electricity it was intended to produce.

On the positive side of the ledger, the reservoir contains trophy trout, salmon, and bass. Its shores are dotted with campsites. Tours of the dam are available during most of the year. Outfitters in Orofino and Ahsahka can provide information on fishing methods and locations, boat rentals, and other activities available on the reservoir.

Return to US 12 by retracing your route to Orofino, crossing the Clearwater and turning right (west). At Ahsahka, opposite the base of the dam, is a small park at the site of Lewis and Clark's canoe camp. Here the explorers stopped in September 1805 to hollow out five canoes to continue their westward journey. They cached supplies and equipment and left their horses with local Nez Perce tribesmen before setting off on October 7, 1805, for the final push down the Clearwater, Snake, and Columbia rivers to the Pacific Ocean.

At the Lenore Rest Area (milepost 27), 13 miles below Ahsahka, is a bend in the river known as Big Eddy. The turbulent, powerful eddy is visible from just past the picnic tables at the west end of the rest area, or from the road just downstream, although there is no safe pullout there. This site was obviously a good fishing hole, since archaeological evidence shows that it was inhabited as long as 10,000 years ago. More recently, it was the site of Slaterville, a town that lasted for about a week of 1861, at the height of the gold rush upstream at Pierce.

The Oregon Steam and Navigation Company (OS&N) sent the steamship *Colonel Wright* upstream to this point with supplies and miners headed for the gold fields. Seth Slater, an entrepreneur from Portland, stepped off the boat, set up his wares, covered by blanket awnings, and declared that this was Slaterville. The next week, when the *Colonel Wright* returned, the water was higher due to spring runoff, and the boat snapped a line in the treacherous eddy just below the landing. The OS&N, fearing for their boat's safety, decided immediately that Lewiston would make a better port than Slaterville, and declined to send any more commerce Slater's way. Only one other boat ever docked at Slaterville, and sensing defeat, Seth Slater climbed aboard and moved himself and his business downstream to Lewiston.

From here to Lewiston, the road is a fast and smooth two-lane highway with broad shoulders and occasional passing lanes. A side trip up ID 3 takes off to the north, 12 miles below Lenore, through the rolling fields and hills of the Palouse to the little towns of Kendrick and Juliaetta. Another 3 miles on US 12 brings you to the junction of US 12 and US 95, Idaho's north-south lifeline. Here this drive leaves US 12 momentarily, heading south on US 95, just 2 miles to the Nez Perce National Historical Park Visitor Center.

Considered by some to have the world's finest small collection of Western Native American artifacts, the center also offers a slide show and a collection of books relating to the history and culture of the Nez Perce and other Western tribes. The park is spread out, with historical sites scattered through Montana, Idaho, Washington, and Oregon. A number of the sites are related to the Nez Perce War of 1877, when the great Chief Joseph led a band of 700 people on an epic journey that began near here and ended in Joseph's defeat near the Canadian border.

Return north on US 95 to US 12. Follow US 12 west toward Lewiston. Just west of the junction of US 95 and US 12 is a small rock arch on the road's north side, just above the road cut. To the Nez Perce these stones represent Ant and Yellowjacket, mythological insects that feature prominently in Nez Perce lore. A territorial squabble between the two insects over some dried salmon led to a brawl. The insects were so enraged that they failed to hear the wise Coyote when he demanded that they stop. When they refused to listen, Coyote turned them into stone.

As the road enters Lewiston, pass the Nez Perce casino and, across the river, the enormous sawmill and wood products plant. At 738 feet, this is the lowest elevation in the state of Idaho. Lewiston is a city famous for the variety of trees that grow here, encouraged by the relatively mild climate. Lewiston and its sister city on the Washington side of the Snake River, Clarkston, sit at the confluence of the Clearwater and the Snake. Up the Snake River from here is Hell's Gate, the lower end of the dramatic Hell's Canyon, the deepest gorge in the United States. Lewiston marks the end of your voyage of discovery along the Lewis and Clark Trail.

If you haven't had enough of Clearwater country, or if your plans call for continuing north on US 95, a short side trip climbs the old highway grade from Lewiston into the rolling Palouse hills north of the city and the Clearwater River. From US 12, just west of the northbound US 95 exit, turn right and begin the climb through the grassy slopes on the north side of the valley. The road, known as the Spiral Highway, twists and turns its way from the river's edge to the plateau above in a little less than 10 miles, gaining more than 1,600 feet of elevation in the process. An overlook at the top of the grade, just before the road ends at US 95, provides an expansive vista of the Clearwater River as it empties into the Snake River. Lewiston and Clarkston straddle the Snake, which emerges from Hell's Canyon just south of Lewiston.

21

McCroskey Skyline Drive

General description: A 24-mile drive on gravel and dirt roads that follows a ridge line with expansive views of the forests and Palouse hills of north-western Idaho and eastern Washington.

Special attractions: The road itself, and the story behind it, is the main attraction on this drive. Virgil McCroskey's tribute to his mother's memory is a wonderful reminder of the power of the human spirit.

Location: The Idaho Panhandle, north of Moscow.

Drive route numbers: Skyline Drive, Mail Route Road, DeSmet Road (Saltice Road).

Travel season: From late April or May, when winter's snowdrifts are cleared from the route, until snow flies again in the fall. The golden colors of the Palouse grain fields from August until harvest make the panorama even more spectacular.

Camping: There are a few campsites in McCroskey State Park. Heyburn State Park offers more extensive camping facilities.

Services: The university town of Moscow, to the south on U.S. Highway 95, has a full range of services, from fast food to fine dining, motels, groceries and automotive services.

Nearby attractions: Appaloosa Horse Club Museum and Heritage Center west of Moscow; athletic and cultural events on the University of Idaho campus; the historic McConnell Mansion in Moscow.

The Drive

This is a short 24-mile drive on gravel and improved dirt roads that are suitable for passenger vehicles, although there are some rough spots and exposed rocks. It hugs the side of Mineral Mountain, meandering back and forth as it proceeds west of US 95 to a series of panoramic views of the Palouse country from vantage points more than 800 feet above the wheat-covered hillocks along the Idaho-Washington border.

The route is known as the Skyline Drive, and it wends its way through Mary Minerva McCroskey State Park. The drive, and the park, are testimony to the proposition that one person, with enough perseverance and dedication, can fulfill a dream, and in the process take on "big government" and win.

Drive 21: McCroskey Skyline Drive

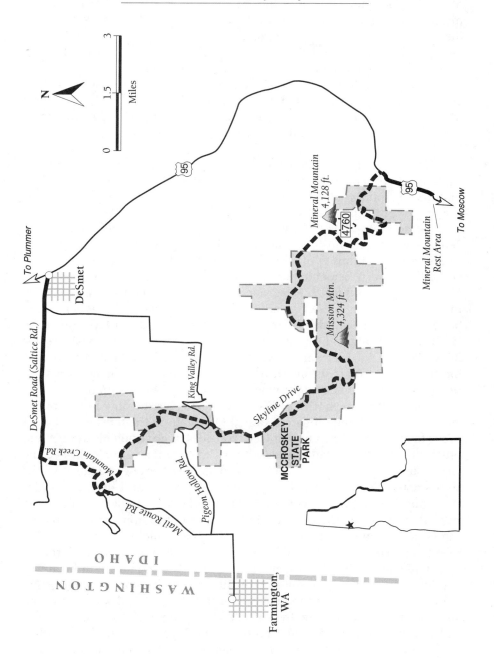

Begin the drive at the Mineral Mountain Rest Area on US 95, just south of the Latah-Benewah county line between Potlatch and DeSmet. Large interpretive signs at the rest area tell the story of Virgil McCroskey and his memorial to his pioneer mother. While in the rest area take the short walk along the hillside above the parking lot. A variety of native trees and plants growing here have been marked with identifying labels.

Head north from the rest area on US 95, and at the crest of the hill, cross the line into Benewah County and turn left immediately into Mary Minerva McCroskey State Park. The turn is not well marked, so look sharp. If you begin to head downhill, you've gone too far. There is no entrance fee for the park or the Skyline Drive.

The road is gravel, and generally is in good shape. It is narrow, so use caution on corners. The entire drive is suitable for all vehicles, including motor homes and trailers, provided that you are prudent. Note your mileage or set your trip odometer to zero at the entrance to the park.

Some years after the Civil War, Mary McCroskey came west from Tennessee with her husband and ten children. They settled in the eastern Washington community of Steptoe, about 20 miles due west of here. Life was difficult out West, and Mary McCroskey died after just two years here. Her son Virgil, born in 1877, became a pharmacist and opened a drug store in Colfax, Washington, a few miles south of Steptoe, and just across the border from Potlatch, Idaho. Virgil was successful, and in 1920 bought the family farm. He apparently made good money in the pharmacy business, for he was able to work the farm and, at the same time, travel extensively during the next 20 years. In his travels, he visited many of the country's national parks, where he seems to have gotten part of his inspiration.

Virgil's fond memories of his mother were inextricably linked to the view of Mission Mountain and Mineral Mountain in the forested hills east of the family farm. When he connected the idea of honoring his mother and other pioneer women with the idea of a park, his own mission in life became clear. Virgil began buying pieces of land as they became available on the slopes above Palmer Butte. He stitched together a parcel here and a plot there until he had finally connected enough land to run a road along the ridge that makes up the park. He built picnic and camping sites along the route, carved out spots from which to enjoy the scenic vistas, and, in 1951, offered the park to the state of Idaho as a gift to memorialize his mother.

Only one problem mars this tale of dedication and love—and that was the surprising reaction of the state of Idaho, which said, in essence, "No thank you; we can't afford to take care of the place." Virgil was undeterred and continued his campaign. In 1955, after four years of cajoling state officials and enlisting the support of such groups as the Boy Scouts, Virgil McCroskey finally was able to grant the state of Idaho this 4,000-acre memorial. The

McCroskey Skyline Drive offers scenic vistas from a high ridge over Palouse country.

state threw one last wrench into the works, however, demanding that Virgil McCroskey, at age 78, agree to maintain the park himself for a period of 15 years. Virgil agreed, and kept up his end of the bargain, making sure that the road was in good repair, that picnic tables were functional, and that trash was removed. Virgil died in 1970 at the age of 93. He had spent the last 15 years of his life fulfilling his commitments and his destiny.

Forest Road 4760 splits off to the right 4.5 miles into the drive, leading to a fire lookout tower atop of Mineral Mountain. Just past mile 6 on the Skyline Drive is Lone Pine Lookout, with expansive vistas to the south and west. As you reach the 8-mile mark, the vistas become more grand as the road straddles the top of the ridge. Views to both the left and the right combine the rich dark green of the ponderosa pine forest with the golden wheat fields below.

At the 10-mile mark, the road forks. Stay to the right here. At mile 12, another viewpoint leads the eye to the west. The road makes a long right turn around the flank of a hillside at mile 13, and the views westward into Washington seem to stretch forever. The Palouse reveals its true nature from this high vantage point. The landscape is not dominated by rivers and streams carving the land into valleys and canyons. In fact, the countryside seems to be made up of random bumps and depressions. This is a vast area of dunes, made up of wind-blown silt that settled here sometime prior to the last ice age. Grasses growing during the wetter climate of the ice ages stabilized the dunes.

At 13 miles, continue straight at the intersection with King Valley Road, which heads off to the right (east), and Pigeon Hollow Road, which heads west, toward Farmington, Washington. The Skyline Drive here is dirt, not the improved gravel found on the rest of the drive. Skyline Drive ends abruptly in 4 more miles, at its junction with Mail Route Road. Turn right on Mail Route Road and head downhill 2 more miles to DeSmet Road, (called Saltice Road on some maps) where a right turn leads to pavement and, in 4 miles, into DeSmet. The drive ends here, at the junction of DeSmet Road and US 95 in DeSmet. From here Coeur d'Alene is 50 miles north, and Moscow is 37 miles south.

DeSmet was the third location of the Jesuit Mission of the Sacred Heart, first established by Father Pierre DeSmet near St. Maries, and then moved to the knoll at Cataldo. In the 1880s the Coeur d'Alene tribe, like many others, was herded onto a small, isolated reservation. The Coeur d'Alene Reservation included the area around DeSmet. The priests of the mission, anxious that the tribe not lose what little land they had been given by the government, urged tribal members to move onto the reservation. The mission was moved here from Cataldo as well, and many of the Coeur d'Alene followed. DeSmet became the center of the tribe's spiritual life, and a magnificent cathedral, which burned in 1939, was the center of DeSmet.

The Coeur d'Alene Tribe has fared about as well as any of the Native American tribes, since they have proven to be sharp businessmen. Coeur d'Alene translates from the French as "Heart of an Awl," indicating that the early fur trappers respected the tribe's tough negotiating stance. In recent years, the tribe has waged a battle for the return to its control of the entirety of Coeur d'Alene Lake. The tribe also has been instrumental in the development of the National Indian Lottery. The tribe's casino at Worley has been a great success, drawing clientele from Spokane and Coeur d'Alene, as well as from more distant locations.

22

Plummer To Potlatch

General description: This is primarily a forest drive, covering 74 miles on two-lane paved roads. Stands of Idaho's magnificent western redcedar and white pines dominate the landscape. Portions of the route have been designated the White Pine Scenic Byway. The second half of the drive features tidy farms in the rolling Palouse hills.

Special attractions: Heyburn State Park at the southern end of Lake Coeur d'Alene; the St. Joe River coursing through Chatcolet and Round lakes; wild rice fields; the lumber town of St. Maries, with its riverfront water park; side trips to the Emerald Creek Garnet Area and the Hobo Cedar Grove; giant white pine trees; mixed forest and dryland farming communities in the Palouse country; the company town of Potlatch.

Location: The north Idaho Panhandle.

Drive route numbers: Idaho Highway 5, Idaho Highway 3, and Idaho Highway 6.

Travel season: These roads are accessible year-round, although heavy winter snows may make winter travel difficult.

Camping: Heyburn State Park offers camping, and a St. Joe National Forest campground is located at the Giant White Pine site on ID 6.

Services: Plummer, St. Maries, and Potlatch all offer limited fuel and grocery services. Coeur d'Alene to the north, and Moscow to the south both offer full services.

Nearby attractions: All the attractions of Coeur d'Alene—the lake, the city, and its museums and outdoor opportunities; gambling at the Coeur d'Alene tribe's casino at Worley; floating on the St. Joe River; the Appaloosa Horse Club Museum and Heritage Center west of Moscow; athletic and cultural events on the University of Idaho campus.

 The Drive

The drive from Plummer south to Potlatch is a celebration of the marvelous forests that characterize northern Idaho. Paralleling the White Pine Scenic Byway, the route passes through dramatic stands of western redcedar and Idaho's state tree, the majestic white pine. Glimpses of the Palouse hills, their rolling dunes covered in wheat, are available on several stretches of the drive. The curious sight of the St. Joe River winding its way through Chatcolet Lake adds to the charm of this pleasant drive.

Drive 22: Plummer to Potlatch

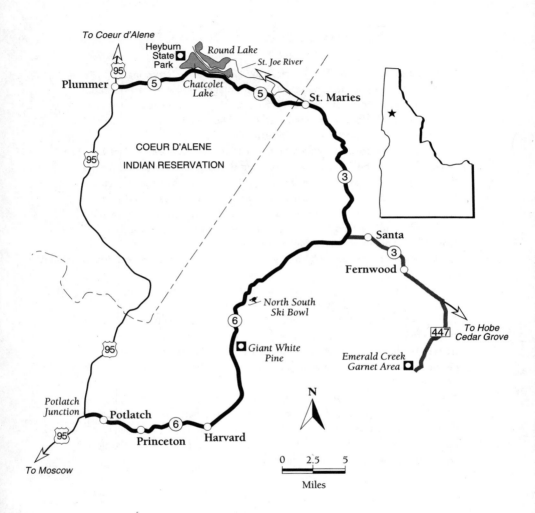

Begin in Plummer, located on U.S. Highway 95, 34 miles south of Coeur d'Alene. Head east on ID 5 across open meadows interspersed with stands of ponderosa pine. Deer are often seen grazing at the edges of the clearings in the early mornings and late in the day. This is the northern edge of the Palouse hill country, a vast region of wind-blown dunes formed in dry, windy conditions many thousands of years ago, and stabilized by the growth of vegetation during more moist periods. The road quickly drops off the plateau and down through the forest, crossing under a railroad trestle near the bottom of the hill, 6 miles from Plummer.

Take an immediate left after the trestle for a short side trip to a small picnic area and boat ramp on the western shore of Chatcolet Lake in Heyburn State Park. Vacation homes are sprinkled all along this shore and around the southern end of the lake. Chatcolet Lake, along with Benewah Lake, Round Lake, and Hidden Lake, is in actuality part of Coeur d'Alene Lake, whose level was raised slightly in 1906 by the construction of Post Falls Dam on the Spokane River west of the city of Coeur d'Alene. Prior to that time, the St. Joe River coursed through this valley, meandering between the shallow lakes. With the slight rise in the water level across the entire system, the natural levees the river had created along both banks became visible as the flooding joined all the bodies of water into one.

Ironically, Heyburn State Park was named for a United States senator who was vehemently opposed to the federal government's involvement in what he considered to be Idaho's affairs. Inspired by an upcoming allotment of land to the Coeur d'Alene tribe, he sponsored a bill in which he proposed that Chatcolet Lake be named a national park. He felt that state parks were "always a source of embarrassment." While he was away from Washington, the bill came to a vote and was modified to allow the state of Idaho to purchase the land, turning it into exactly what he feared most.

Return to ID 5 and head east. At Rocky Point, 2 miles ahead, is a picnic area, a marina, and a small museum housed in a log cabin. In front of the cabin sits a carved stone sign, dedicated to the Civilian Conservation Corps workers who built many of the park's facilities in the 1930s. The sign had originally been placed on the roadside, but had been vandalized and pushed down a hill sometime in the 1960s. Found in the thick undergrowth some two decades later, it was brought to this site and rededicated.

Continuing east on ID 5, the course of the St. Joe River through the lakes is clearly visible. Off to the left (north) of the road, you will see Chatcolet Lake (on the left) and Round Lake (on the right). One of Idaho's more unusual crops is grown in the marshy waters between here and St. Maries (and along ID 3 north of town). Wild rice flourishes in these wet lowlands, and is one of the more popular products of the region.

After winding past Benewah Lake, the road enters St. Maries (pronounced *Saint Marys*), passing Mullan Trail Park on the left side of the road. Overlooking the park is a statue of Captain John Mullan, the army engineer whose military road from Walla Walla, Washington, to Montana was first routed through this valley. After two years of struggling with the damage wrought by seasonal flooding, of chopping trees to build corduroy roads (made of logs laid side to side across boggy ground), and of carving out hillsides to avoid the worst swamps, Mullan rerouted his road to pass north

The fertile, rolling hills of the Palouse between Plummer and St. Maries.

of Coeur d'Alene Lake, some 20 miles north of St. Maries.

The elementary school on the right, guarded by a giant lumberjack mascot, will take you back many years. Notice the entrances to the building—one for girls, one for boys, each clearly labeled in block letters carved into the stone. The school was built in the 1920s, but no one in town can remember when the separate entrances were last used.

St. Maries is a working town of 2,400 people. It is easy to see that timber is the primary industry here, but on bright, warm summer days work is forgotten at the Aqua Park along the St. Joe River, a great old-fashioned swimming hole for visitors and the local kids alike.

Take ID 3 south from the center of St. Maries, crossing the St. Maries River before climbing out of the valley through a narrow canyon of basalt outcrops. The road reaches a plateau and heads over, down, up, across, and down again before returning to the river 12 miles later. After 2 more miles, the highway meets ID 6.

For a side trip to two of Idaho's best-kept secrets, stay on ID 3. The first is the Emerald Creek Garnet Area, where anyone with the urge to get incredibly muddy can hunt for the state gemstone, the star garnet, found in only two places in the world. From a junction south of Fernwood, 6 miles south of the ID 3/ID 6 junction, take Forest Road 447 for 8 miles, and then

School mascot in St. Maries.

hike about half a mile to the garnet hunting grounds. Daily permits for garnet mining are issued from an information center at the site between Memorial Day and Labor Day. For more information, contact the ranger station in St. Maries.

The other destination on this side trip is the Hobo Cedar Grove, a 240-acre stand located on steep slopes northeast of Clarkia. At Clarkia, 10 miles south of Fernwood, take FR 321 (Merry Creek Road) about 8 miles to a short side road (FR 1903) that leads to the grove and a nature trail.

If you've taken these side trips, return north on ID 3 to its junction with ID 6 and rejoin the tour. Head west on ID 6 through terrain that is not as heavily forested, and not as steep, as the regions to the north. Hills here are a bit more rounded, with patches of open meadows. West of the junction 6 miles is the town of Emida, named for three pioneer families—the Easts, the Millers, and the Dawsons. Forest clearcuts in the area are reminders of earlier, less selective logging practices.

Continuing on beyond Emida, the forest thickens as it climbs to the Palouse Divide and the nearby North South Ski Bowl, a small local ski area with a 500-foot vertical drop. A sharp descent through towering western redcedars and white pine levels out near a giant white pine, located next to a campground named, appropriately enough, Giant White Pine Campground. This noble specimen provides only a hint of the gargantuan trees that were once found throughout the Idaho Panhandle's forests. The 400-year-old tree stands 188 feet tall and has a circumference of 20 feet. Estimates are that the behemoth would yield 13,000 board-feet of lumber, were anyone callous enough to cut it down.

The temptation to cut white pine was too much for many loggers to resist, since it is one of the most highly prized of the softwoods. White pine is used extensively in window frames and doors because of its resistance to warping, its attractive grain, and light weight. Much of the early demand for the white pine was for a more mundane purpose, however, and millions of board-feet went up in smoke as wooden matches.

The campground is also the site of a small marker honoring Charlie Sampson, a Boise businessman who took on an unusual challenge. Sampson owned a music store in Boise, and one day in 1914 he became lost in the country south of Boise while returning from a delivery. Frustrated by the lack of road signs, Charlie took buckets of orange paint on his travels and began to mark "Sampson Trails," routes back to Boise from points all over the Northwest. In places his markings included an advertisement for his music store, but advertising was not his primary motivation. For 20 years grateful travelers sent Charlie letters of appreciation for his efforts.

The government agencies in charge of highway signage must have been a bit embarrassed by Charlie's usurping their responsibility, since they tried to have him stopped as a vandal. The state legislature saw through their game, however, and passed a resolution granting Charlie Sampson the "right and privilege of marking and maintaining the Sampson Trail on state and federal highways." Though Sampson died in 1935, faint traces of his markings are still visible on rocks in scattered parts of the state.

Down ID 6, a few miles past the Giant White Pine Campground, the forest opens up into a small valley along Meadow Creek and the Palouse River. Grazing cattle and red barns complete the pastoral scene. The small villages of Harvard and Princeton, named for Eastern universities, were links in a chain of stations on the Washington, Idaho, and Montana Railroad. Other nearby stations were Wellesley, Yale, Vassar, Cornell, and Purdue.

Potlatch, the quintessential "company town," lies 3 miles past Princeton. The Potlatch Lumber Company built the entire town and owned all the land and buildings, including homes, schools, and churches. As the road descends the hill through town, the homes on the left just before the railroad station at the bottom of the hill have been preserved as the Nob Hill Historic District. The large building on the right as the road turns north was an employee gymnasium. It is currently reincarnated as a small restaurant and antique shop. The meadow west of town was the site of the Potlatch Lumber Mill. Pieces of concrete foundations are still visible in the meadows.

At their peak between 1908 and 1927, timber operations here processed 130 million board-feet per year, mostly western white pine. The percentage of white pine coming through the mills of north Idaho today is a mere fraction of those totals.

The drive ends at the junction of ID 6 and US 95, 2 miles west of Potlatch. From here, Moscow is 17 miles south and Coeur d'Alene 70 miles north. Both towns offer complete tourist services.

23

Lake Coeur d'Alene Loop

General description: A 90-mile country drive, almost entirely on two-lane paved roads following the east shore of Lake Coeur d'Alene from north to south, then along the Coeur d'Alene River valley and up Fourth of July summit back to the city of Coeur d'Alene.

Special attractions: The city of Coeur d'Alene itself, with its museums and waterfront park; the Coeur d'Alene Resort and its famous floating golf green; Lake Coeur d'Alene, named one of the world's five most beautiful alpine lakes; the town of Harrison; the possibility of sighting ospreys, eagles, and other birds in the Coeur d'Alene River valley; the Mullan Tree at the top of Fourth of July Summit.

Location: Northern Idaho Panhandle.

Drive route numbers: Coeur d'Alene Lake Drive, Idaho Highway 97, Idaho Highway 3, Interstate 90.

Travel season: The best time to travel along Lake Coeur d'Alene is between April and October. Winter travel is possible, and presents a good chance of spotting bald eagles on the lake.

Camping: National Forest campgrounds are located at Beauty Bay and Bell Bay, and commercial campgrounds at Wolf Lodge Bay and Arrow Point.

Services: Coeur d'Alene offers the full range of visitor services. There are only very limited services elsewhere along the route.

Nearby attractions: Silverwood Amusement Park; hiking at Tubbs Hill; gambling at the Coeur d'Alene Indian Reservation casino at Worley; lake excursions on Coeur d'Alene Lake; Crane House Museum in Harrison; historic Cataldo Mission; Heyburn State Park; the Emerald Creek Garnet Area.

 ## The Drive

Lake Coeur d'Alene has been called the world's most beautiful lake. From its icy, crystal blue waters to the high bluffs and forested hills that surround it, and from its dramatic rocky shorelines to the intensity of its sunsets, this lake has it all. The city of Coeur d'Alene is a bonus. The elegant Coeur d'Alene Resort dominates the city's shoreline, with a floating board-walk that stretches 3,300 feet around a marina filled with expensive water toys. Its golf course, located a short distance away, has been recognized as

Drive 23: Lake Coeur d'Alene Loop

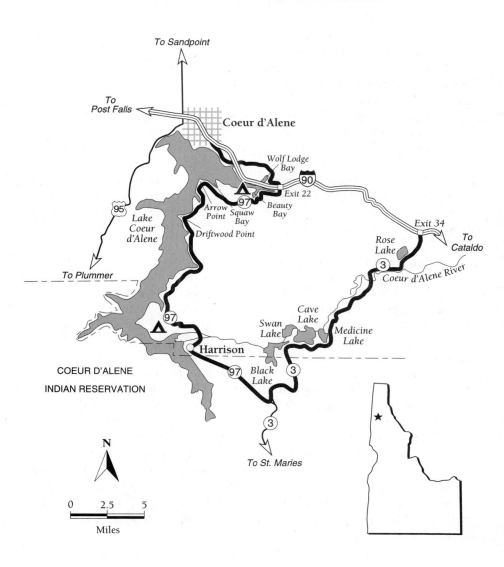

one of the best resort courses in the country. The par-three 14th hole is distinguished by a putting green that floats offshore. Players take a small boat out to sink their putts.

Coeur d'Alene was first settled as a military fort in 1878 by General William Tecumseh Sherman of Civil War fame. Sherman set up forts to quell the rising tide of native troubles that had led to the defeat of General Custer at the Little Bighorn in 1876, and to the flight of Chief Joseph's band of Nez Perce in 1877. Some of Fort Sherman's original buildings are now used by North Idaho College, a two-year institution that occupies a portion of the old fort's original site. The Museum of North Idaho and a city park and beach also occupy the grounds, just west of the resort. A double-decker bus tour of the city begins and ends near the museum during summer.

This drive follows the lake from its north end in Coeur d'Alene down its eastern shore to Harrison, on the southeastern shore, where the Coeur d'Alene River empties into the lake. From there, the drive traverses a ridge before heading up the Coeur d'Alene River and back to Coeur d'Alene on I-90, 28 miles east of Coeur d'Alene.

Begin in Coeur d'Alene's east end, turning south off Sherman Avenue onto Coeur d'Alene Lake Drive. After three quarters of a mile, turn right on Potlatch Hill Road. Pull off carefully, immediately before the bridge that loops left over Coeur d'Alene Lake Drive. From here you get a good view of the floating green on the golf course of the Coeur d'Alene Resort. Turn around and return to Coeur d'Alene Lake Drive. Turn right and continue south another 2 miles along the lakeshore to the dramatic view of the Veteran's Memorial Centennial Bridge, dedicated in 1990. The graceful, brilliant white bridge on I-90 sits high above the lake, spanning the head of Bennett Bay.

Follow Coeur d'Alene Lake Drive along the lakeshore. From the crossing of little Bennett Creek, measure 0.7 miles to a junction with East Yellowstone Trail. Take East Yellowstone Trail, going straight at a junction with Sunnyside Road, 4 miles ahead. The road turns to gravel, and the number of homes lining the road drops dramatically as the route rounds the end of little Blue Creek Bay. After about a mile of gravel, the pavement returns. In another mile, the road reaches I-90 at Wolf Lodge Bay. The concentration of bald eagles here in the winter months makes this arm of the lake popular with birders.

Cross I-90, picking up ID 97 on the south side of the highway. This is the beginning of the Coeur d'Alene Scenic Byway, one of 14 designated scenic byway routes in the state. Following the curves of the lakeshore, the road reaches Beauty Bay after 2 miles, then climbs across a forested plateau for 4 miles before returning to the lake at Squaw Bay and Arrow Point, directly south across the lake from the city of Coeur d'Alene. The road dips and soars past Echo Bay and Gotham Bay. At Driftwood Point the vista opens

Catamaran on Lake Coeur d'Alene.

Abandoned farmhouse near Harrison on Lake Coeur d'Alene.

up to a view down the lake's main body.

Lake Coeur d'Alene is an indirect product of the great glaciers that crawled down through the Purcell Trench as recently as 20,000 years ago. The lake was formed when the glacial debris at the glacier's toe dammed the river that flowed through this channel. The lake backed up behind that natural dam, but the lake was not carved by glacial activity. The lake has an area of 50 square miles, and extends 32 miles from one end to the other.

Steamboats played an important role in the early days of development in the Coeur d'Alene mining district. A sternwheeler plied the lake's waters as early as 1880. When gold was discovered at Kellogg in 1885, the steamers ferried miners and equipment from Fort Sherman, on the site of the future city of Coeur d'Alene, south past Harrison and up the Coeur d'Alene River to Cataldo Landing. By the turn of the century, passenger excursions were keeping an ever-growing fleet of steamships profitable. On a pleasant Sunday morning, it was common for there to be as many as 2,500 people on the Coeur d'Alene docks for a day on the lake.

Now the road passes a series of small bays—Turner Bay, Carlin Bay, Half Round Bay, Powderhorn Bay—before turning away from the lake again, 10 miles from Driftwood Point, and cresting a small hill before dropping into the valley that holds the mouth of the Coeur d'Alene River and the town of Harrison.

Harrison was given its name out of gratitude to President Benjamin Harrison, who granted early entreprenuers a slice of the Coeur d'Alene reservation for a lakeshore development in 1889. The townsite soon had sawmills, a railroad line leading to the mines at Wallace and Kellogg, and a reputation as a place to blow off steam. Things were so wild that, in 1904, the citizenry led a successful campaign to outlaw saloons. In the summer of 1917 a voracious fire consumed one of the town's sawmills along with a sizable portion of the town itself. The sawmills were never rebuilt, and the town has led a quiet existence ever since.

About a mile past Harrison, the road leaves the lakeshore for the last time, entering the Coeur d'Alene Indian Reservation and heading across the rolling meadows and open fields of Harrison Flats. The height of the reflector posts along the road's edge provides an indication of the amounts of snow this portion of Idaho receives every winter. The end of ID 97 is reached 8 miles from Harrison, at an intersection with ID 3.

Turn left here, heading north on ID 3. Six miles from the junction, after winding around a low hill, the road drops into the valley of the Coeur d'Alene River at Swan Lake. An overlook here provides a vista of Black Lake to the left, Swan Lake, and, to the right, Cave Lake. All of the lakes sit on the broad, flat, and swampy valley floor. Close to here was the original site of the mission that moved to Cataldo in the 1840s because of the difficulties of spring flooding.

As the road hugs the shoreline of Cave Lake and Medicine Lake, look for the large, untidy nests of ospreys, usually located at the top of a dead tree or on a utility pole. In some places nesting has been facilitated by the strategic placement of poles with a small platform on top. Some of these huge nests are located right at the edge of the road.

The road crosses the Coeur d'Alene River 8 miles beyond Cave Lake near a stretch of lovely vacation homes and stately cottonwood trees. The road cuts through the flood plain here. Look for signs of recurrent high water—sand bars and driftwood—along this stretch. The road leaves the river at the tiny settlement of Rose Lake. Continue 3 miles north on ID 3 to I-90, which marks the end of the Coeur d'Alene Scenic Byway. Head west on I-90. At Exit 28, at the summit of Fourth of July Pass, follow the signs to the site of the Mullan Tree, named for John Mullan, the military surveyor who laid out a route through this area in 1861. Return to I-90 and glide down the hill 6 miles to the east end of Lake Coeur d'Alene. Another 7 miles takes you back to the city of Coeur d'Alene.

24

The Mullan Road

General description: This 99-mile drive begins in Coeur d'Alene, climbs Fourth of July Summit and visits the Mullan Tree. From there, it travels to the oldest building in Idaho, the pale yellow Cataldo Mission, before heading to the mining towns of Kellogg and Wallace. The drive balances out the highway miles with some narrow gravel roads over Dobson Pass and Kings Pass, the location of some of the earliest prospecting in the Coeur d'Alene mining district. The return loop to Interstate 90 follows the North Fork of the Coeur d'Alene River through a quiet valley.

Special attractions: The town of Coeur d'Alene and its namesake lake; the historic Mullan Tree; the tranquil beauty of the Cataldo Mission; Kellogg—the town founded by a jackass; Silver Mountain Ski Resort; wonderful Wallace, with its historic buildings and museums; the eclectic Spragpole Inn in Murray; and a serene riverside drive along the Coeur d'Alene River.

Location: Northern Idaho Panhandle.

Drive route numbers: Interstate 90, Nine Mile Canyon Road (Coeur d'Alene National Forest Road 456), Kings Pass Road (Delta-Murray Road, or Forest Road 605), Pritchard Creek Road (Forest Road 9).

Travel season: The interstate portion of this drive is accessible year-round. The stretch north of Wallace and back to Kingston should only be driven in good weather. Portions may be closed due to heavy snows, and travel in extremely wet weather is not recommended in any season.

Camping: Commercial campgrounds are available at the east end of Lake Coeur d'Alene, and at Cataldo, Pinehurst, Osburn, and Silverton. Coeur d'Alene National Forest campgrounds are located nearby at Beauty Bay on Lake Coeur d'Alene and on the North Fork of the Coeur d'Alene River.

Services: Coeur d'Alene offers a full range of tourist services, and services are also available at Kellogg and Wallace.

Nearby attractions: Silverwood Amusement Park; the Fort Sherman Museum and Museum of North Idaho; the Wild Waters water park; and boat cruises on Lake Coeur d'Alene.

The Drive

Begin on I-90 in Coeur d'Alene and head east. As the road begins to climb past Sherman Avenue, a quick peek to your right will provide a glimpse of the famous floating green on the Coeur d'Alene Resort golf course. Players

Drive 24: The Mullan Road

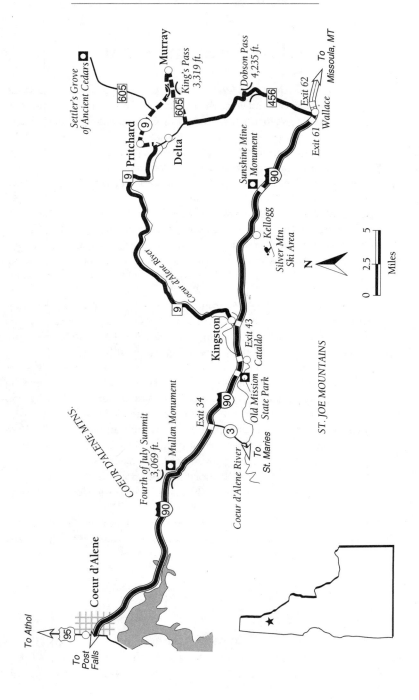

have to take a small boat to reach the green and hole out their shots.

As the road climbs, hugging the hillside, passengers on the right side will have great views of Coeur d'Alene Lake. The highway crosses the graceful Veterans Memorial Centennial Bridge before dropping back down to lake level and following Wolf Lodge Bay to the lake's east end.

I-90 enters dark, narrow Cedar Canyon and begins the ascent to Fourth of July Summit, 3,069 feet above sea level, almost 900 feet above the lake's level. At the summit, Exit 28, leave the highway, and follow the signs to the Mullan Tree Historic Site, about 200 yards north of the bridge over the highway. A short walkway leads through a small grove of giant white pines to a stump, enclosed by a small fence.

Captain John Mullan was a U.S. Army surveyor and engineer who was assigned the task of laying out a wagon road between Fort Benton in Montana and Fort Walla Walla in Washington. The first attempt went around the south end of Lake Coeur d'Alene, but boggy ground with a tendency to flood made it necessary to reroute the road around the north end of the lake. Mullan and his crew reached this point on July 4, 1861, and celebrated the milestone by carving the date into a large white pine here in this grove, along with the initials "M.R.," which stood for "Military Road." The tree was badly damaged in a windstorm in 1962, and is preserved in the Museum of North Idaho in Coeur d'Alene. A marker here designates the Mullan Road as a National Civil Engineering Landmark, and a statue of Mullan is located near the site.

Mullan's road was heavily damaged by severe flooding the year after its completion, and never received a great deal of traffic. The road was also intended to be the route of the Great Northern Railway, but the lure of large stands of valuable timber on an alternate route to the north of Lake Pend Oreille caused the railroad to select the other path. Mullan's route was well chosen, however, and ultimately became the choice for the construction of I-90.

U.S. Highway 10 followed this route before the interstate was constructed. Early travelers looked forward to their arrival at this summit. To those heading west, it meant that they had conquered their last major mountain obstacle. The summit was also home to a dancing bear, whose antics entertained bored and weary travelers. The bear didn't hurt business at the restaurant run by its owners, either!

From the Mullan Tree site, return to I-90 and continue east, down a sharply pitched descent of 5 miles. Exit 34 leads to the Lake Coeur d'Alene Scenic Byway (See Lake Coeur d'Alene Loop). Continue another 5 miles east on I-90 to Exit 39 at Old Mission State Park. Situated on a low hill here is Cataldo Mission of the Sacred Heart, the state's oldest building.

Jesuits led by Father Pierre Jean DeSmet, a missionary who was one of

The church at Cataldo Mission is the oldest building in Idaho.

the West's most important early arrivals, established a mission in the valley of the St. Joe River south of here in 1842. The same weather that flooded Mullan's first road also led the missionaries to move their mission from the swampy valley southeast of Lake Coeur d'Alene to this site in 1846, and to seat their mission church atop this peaceful knoll.

Designed by Father Antonio Ravalli in the Greek Revival style, the church has walls that are more than a foot thick. All interior elements are carved of wood, and hinges and candleholders were all hand-crafted on the site. The parish house next door was a later addition, and it has been preserved to provide an insight into the lives of these selfless missionaries.

A slide show and exhibits in the visitor center at the base of the hill provide more information about the mission, which was moved again in 1877 to DeSmet, south of Lewiston, abandoning the stately church building. Also on the grounds are picnic tables and a small grassy park. The mission church sits above the Coeur d'Alene River, a body of water that carried away vast amounts of toxic materials from the mines upstream, including wastes that overflowed holding ponds during severe flooding in 1915. Signs in the park warn of the dangers of contamination, suggesting that visitors not eat on the ground, drink the water, or play in areas of bare soil.

Return to I-90 and head east once again, passing a series of small mining communities. This is the Silver Valley, aptly named to reflect the incredible amounts of silver that have been pulled from the ground here. Up the valley 11 miles east of the mission church is Kellogg, the town founded by a jackass. The legend says that Noah Kellogg was prospecting above the present townsite in 1885 when his jackass wandered off. When Kellogg finally found the animal, it was grazing near an outcrop of galena, a lead ore. Kellogg had the ore assayed, and it proved to be a remarkably rich find. The discovery led to the opening of Bunker Hill Mine, which, along with the district's other mines, has produced an unbelievable amount of gold, silver, lead, and zinc. In the first hundred years of operations these mines have yielded more than 507,000 ounces of gold and more than 1 billion ounces of silver. Add to that 31,000 tons of lead, 4,000 tons of copper, and 3,300 tons of zinc. The yield from these mines is greater than that of all other mines in Idaho combined.

Economic conditions have reduced the presence of the Bunker Hill Company significantly in recent years, and the town has had to look to other means of survival. Many company facilities have closed, and some remaining ones are being put to new uses. The Staff House is now the home of the Shoshone County Mining and Smelting Museum.

A nicely scrubbed business district, with a number of freshly restored storefronts from the town's heyday, gives the town the look of an eager suitor, hopeful of finding a marriage that will work. Quirky welded and painted metal sculptures of subjects as diverse as knights and dragons, wildlife, locomotives, miners and mules, the Red Baron, and Don Quixote are sprinkled throughout the town. Wandering the streets is a wonderful way to discover these offbeat creations. It's fun to try to identify the pieces of scrap metal used in the construction. Old auto parts, plumbing supplies, and mining and railroad equipment are all integrated into the artwork.

The Silver Valley has recently begun to profit from white gold—the heavy snows that fall on Kellogg Peak and the ski resort of Silver Mountain. A high-speed gondola carries skiers 3.1 miles up the slopes above Kellogg to ski runs carved from the slopes of Kellogg Peak. The gondola has helped

Whimsical sculptures of scrap iron are scattered throughout Kellogg.

transform Kellogg into a destination resort. More restaurants and hotels are added each year, as the ski area grows more popular.

Back on I-90, head east for 3.5 miles to Exit 54. Cross under the highway to the monument on the north side of the road. In 1972, a fire 3,700 feet below the surface of the Sunshine Mine, located 4 miles south of here on Big Creek, took the lives of 91 miners. The disaster impacted everyone in the valley, and this statue of a miner drilling skyward is a constant reminder of the dangers of work underground. The miner's headlamp is always on, the equivalent of an eternal flame.

The Sunshine Mine is more than a mile deep and has more than 100 miles of tunnels. Other mines in the district venture even farther into the bowels of the earth, as much as 8,000 feet or more, following the rich veins of silver-bearing ores.

Continue on I-90 to Wallace, 7 miles ahead, where a mine tour offers the opportunity to venture down into the Sierra Silver Mine for an hour-long, guided exploration of this underground world.

For those with different interests, or perhaps a touch of claustrophobia, Wallace also offers the Northern Pacific Depot Railroad Museum, housed in a classic depot building, and the Oasis Bordello Museum. This site was home of one of the last legal brothels in the United States, open until 1988.

The Oasis Bordello Museum at Wallace is a quirky attraction.

The bordello is a surprisingly entertaining museum, albeit one that makes some people feel a bit uncomfortable. Some of the rooms look as though they haven't been disturbed since the bordello officially closed.

Wallace, like other Idaho cities and towns, retains a good number of stately old homes and commercial buildings, many of which have been lovingly restored. The entire central business district has been designated a National Historic District, and the brick buildings here are a testament to the town's early wealth. A disastrous fire in 1888 destroyed the first wooden buildings in town, and the town's businessmen resolved to protect themselves from another disaster. Another fire in 1910 managed to destroy about a third of the town, but many of the brick structures were spared. The town was destroyed again, on film, in the adventure movie *Dante's Peak*, which was filmed in Wallace in 1995.

The drive leaves the interstate here at Wallace, heading north on Sixth Street to the paved two-lane Ninemile Canyon Road (FR 456) that ascends heavily forested Dobson Pass before dropping into the Beaver Creek valley. The nearby town of Burke, in the next valley to the east, had its moment in the spotlight many years ago when *Ripley's Believe It or Not* described the streets as being so narrow that residents had to close their shutters whenever a train came by. This drive bypasses Burke and heads instead for the ghost town of Delta, 13 miles northwest of Wallace. Turn right at Delta and travel for 6 miles, on a good gravel road over Kings Pass, to Murray. Use caution in wet or cold weather; the road is narrow and steep in places.

As the road enters Murray, once the Shoshone County seat, it passes the stately Murray Cemetery, on a hillside to the right. Coming down the hill, the scars from a voracious gold dredge that once churned up Pritchard Creek are visible. This was the scene of a minor gold rush in early 1996 as winter flooding and a road construction project stirred up the old tailings and dredged material. The discovery of a 10-ounce gold nugget was enough to set off a flurry of activity, and gold fever brought hundreds of fortune hunters with metal detectors to the valley. A shop in Murray sells gold pans and other equipment for weekend prospectors. Be aware of existing claims before venturing out to make your fortune. Claim jumpers are not treated any better these days than they were 100 years ago.

Murray is the home of the Spragpole Inn, one of the more eclectic establishments to be found anywhere. Housed in an old wooden storefront, the inn offers a place for locals to watch a football game and enjoy a beer and a cheeseburger. The inn also serves as the unofficial museum of the area, with mining memorabilia, mineral samples and whiskey bottles displayed casually in a back room. It also gives the visitor a taste of the story of Molly B'Damm, as Maggie Hall was known.

Maggie arrived from New York, her reputation already soiled by her marriage to a fellow named Burdan, who turned out to be a pimp. She had left him and headed to Murray to profit from the gold fever, opening a saloon. Molly B'Damm was the miner's playful contraction of her full name, Maggie Burdan Hall. She was a favorite of the locals, being kind and generous, and offering assistance to those who fell ill. Molly knew how to make money, allowing miners to sprinkle her bath water with gold dust for the privilege of washing her back, among other things. When Maggie died of pneumonia in 1881 at the age of 35, the entire town turned out to mourn.

Leave Murray on the Pritchard Creek Road (FR 9) and head downstream past more of the devastation caused by the all-consuming dredge operations. A 5-mile side trip begins 3 miles from Murray. Turn right up FR 805 and the West Fork of Eagle Creek to the Settler's Grove of Ancient Cedars. A footpath winds through the majestic 183-acre stand of old-growth redcedar.

Return to FR 9. Down the road, about 3 miles ahead, is Pritchard, another of the many small former mining communities that are just barely hanging on to their existence in the north Idaho woods. Pritchard was always more of a support community than an actual mining town. Horse-drawn barges were sent up the Coeur d'Alene River from Cataldo to here with machinery and supplies. As early as 1885, four sawmills near Pritchard provided lumber for mine buildings and mine timbers. It was said that some of the mines here were so extensive that there was more timber underground than there was growing above it.

At Pritchard, bear left where Pritchard Creek joins the Coeur d'Alene River. At a T intersection 2 miles ahead, turn right toward Kingston, which lies 22 miles ahead on I-90, below Cataldo. From the end of FR 9 at I-90, Coeur d'Alene is 30 miles west, and Wallace is 18 miles east.

25

Oldtown to Lake Pend Oreille

General description: This is a low-key, 40-mile drive on paved back roads through the pastoral north country. It runs straight as an arrow from Oldtown to Blanchard before turning to Spirit Lake and going on to the southern end of Lake Pend Oreille, with a visit to the historic naval base that is now part of Farragut State Park.

Special attractions: Spirit Lake; peaceful hay meadows and country scenes; a chance to reminisce with World War II veterans at a former naval recruit training base; scanning the slopes across chilly Lake Pend Oreille for mountain goats.

Location: Northern Idaho panhandle.

Drive route numbers: Idaho Highways 41 and 54, U.S. Highway 95.

Travel season: The entire route is paved, two-lane highway, and is accessible year-round. The drive is best taken between April and October, while the hay crops are growing around Blanchard.

Camping: Campsites are available at the boat ramp at Albeni Cove, just south and east of Oldtown, and at Farragut State Park.

Services: Motels, restaurants, gas, and groceries are available at Newport, Washington, and Oldtown, Idaho. Limited services can be found at Blanchard, Spirit Lake, Athol, and Bayview.

Nearby attractions: Albeni Falls Dam; Priest Lake; Silverwood Amusement Park; and Coeur d'Alene.

 The Drive

Begin at the Washington-Idaho state line, which runs between the twin communities of Newport, Washington, and Oldtown, Idaho. Newport is known as the "City of Flags," and lives up to that name with banners flying along both sides of the road. The theme is carried over onto the Idaho side, where the bridge across the Pend Oreille River is festooned with gaily flapping flags.

Head south on ID 41 in Oldtown. Before turning left to crest a small hill, the road serves as the unofficial border between the two states. For a diversion before leaving Oldtown, turn left at East Fourth Street South, which becomes Albeni Cove Road. It leads to a picnic and river access area at Albeni Cove, 2 miles from town. The location is directly across from the

Drive 25: Oldtown to Lake Pend Oreille

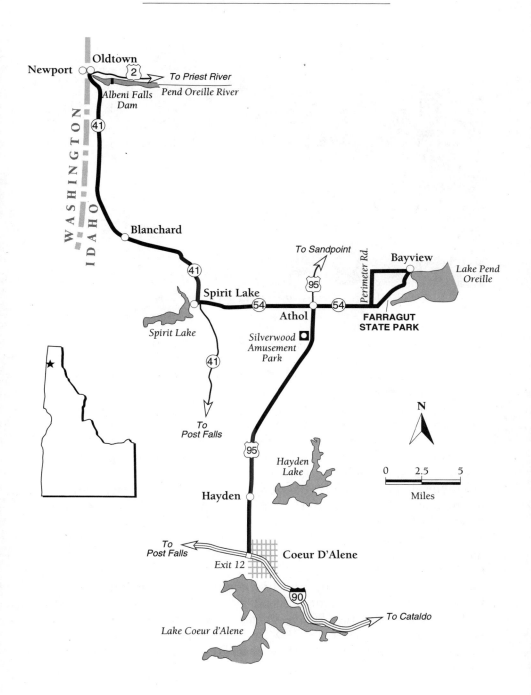

A railroad bridge reflected in the calm waters above Albeni Falls Dam.

Albeni Falls Dam Visitor Center, located on US 2. Retrace your route to return to the scenic drive.

Continue south on ID 41, which runs for 10 miles through a forest of lodgepole pine before making a long left turn into Blanchard, 13 miles from Oldtown. The lodgepole's name reflects its straight, tall growth, and the road here is just as straight as the trees in the surrounding forest.

The town of Spirit Lake lies just over the Kootenai County line, 6 miles past Blanchard. Turn right from ID 41 onto Maine Street past a block of stately old storefronts and down a small hill to a pocket-sized beach and picnic site on the north end of quiet Spirit Lake. Beyond the beach along the north shore are a number of private homes, and a small resort at Silver Beach. The forested north shore road has only limited views of the lake.

Return to ID 41 and continue south another mile before turning left on ID 54. The road makes a turn and then heads straight across the floor of the Purcell Trench, a broad valley created by vast geological forces, then filled and smoothed with glacial debris. The forests are a mixture of open, harvested stands and meadows, interspersed with thicker stands of uncut timber. After 7 miles, the road arrives at Athol and crosses US 95 at a very busy intersection.

Farragut State Park is 4 miles past Athol, on the shores of Lake Pend Oreille. Farragut's wide roads and general layout are reminiscent of a military base, and with good reason. This was the site of a naval recruit training facility. Between 1942 and 1946 more than 290,000 recruits were trained here, many of them arriving by train from the big cities of the East Coast. These young men were impressed by the mountains and the magnificent scenery of Idaho, and many of them returned to visit or to settle down after their service time was complete.

In the park's main visitor center, there are hundreds of group photographs of the young fresh-faced recruits, each labeled with dates and unit numbers. Almost any day in the summer tourist season, you can see men in their late sixties and seventies scanning the photographs, and finding pictures of themselves and their long-forgotten fellow sailors. Ask them about their experiences here, and be prepared to listen to some wonderful reminiscences of their "great adventure." The park has several campgrounds and picnic areas, and even a small airfield for radio-controlled aircraft.

Follow the signs to the Willow Day Use Area in Farragut Park, where high-powered telescopes are set up to spot mountain goats grazing on the cliffs below Bernard Peak, across Idlewild Bay. These timid creatures are generally very difficult to see, since they shy away from human contact, but they feel safe from harm across the open waters of Lake Pend Oreille. Look for them high on the slopes—small patches of white slowly feeding or calmly enjoying the view from their lofty perches.

Continue through the park to Bayview, a postcard-pretty setting at the head of generically named Scenic Bay. The Navy still operates a facility here, officially named the Naval Surface Warfare Research Center. The facility's activities are kept under tight wraps, but the research done here, facilitated by the lake's 1,200-foot depth, involves deep water acoustic testing and remotely controlled submersible craft.

Bayview has several nice restaurants, making this a good place to spend a bit of time and enjoy the views of the lake. ID 54 ends here, but it is easy to follow the local road as it turns away from the lake. Follow the signs for Athol. The road parallels a long perimeter fence that surrounds the state park. At the end of the fence, turn left (south) and pick up the fence again, on your left, as the road climbs a small hill. This is Perimeter Road (another obvious name). It rejoins ID 54 at a traffic circle at the park's entrance. Bear right to return the 4 miles to Athol.

From here, it is 3 miles south on US 95 to the Silverwood Amusement Park and another 16 miles south to Interstate 90 at Coeur d'Alene.

26

Priest Lake

General description: A 110-mile drive through heavy forests on two-lane paved roads and improved gravel roads to isolated Priest Lake in the northern Idaho panhandle. Glimpses of the lake give way to expansive views as the route travels up the lake's east shore.

Special attractions: Albeni Falls Dam; the progressive timber town of Priest River; the quiet serenity of the northern Idaho forest; Priest Lake, with its lunker fish lurking below the surface.

Location: Far northern Idaho Panhandle.

Drive route numbers: U.S. Highway 2, Idaho Highway 57, Coolin Road and East Side Road.

Travel season: This route is best traveled in late spring (after the snow is gone), and in summer and early fall. Due to the isolation of the region, off-season travel is not recommended.

Camping: A Kaniksu National Forest campground is located near the intersection of ID 57 and Coolin Road, and camping is available in the Indian Creek Unit of Priest Lake State Park, on the lake's east side. USDA Forest Service campgrounds available up the lake's western shore include Beaver Creek, Reeder Bay, Luby Bay, and Osprey.

Services: Newport, Washington, its sister city Oldtown, Idaho, and the town of Priest River offer all tourist services. Limited services are available at Coolin, on Priest Lake's southeast shore.

Nearby attractions: Sandpoint and Lake Pend Oreille; Schweitzer Mountain Ski Area; Silverwood Amusement Park; Farragut State Park.

 The Drive

This drive takes you into a remote corner of the Idaho Panhandle—a region thick with coniferous forests, which also cradles the pristine beauty of Priest Lake. The lake is the smallest of the three large bodies of water in the north country, but it is no less inviting and no less attractive than either Lake Coeur d'Alene or Lake Pend Oreille.

Begin the drive on the Washington-Idaho border at the town of Newport, Washington, and its Idaho counterpart, Oldtown. For all practical purposes, Newport and Oldtown are a single settlement which just happens to have a state line drawn down its center.

Drive 26: Priest Lake

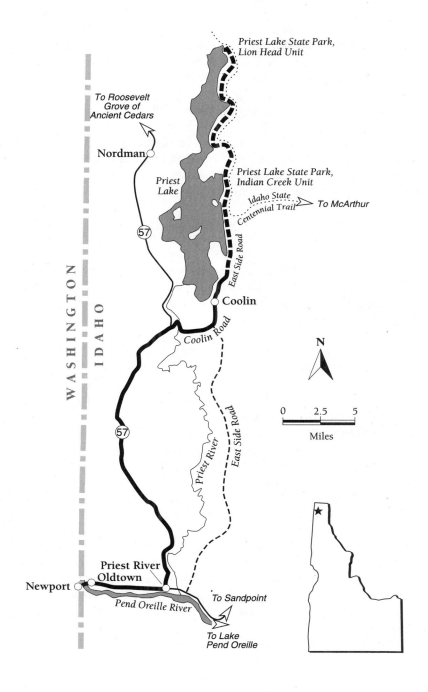

Priest Lake State Park, Lion Head Unit

To Roosevelt Grove of Ancient Cedars

Nordman

Priest Lake

Priest Lake State Park, Indian Creek Unit

Idaho State Centennial Trail

To McArthur

57

East Side Road

Coolin

Coolin Road

N

0 2.5 5
Miles

WASHINGTON

IDAHO

Priest River

East Side Road

57

Priest River Oldtown

Newport

Pend Oreille River

To Sandpoint

To Lake Pend Oreille

Head east from Oldtown on US 2 along the Pend Oreille River, stopping at the Albeni Falls Dam overlook after 2 miles. The dam was built in the 1950s, and now controls the level of water in all of the Pend Oreille River upstream, as well as the level of Lake Pend Oreille and the Clark Fork River for some distance above its mouth on the east side of the lake. The small door at the base of the dam on the near side of the river is a log chute, an opening in the dam which allowed floating logs to be channeled down the river.

Prior to the building of the dam, waterfalls did exist here. In 1887, Albeni Poirier, a Frenchman who lived in Blanchard, Idaho, 15 miles south of the site, built a log cabin at the falls. The scenic cascades were popular with sightseers even then, and Poirier eventually built a hotel, restaurant, dance hall, and saloon. After the Great Northern rail line was built through here in 1892, excursions from Spokane regularly brought visitors to see the falls.

Continue into the town of Priest River. This community of more than 1,500 people was supported almost entirely by the lumber industry for many years. Now, with economic and environmental concerns causing a different approach to timber harvests, the town has had to find new ways to survive. Timber is still the economy's primary base, but the need to diversify has led the town to take a long, hard look at itself. The result is a number of small businesses that enhance and expand its economic base. Take a short drive down Main Street (a right turn off US 2) to see the nicely restored buildings from the town's glory days. At the end of Main Street is a small museum, the Keyser House, with exhibits that expand on the town's long-standing timber industry connections.

Once you have explored Priest River, return to the highway and backtrack (west) a short distance to a stoplight and head north on ID 57. The road travels through thick, almost luxuriant forests that allow only fleeting glimpses of the surrounding low hills. The forests here are a patchwork of federal, state, and private land holdings, dominated by the Kaniksu National Forest, managed as part of the Idaho Panhandle National Forests.

The road crosses the Lower West Branch of the Priest River 8 miles from Priest River, and then the Upper West Branch in 10 more miles. Another 2 miles past that crossing there is a junction, and a decision to be made. A side trip continues on ID 57 and leads 18 miles through more forest to the town of Nordman, the only settlement on the western side of Priest Lake. The route is heavily forested, but short spurs lead to views of the lake at Outlet Bay and Nordman. North of Nordman 14 miles is the 20-acre Roosevelt Grove of Ancient Cedars. If you take this side trip, inquire in Nordman for directions and road conditions.

The main drive leaves ID 57 at its junction with Coolin Road and follows Coolin Road to the right and down a long hill, entering Priest Lake State Park and Priest Lake State Forest, arriving at the vacation village of Coolin after 5 miles. Coolin sits at the southern edge of Priest Lake, which has remained hidden in the thick forests until this point. If you wish to satisfy yourself that there really is a lake, explore the little village ahead and to your left. Otherwise turn right onto East Side Road. After traveling almost 4 miles north, past vacation homes and more forest (and not seeing a lake!), the road passes the end of a grassy aircraft landing strip with white-painted rocks marking the edges of the runway. In another mile the lake finally comes into view at Cavanaugh Bay. Ahead is the full expanse of the 25-mile-long lake. Priest Lake is famed for the record trout that have been pulled from its depths, including several world record specimens.

Another 6 miles brings you to the Indian Creek Unit of Priest Lake State Park, which has a general store, camping, and a marina. This is the largest tourist facility on this side of the lake. In the park is a preserved section of an old log flume, a wooden channel used to float timber down steep hills. Diamond Match Company built the 3.5-mile-long flume here in 1946 at a cost of $30,000 per mile to carry logs down Indian Creek and into Priest Lake. The timber would be stored on the lake, and then in the spring, when water levels were high, a tug would tow booms of logs south to the lake's outlet. From there, the logs would be floated down the Priest River to the mills. The flume operated for only six years, until 1952.

The drive continues up the east shore of Priest Lake from the Indian Creek area, turning away from the lake for 3 miles across the neck of a peninsula alongside Indian Creek. The road parallels the lakeshore all the way to the north end of the lake and the Lionhead Unit of the state park. Also parallel to the lakeshore is the Idaho State Centennial Trail, a non-motorized hiking route that extends the length of the state, from the Canadian border to Nevada.

Upper Priest Lake is no more than 2 miles beyond the north end of the larger lake, but it is inaccessible by passenger automobile. It is possible to continue north on this road for many miles, and eventually to connect with USDA Forest Service roads on the west side of the two lakes, or to head north and east over the Selkirk Crest on back roads to the town of Porthill on the Canadian border. Do not attempt either of these alternate routes without having made local inquiries and verifying that you and your vehicle are adequately prepared for backcountry conditions.

The drive ends here at the north end of Priest Lake. From here, retrace your tracks to Priest River, about 50 miles to the south.

27

Moyie Falls to Cabinet Gorge

General description: This 80-mile drive follows two-lane paved highways as it traverses the Purcell Trench and passes through a pair of historic towns. After visiting Sandpoint, it continues along the shore of one of Idaho's "gems"—Lake Pend Oreille, and winds up at Cabinet Gorge on the Montana border.

Special attractions: Moyie Falls and the 450-foot-high Moyie River Bridge; the historic communities of Bonners Ferry and Sandpoint; the Purcell Trench, a unique geological feature that defines the landscape; the possibility of spotting moose near McArthur Lake and on the Pack River; the hillside community of Hope; Cabinet Gorge Dam.

Location: Northern Idaho Panhandle.

Drive route numbers: U.S. Highways 2 and 95, Idaho Highway 200.

Travel season: The entire drive is on all-season roads, and passes within miles of ski slopes at Schweitzer Mountain Resort, but the best times to travel are during late spring, summer, and fall.

Camping: There are commercial campgrounds south of Bonners Ferry, at Sagle, south of Sandpoint, and near Trestle Creek on the shore of Lake Pend Oreille. Kaniksu National Forest campgrounds are located at various points along the shore of Lake Pend Oreille.

Services: Both Bonners Ferry and Sandpoint offer a full range of tourist services.

Nearby attractions: Kootenai National Wildlife Refuge and Island Pond Wildlife Trail, both west of Bonners Ferry; skiing at Schweitzer Mountain Resort; the Bonner County Historical Museum; bicycling across the Long Bridge; Priest Lake State Park; Round Lake State Park.

 The Drive

The drive begins at Moyie Springs and heads south through the historic town of Bonners Ferry and along the Purcell Trench to Sandpoint, on the northern shore of 1,100-foot-deep Lake Pend Oreille. From there, follow the lakeshore to Hope, a hillside town with a grand view, and on to the Montana border at Cabinet Gorge Dam.

Begin at the east end of the Moyie River Bridge on US 2, just east of Moyie Springs, and 12 miles west of the Montana border. Park at the overlook on the south side of the road for a good look at this 450-foot-high span, the second-highest bridge in Idaho. Upstream from the bridge a

Drive 27: Moyie Falls to Cabinet Gorge

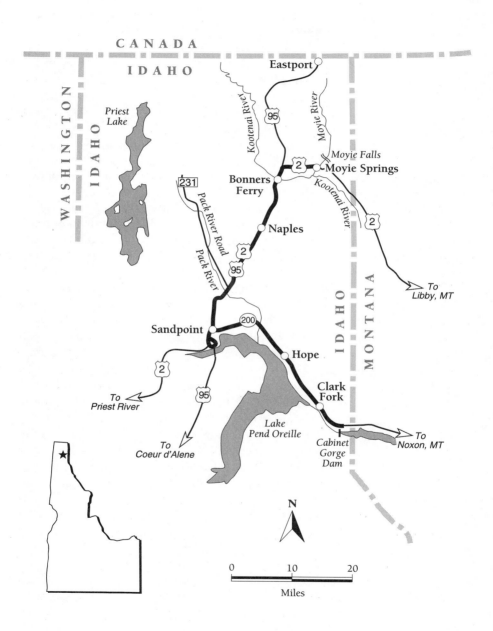

half mile is Moyie Falls, a 100-foot cataract. The water flow is highly seasonal: spring runoff chokes the falls with water, but the flow tapers off and becomes quite irregular later in the season. The Moyie Dam, just above the falls, controls the flow of water to the falls. The 212-foot concrete structure was built by the city of Bonners Ferry in 1949.

Head west on US 2 through Moyie Springs and turn left (south) at the junction with US 95. The road angles off the plateau into the valley of the Kootenai River and then into Bonners Ferry. Just across the bridge, turn right and visit the visitor center. Good information on food, lodging, and activities in the surrounding area is available from the friendly volunteer staff at this, and at visitor centers throughout the state. Boundary County has a wealth of activities for the active traveler, including fishing and hunting, bird watching at the nearby Kootenai National Wildlife Refuge, and hiking. In the winter, snowmobiling and cross-country skiing are popular outdoor activities.

Bonners Ferry got its start in 1864, as the location of a ferry for gold miners heading up to Wild Horse Creek in British Columbia. Edwin Bonner, in an astute business move, secured a license for the service from the territorial legislature, and charged $1.50 per pack animal and fifty cents per person for his services.

Continuing south on US 2/95 from Bonners Ferry, the road skirts the eastern edge of the Purcell Trench. The trench is a broad, straight valley running roughly north and south from British Columbia to a point between Sandpoint and Coeur d'Alene. Geologists think it was formed some 50 to 70 million years ago when a large dome of granitic magma rose up in this area. A large mass of the rocks that had overlain the eastern flank of the granite dome slid off to the east, forming the Cabinet Mountains and the Purcell Mountains, whose rock is much older than that found in the Selkirks to the west. The trench was the seam between the granite dome to the west and the ranges to the east. The trench ultimately was filled and leveled by the many episodes of glaciation that occurred here at regular intervals. The depth of the fill has obliterated any evidence of intervening changes in the time between 50 million years ago and 20,000 years ago—a very sizable gap in the geologic record.

As the road climbs a hill south of Bonners Ferry, a panoramic view of the Purcell Trench across a golf course provides a clearer picture of all this geologic activity. Small ponds dot the flat surface smoothed by glacial flows, all contained by the hills on either side of the trench's floor.

The road negotiates a steep hill and drops back down through a mixed forest of cedar, fir, and spruce. The small settlement of Naples appears 10 miles south of Bonners Ferry. Though it looks nothing like Italy, it was named by homesick Italian workers here laying rail for the Great Northern Railroad in the 1890s. Back in the forest near Naples is Ruby Ridge, site of a

Moyie River Bridge east of Bonners Ferry.

controversial FBI shoot-out in 1992.

The relatively flat reaches along the highway here collect snowmelt and rainwater, making the ground in many places soft and marshy. This creates ideal habitat for moose, particularly around McArthur Lake, 5 miles south of Naples, and along the Pack River farther south. The Idaho State Centennial Trail, a footpath that winds from the Canadian border to the Nevada state line, crosses the highway just north of McArthur Lake.

The Pack River crosses the road about 10 miles north of Sandpoint. A wonderful side trip through beautiful forest country takes the Pack River Road northwest from the highway just north of the river crossing. The upper Pack River drainage is home to one of the rarest mammal species in the contiguous United States. A herd of mountain caribou, estimated to number about 30 animals, inhabits the area. They are the last remaining band of wild caribou in the lower 48 states. The flanks of the Selkirks in this region are also home to the grizzly bear, a larger, more ferocious cousin of the black bears that are common in mountainous regions throughout the state.

Continue down the highway, passing the turnoff to Schweitzer Mountain Resort and into Sandpoint. The Sandpoint Visitor Center is on your left, a half mile or so past the junction with ID 200, the highway which skirts the north and east shores of Lake Pend Oreille. Continue from here into town, with its comfortable, small-town main street. Get out and walk, past some of the many interesting craft shops. The town has a homey feel to it, pulling together such disparate elements as loggers, artists, and skiers. The skiers are here to try out Schweitzer Mountain's 300 inches of snow. The Cedar Street Bridge Market is just what its name says—a collection of nice shops in a two-story center built atop a bridge across Sand Creek. The market has become a symbol of Sandpoint, appearing on postcards along with pictures of the lake and the ski area. The mail-order company that runs the market also provides employment to a major portion of Sandpoint's workforce.

After refreshing yourself in Sandpoint, return north on the highway leaving town. Bear right on ID 200 where it intersects US 2/95. The remainder of the journey will be along the Pend Oreille Scenic Byway, which runs 33 miles from here to the Montana state line at Cabinet Gorge.

Pass through the settlements of Ponderay, whose name echoes the pronunciation of Lake Pend Oreille, and Kootenai, named for the Native American tribe that called this area home. The road leaves the lakeshore here, crosses the mouth of the Pack River at a golf course that is very popular with the local moose, and returns to the lakeshore. Ahead lie the camping and boat launch facilities at Trestle Creek, and 5 miles farther the impossibly steep hillside towns of Hope and East Hope. The views from here across the northern end of Lake Pend Oreille are nothing short of stupendous, particularly when one of the glorious north Idaho sunsets flames across the western skies.

The Northern Pacific (now Burlington Northern) rail line that this drive parallels from Sandpoint to Cabinet Gorge was built in 1881–1882. Chinese laborers did most of the heavy work, as was common with many western rail projects of the time. A small Chinese settlement at Hope remained after the rails were laid, and a small cemetery at the west end of Hope holds the remains of a number of the early Chinese inhabitants. Most Chinese immigrants to the West fervently wished to return to China, and believed that their remains would not be at rest unless they were shipped to China. This Chinese cemetery is therefore a bit of a rarity.

Take the short frontage road (Business Route 200) that leaves ID 200 at Hope. Between Hope and East Hope, alongside the frontage road, stands a historical marker commemorating one of the most remarkable (and one of the least well-known) of all the early explorers of the vast territory that was to become Idaho. David Thompson learned the skills of surveying, trapping, and trading while apprenticed to the Hudson's Bay Company. After completing his apprenticeship, Thompson quickly became a partner in the North West Company, a rival outfit based in Montreal.

In 1807, less than a year after the completion of Lewis and Clark's successful expedition, Thompson explored the upper reaches of the Columbia River system, including the Kootenai and Clark Fork rivers. He built a trading post called Kullyspell House near here on Memaloose Point. From this post he and his men traded with the tribes of the region, including the Flathead, Coeur d'Alene, and Kalispell tribes. Kullyspell House was the first European settlement in Idaho. The remains of the post are on private property on the Hope Peninsula, and are not accessible.

Across the water is Pearl Island, which has a large resident population of deer, protected from wandering predators by the lake's waters. A right turn onto the Hope Peninsula takes you past some wonderful vacation homes, and gets you up close and personal with some of the most tame deer you would ever hope to see.

Continue east on BR 200 and rejoin ID 200, heading southeast. The road quickly arrives at the main inlet for Lake Pend Oreille, the Clark Fork River. The level of the water here at the river's mouth, as well as in the lake and in the Pend Oreille River west of Sandpoint, is controlled by the Albeni Falls Dam, miles away near the Washington border.

The lumber and mining town of Clark Fork slumbers peacefully 8 miles east of Hope. Be especially cautious as you pass through the town, since the highway is very narrow here. Clark Fork is also home to a fish hatchery. To visit it turn left on Spring Creek Road at the west end of town. The hatchery lies 1.5 miles up the road. If you visit the hatchery, turn left on

Cabinet Gorge Dam.

your return to the highway. The next 6 miles of highway are flanked by high palisades of sedimentary rock. Look for polished horizontal grooves in the rock that lines the road. The grooves were made by stones and gravel embedded in the huge glaciers that once filled this valley. As the glacier moved along, the debris embedded in its flanks slowly buffed and etched the rock formations it passed.

The greatest prehistoric flood known to modern geologists occurred in this valley. Giant fingers of glacial ice thousands of feet thick flowed through northern Idaho 20,000 years ago. The ice blocked the flow of the Clark Fork, creating a body of water known as Glacial Lake Missoula. More than 2,000 feet deep, it contained more than 500 cubic miles of water, half the volume of Lake Michigan. When the ice dam broke, as it did several times, the water poured through the neck of Idaho, past the site of present-day Spokane, Washington, and into the Columbia River. Scientists estimate that the peak flow of the flood was the equivalent of ten times the flow of all the world's rivers.

Just before the Montana border, a gravel road leads about a half mile to the impressive site of Cabinet Gorge Dam. The sheer walls of the gorge—carved out by the repeated floods—led Washington Water Power to build this 208-foot-high arched dam in 1952. The impoundment holds back 24 miles of water, all but the last half mile of it in Montana.

Appendix
For More Information

Drive 1

Bear Lake State Park
P.O. Box 297
Paris, ID 83261
(208) 945-2790

Southeastern Idaho Travel Council
c/o Lava Hot Springs Foundation
P.O. Box 668
Lava Hot Springs, ID 83246
(800) 423-8597

Drive 2

Caribou National Forest
Federal Building, Suite 282
250 South Fourth Avenue
Pocatello, ID 83201
(208) 236-7500

Bear Lake National Wildlife Refuge
P.O. Box 9
370 Webster
Montpelier, ID 83254
(208) 847-1757

Grays Lake National Wildlife
   Refuge
74 Grays Lake Road
Wayan, ID 83285
(208) 574-2744

Bear Lake State Park
P.O. Box 297
Paris, ID 83261
(208) 945-2790

Southeastern Idaho Travel Council
c/o Lava Hot Springs Foundation
P.O. Box 668
Lava Hot Springs, ID 83246
(800) 423-8597

Drive 3

Targhee National Forest
420 North Bridge Street
P.O. Box 208
St. Anthony, ID 83445
(208) 624-3151

Harriman State Park
HC 66, Box 500
Island Park, ID 83429
(208) 558-7368

Henrys Lake State Park
HC 66, Box 20
Island Park, ID 83429
(208) 558-7532

Yellowstone/Teton Territory Travel
   Committee
P.O. Box 50498
Idaho Falls, ID 83402
(800) 634-3246
(208) 523-1010

Drive 4

Camas National Wildlife Refuge
HC 69
Box 1700
Hamer, ID 83425
(208) 662-5423

Targhee National Forest
420 North Bridge Street
P.O. Box 208
St. Anthony, ID 83445
(208) 624-3151

Harriman State Park
HC 66, Box 500
Island Park, ID 83429
(208) 558-7368

Bureau of Land Management
Idaho Falls District Office
1405 Hollipart Drive
Idaho Falls, ID 83401
(208) 524-7500

Drive 5

Craters of the Moon National
   Monument
P.O. Box 29
Arco, ID 83213
(208) 527-3257

Drive 6

Massacre Rocks State Park
3592 North Park Lane
American Falls, ID 83211
(208) 548-2672

South Central Idaho Travel
   Committee
858 Blue Lakes Boulevard North
Twin Falls, ID 83301
(800) 255-8946

Twin Falls Chamber of Commerce
858 Blue Lakes Boulevard North
Twin Falls, ID 83301
(208) 733-3974

Bureau of Land Management
Burley District Office
15 East, 200 South
Burley, ID 83318
(208) 677-6641

Drive 7

Hagerman Fossil Beds National
   Monument
221 North State Street
P.O. Box 570
Hagerman, ID 83332
(208) 837-4793

Malad Gorge State Park
1074 East 2350 South
Hagerman, ID 83332
(208) 837-4505

South Central Idaho Travel
   Committee
858 Blue Lakes Boulevard North
Twin Falls, ID 83301
(800) 255-8946

The Nature Conservancy
P.O. Box 165
Sun Valley, ID 83353
(208) 726-3007

Drive 8

Sawtooth National Forest
2647 Kimberley Road East
Twin Falls, ID 83301
(208) 737-3200

Sawtooth National Recreation Area
Star Route (Highway 75)
Ketchum, ID 83340
(208) 726-7672

Sun Valley/Ketchum Chamber of
Commerce
P.O. Box 2420
Sun Valley, ID 83701
(208) 726-3423
(800) 634-3347

Stanley/Sawtooth Chamber of
Commerce
P.O. Box 8
Stanley, ID 83278
(208) 774-3411

Bureau of Land Management
Shoshone District Office
P.O. Box 2-B
400 West F Street
Shoshone, ID 83352
(208) 886-2206

Drive 9

Salmon-Challis National Forest
Highway 93 South
P.O. Box 729
Challis, ID 83467
(208) 756-2215

Sawtooth National Recreation Area
Star Route (Highway 75)
Ketchum, ID 83340
(208) 726-7672

Stanley/Sawtooth Chamber of
Commerce
P.O. Box 8
Stanley, ID 83278
(208) 774-3411

Drive 10

Salmon-Challis National Forest
Highway 93 South
P.O. Box 729
Challis, ID 83467
(208) 756-2215

Land of the Yankee Fork State
Park
P.O. Box 1086
Challis, ID 83226
(208) 879-5244

Drive 11

Sun Valley/Ketchum Chamber of
Commerce
P.O. Box 2420
Sun Valley, ID 83701
(208) 726-3423
(800) 634-3347

Drive 12

Salmon National Forest
Highway 93 North
P.O. Box 729
Salmon, ID 83467
(208) 756-2215

Bureau of Land Management
Salmon District Office
P.O. Box 430
Hwy 93 South
Salmon, ID 83467
(208) 756-5400

Drive 13

Bureau of Land Management
Boise District Office
3948 Development Avenue
Boise, ID 83705
(208) 384-3300

Bruneau Dunes State Park
HC 85, Box 41
Mountain Home, ID 83647
(208) 366-7919

Three Island Crossing State Park
P.O. Box 609
Glenns Ferry, ID 83623
(208) 366-2394

Nampa Chamber of Commerce
1305 Third Street south
Nampa, ID 83278
(208) 466-4641

Drive 14

Boise National Forest
1750 Front Street
Boise, ID 83702
(208) 373-4100

Southwest Idaho Travel
  Association
P.O. Box 2106
Boise, ID 83701
(800) 635-5240

Stanley/Sawtooth Chamber of
  Commerce
P.O. Box 8
Stanley, ID 83278
(208) 774-3411

Boise Convention and Visitors
  Bureau
168 North Ninth Street
P.O. Box 2106
Boise, ID 83702
(800) 635-5240
(208) 344-7777

Drive 15

Payette National Forest
106 West Park Street
P.O. Box 1026
McCall, ID 83638
(208) 634-8151

Idaho Department of Parks and
  Recreation
P.O. Box 83720
Boise, ID 83720-0065
(208) 334-4199
(Park-N'-Ski Information)

Ponderosa State Park
P.O. Box A
McCall, ID 83638
(208) 634-2164

Drive 16

Payette National Forest
106 West Park Street
P.O. Box 1026
McCall, ID 83638
(208) 634-8151

Hell's Canyon National Recreation
  Area
P.O. Box 832
Riggins, ID 83549
(208) 628-3916

Drive 17

Payette National Forest
106 West Park Street
P.O. Box 1026
McCall, ID 83638
(208) 634-8151

Hell's Canyon National Recreation
  Area
P.O. Box 832
Riggins, ID 83549
(208) 628-3916

Drive 18

Nez Perce National Forest
Route 2, Box 475
Grangeville, ID 83530
(208) 983-1950

Drive 19

Clearwater National Forest Visitor
  Center
12730 U.S. Highway 12
Orofino, ID 83544
(208) 476-4541

Drive 20

Nez Perce National Historic Park
P.O. Box 93
Highway 95
Spalding, ID 83551
(208) 843-2261

Dworshak State Park
P.O. Box 2028
Orofino, ID 83544
(208) 476-5994

North Central Idaho Travel
  Association
2207 E. Main
Lewiston, ID 83501
(208) 743-3531

Drive 21

Heyburn State Park (McCroskey)
Route 1, Box 139
Plummer, ID 83851
(208) 686-1308

Drive 22

Heyburn State Park
Route 1, Box 139
Plummer, ID 83851
(208) 686-1308

Drive 23

Idaho Panhandle National Forests
(Coeur d'Alene National Forest)
(Kaniksu National Forest)
3815 Schreiber Way
Coeur d'Alene, ID 83814
(208) 765-7223

Old Mission State Park
P.O. Box 30
Cataldo, ID 83810
(208) 682-3814

Coeur d'Alene Convention and
  Visitors Bureau
202 Sherman Avenue
P.O. Box 1088
Coeur d'Alene, ID 83816
(208) 664-0587

North Idaho Travel Committee
P.O. Box 877
Coeur d'Alene, ID 83814
(208) 769-1537

Farragut State Park
E. 13400 Ranger Road
Athol, ID 83801
(208) 683-2425

Drive 24

Idaho Panhandle National Forests
(Coeur d'Alene National Forest)
(Kaniksu National Forest)
3815 Schreiber Way
Coeur d'Alene, ID 83814
(208) 765-7223

Old Mission State Park
P.O. Box 30
Cataldo, ID 83810
(208) 682-3814

Coeur d'Alene Convention and
   Visitors Bureau
202 Sherman Avenue
P.O. Box 1088
Coeur d'Alene, ID 83816
(208) 664-0587

North Idaho Travel Committee
P.O. Box 877
Coeur d'Alene, ID 83814
(208) 769-1537

Drive 25

Idaho Panhandle National Forests
(Coeur d'Alene National Forest)
(Kaniksu National Forest)
3815 Schreiber Way
Coeur d'Alene, ID 83814
(208) 765-7223

Drive 26

Idaho Panhandle National Forests
(Coeur d'Alene National Forest)
(Kaniksu National Forest)
3815 Schreiber Way
Coeur d'Alene, ID 83814
(208) 765-7223

Priest Lake State Park
Indian Creek Bay, #423
Coolin, ID 83638
(208) 443-2200

Drive 27

Idaho Panhandle National Forests
(Coeur d'Alene National Forest)
(Kaniksu National Forest)
3815 Schreiber Way
Coeur d'Alene, ID 83814
(208) 765-7223

Bureau of Land Management
Coeur d'Alene District Office
1808 North Third Street
Coeur d'Alene, ID 83814
(208) 769-5000

Index

Page numbers appearing in italics refer to photos.

About the Author

Bob Clark is a Colorado native by birth, and a Westerner by temperament. His ancestors followed the Erie Canal westward to Michigan, and continued on to Wyoming to work on the transcontinental railroad. His grandfather prospected for uranium in the Wyoming deserts, and his grandmother could spot a half-buried arrowhead in a dry creekbed at fifty paces. Both of them could hunt and fish like mountain men, and they gave Bob his love of the wide open Western spaces.

Clark worked for many years in the electronics industry, and has his MBA degree from the University of Colorado. Twelve years of parochial school taught him grammar and spelling, although the lure of spell-checking software has been irresistible. He has been married for 25 years, and has two energetic, enthusiastic children. This is his first book.

The author at the site of the famed Mullan Tree.

FALCONGUIDES ®Leading the Way™

FALCONGUIDES are available for where-to-go hiking, mountain biking, rock climbing, walking, scenic driving, fishing, rockhounding, paddling, birding, wildlife viewing, and camping. We also have FalconGuides® on essential outdoor skills and subjects and field identification. The following titles are currently available, but this list grows every year. For a free catalog with a complete list of titles, call FALCON® toll-free at 1-800-582-2665.

SCENIC DRIVING GUIDES

Scenic Driving Alaska and the Yukon
Scenic Driving Arizona
Scenic Driving the Beartooth Highway
Scenic Driving California
Scenic Driving Colorado
Scenic Driving Florida
Scenic Driving Georgia
Scenic Driving Hawaii
Scenic Driving Idaho
Scenic Driving Indiana
Scenic Driving Kentucky
Scenic Driving Michigan
Scenic Driving Minnesota
Scenic Driving Montana
Scenic Driving New England
Scenic Driving New Mexico
Scenic Driving North Carolina
Scenic Driving Oregon
Scenic Driving the Ozarks
Scenic Driving Pennsylvania
Scenic Driving Texas
Scenic Driving Utah
Scenic Driving Virginia
Scenic Driving Washington
Scenic Driving Wisconsin
Scenic Driving Wyoming
Scenic Driving Yellowstone and
  the Grand Teton National Parks
Scenic Byways East & South
Scenic Byways Far West
Scenic Byways Rocky Mountains
Back Country Byways

HISTORIC TRAIL GUIDES

Traveling California's Gold Rush Country
Traveling the Lewis & Clark Trail
Traveling the Oregon Trail
Traveler's Guide to the Pony Express Trail

WILDLIFE VIEWING GUIDES

Alaska Wildlife Viewing Guide
Arizona Wildlife Viewing Guide
California Wildlife Viewing Guide
Colorado Wildlife Viewing Guide
Florida Wildlife Viewing Guide
Indiana Wildlife Vewing Guide
Iowa Wildlife Viewing Guide
Kentucky Wildlife Viewing Guide
Massachusetts Wildlife Viewing Guide
Montana Wildlife Viewing Guide
Nebraska Wildlife Viewing Guide
Nevada Wildlife Viewing Guide
New Hampshire Wildlife Viewing Guide
New Jersey Wildlife Viewing Guide
New Mexico Wildlife Viewing Guide
New York Wildlife Viewing Guide
North Carolina Wildlife Viewing Guide
North Dakota Wildlife Viewing Guide
Ohio Wildlife Viewing Guide
Oregon Wildlife Viewing Guide
Puerto Rico & the Virgin Islands
  Wildlife Viewing Guide
Tennessee Wildlife Viewing Guide
Texas Wildlife Viewing Guide
Utah Wildlife Viewing Guide
Vermont Wildlife Viewing Guide
Virginia Wildlife Viewing Guide
Washington Wildlife Viewing Guide
West Virginia Wildlife Viewing Guide
Wisconsin Wildlife Viewing Guide

■ *To order any of these books, check with your local bookseller*
*or call FALCON ® at **1-800-582-2665**.*
Visit us on the world wide web at:
www.falcon.com

FALCON®

FALCONGUIDES® Leading the Way™

FALCON®

FALCONGUIDES ® Leading the Way™

FIELD GUIDES
Bitterroot: Montana State Flower
Canyon Country Wildflowers
Central Rocky Mountains
 Wildflowers
Chihuahuan Desert Wildflowers
Great Lakes Berry Book
New England Berry Book
Ozark Wildflowers
Pacific Northwest Berry Book
Plants of Arizona
Rare Plants of Colorado
Rocky Mountain Berry Book
Scats & Tracks of the Pacific
 Coast States
Scats & Tracks of the
 Rocky Mountains
Sierra Nevada Wildflowers
Southern Rocky Mountain
 Wildflowers
Tallgrass Prairie Wildflowers
Western Trees
Wildflowers of Southwestern
 Utah

FISHING GUIDES
Fishing Alaska
Fishing the Beartooths
Fishing Florida
Fishing Georgia
Fishing Glacier National Park
Fishing Maine
Fishing Montana
Fishing Wyoming
Fishing Yellowstone
 National Park
Trout Unlimited's Guide to
 America's 100 Best Trout
 Streams
America's Best Bass Fishing

BIRDING GUIDES
Birding Georgia
Birding Illinois
Birding Minnesota
Birding Montana
Birding Northern California
Birding Texas
Birding Utah

MORE GUIDEBOOKS
Backcountry Horseman's
 Guide to Washington
Camping Arizona
Camping California's
 National Forests
Camping Colorado
Camping Oregon
Exploring Canyonlands &
 Arches National Parks
Exploring Hawaii's Parklands
Exploring Mount Helena
Exploring Southern California
 Beaches
Family Fun in Montana
Family Fun in Yellowstone
Hiking Hot Springs of the Pacific
 Northwest
Recreation Guide to WA
 National Forests
Touring Arizona Hot Springs
Touring California & Nevada
 Hot Springs
Touring Colorado Hot Springs
Touring Montana & Wyoming
 Hot Springs
Trail Riding Western Montana
Wilderness Directory
Wild Montana
Wild Utah
Wild Virginia

ROCKHOUNDING GUIDES
Rockhounding Arizona
Rockhounding California
Rockhounding Colorado
Rockhounding Montana
Rockhounding Nevada
Rockhound's Guide to New
 Mexico
Rockhounding Texas
Rockhounding Utah
Rockhounding Wyoming

HOW-TO GUIDES
Avalanche Aware
Backpacking Tips
Bear Aware
Desert Hiking Tips
Hiking with Dogs
Hiking with Kids
Leave No Trace
Mountain Lion Alert
Reading Weather
Route Finding
Using GPS
Wild Country Companion
Wilderness First Aid
Wilderness Survival

WALKING
Walking Colorado Springs
Walking Denver
Walking Portland
Walking Seattle
Walking St. Louis
Walking San Francisco
Walking Virginia Beach

■ *To order any of these books, check with your local bookseller*
*or call FALCON ® at **1-800-582-2665**.*
Visit us on the world wide web at:
www.falcon.com

FALCON GUIDES ® Leading the Way™

---

www.Falcon.com

Since 1979, Falcon® has brought you the best in outdoor recreational guidebooks. Now you can access that same reliable and accurate information online.

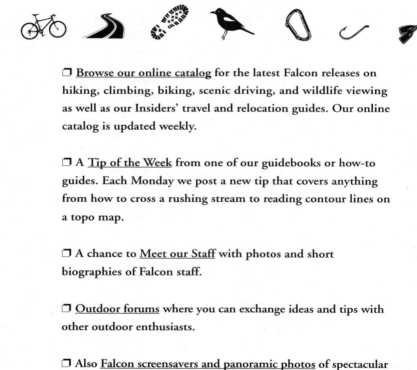

❏ <u>Browse our online catalog</u> for the latest Falcon releases on hiking, climbing, biking, scenic driving, and wildlife viewing as well as our Insiders' travel and relocation guides. Our online catalog is updated weekly.

❏ A <u>Tip of the Week</u> from one of our guidebooks or how-to guides. Each Monday we post a new tip that covers anything from how to cross a rushing stream to reading contour lines on a topo map.

❏ A chance to <u>Meet our Staff</u> with photos and short biographies of Falcon staff.

❏ <u>Outdoor forums</u> where you can exchange ideas and tips with other outdoor enthusiasts.

❏ Also <u>Falcon screensavers and panoramic photos</u> of spectacular destinations.

And much more!

 Plan your next outdoor adventure at our web site. Point your browser to www.Falcon.com and get FalconGuided!

FALCON®